KILLER CASE FILES

60 SHOCKING STORIES OF MURDER AND MAYHEM VOLUME 3

JAMIE MALTON

MP
Malton Publishing LLC
MaltonPublishing.com

ISBN 978-1959137207

WORD OF WARNING

The details written in these stories come directly from eyewitness accounts, interviews, court transcripts, crime scenes, and autopsy reports. Due to the graphic nature of the crimes featured in *Killer Case Files* which include: murder, domestic violence, sexual assault, hate crimes, sex work, incest, mental illness, child abuse, animal abuse, abduction, suicide, mutilation, and necrophilia reader discretion is advised.

BEYOND THE BOOKS

Thank you for reading *Killer Case Files: 60 Shocking Stories Of Murder and Mayhem* Volume 2.

Beyond The Books

With my *Killer Case Files Series,* I'm trying to do something extra for readers that is beyond the normal book experience.

Sometimes a case can grab you in the gut and make you want to go down the rabbit hole a little further. So I've curated the best information from my research and made a "Case File" for each story in each volume. All of the case files are located on my website JamieMalton.com. This is where readers can see the face of the killer, see the faces of victims, learn how the crime was reported in the media, and see the additional crime scene, trial, and evidence photos. No email sign-up is required.

Bonus Story
As a thank you for being one of my readers, each volume also includes a bonus story and bonus case file again available on my website.

If you decide to join my mailing list (and I hope you will) you'll be the first to hear about case updates and my new volumes. You'll also have my direct email address. If you have something to tell me, just hit 'reply', and you'll be in my personal inbox. I read 100% of those emails. I hope to see you there!

Why I Write
The sudden loss of an innocent victim to crime is always hard to take. They are silenced, and families are left to piece together their final moments, grieve their loss and navigate the system of justice. In some cases, the families receive no justice for decades.

By writing the *Killer Case Files* series, I am able to donate some of the revenue from book sales to organizations that help solve cold cases by funding private DNA tests. As forensic technologies improve, there is now hope and closure for the families of victims who never received justice.

Please let me know how you liked this volume.

Sincerely,

Jamie Malton

KILLER CASE FILES: VOLUME 7

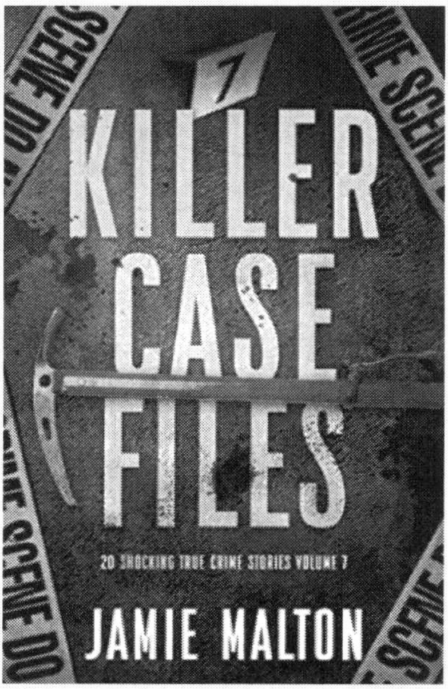

MASTER MANIPULATOR

> "Knoefel picked out the 10-inch serrated kitchen knife and showed her how to plunge it in once and twist."
>
> MARYSVILLE JOURNAL-TRIBUNE
> JULY 16TH, 2014

In one man, there exists a combination of cowardice, malice, and greed. This same man exploits and manipulates a teenager with a tragic life history, coercing her into ruthlessly committing a violent murder of one of her own family members.

LISA KNOEFEL

Lisa Knoefel was born in 1971, in Reynoldsburg, Ohio. She moved to Willoughby Hills, a suburb of Cleveland, in 2000. By 2012, she was living in a lovely family home with her second husband, Kevin, who was one year older than her. Lisa had one daughter from her previous marriage — Megan, born in 1999. Kevin and Lisa had their first and only child together, Hailey, in 2009.

Lisa was a social worker employed by the Cuyahoga County Department of Children and Family Services. She was trained to help with incest cases. Kevin worked as a truck driver and was often away from home. In the summer of 2011, the family decided to foster Sabrina Zunich, a troubled sixteen-year-old.

SABRINA ZUNICH

Sabrina Zunich was born in 1994, in Cleveland, Ohio. Her parents, Mark Zunich and Susan Edwards, battled alcohol and drug addiction and abandoned the girl when she was three. Sabrina's grandmother took care of her for some time but Sabrina would steal from her and get into fights at school.

No other relatives wanted Sabrina, so she ended up in the foster system in 2010 at the age of 16. Sabrina's family had a history of mental illness. Her father was a paranoid schizophrenic and refused treatment for his illness. When

Sabrina joined the Knoefel family, she was taking nine different medications to deal with several mental health conditions. She was diagnosed with attention deficit hyperactivity disorder, oppositional defiant disorder, bipolar depression, insomnia, and anxiety.

SABRINA'S LIFE WITH THE KNOEFEL FAMILY

Sabrina moved in with the Knoefels in July 2011. That same year, her biological father died from a drug overdose. However, Sabrina was starting to get better. She enrolled in school in the Fall and behaved exceptionally well. Her grades were average, but the teen paid attention in class, which was important. She also got along with her foster sisters, Megan and Hailey.

Since she was close to turning eighteen, Sabrina asked her foster family if she could stay with them until high school graduation, and Lisa and Kevin were more than happy to say yes. Sabrina's behavior started to change after that. Lisa noticed she was more aggressive with her older daughter, Megan. The two would often fight over little Hailey.

Sabrina's school friends would later say she told them Lisa only cared about her biological children and that she felt more connected to Kevin, the only person who liked her in that household, according to Sabrina. Around that time, Lisa, who was a trained social worker, noticed a subtle connection between her husband, Kevin, and Sabrina. She confided in a friend that she saw looks and overheard conversations between them that implied a closeness that wasn't there before.

A DOMESTIC DISPUTE

On September 15, 2012, the police were called to the Knoefel residence. Kevin met them outside, saying he had contacted them because of a fight with his wife, Lisa. The couple argued about the behavior of Lisa's daughter from her previous marriage, Megan. Kevin grabbed Megan by the back of her neck and escorted her room.

When Lisa saw that, she started screaming at Kevin that he was choking the girl. Kevin then contacted the authorities to document the incident in case the two divorced one day and Lisa tried to get full custody of their daughter Hailey.

Lisa and Kevin seemingly patched things up the following month and joined their friends for a weekend nature getaway. The two families went camping, and Kevin confided in a male friend that he was considering divorcing Lisa. Disturbingly, Kevin showed him photos of Sabrina from a fashion photoshoot. Kevin also told his friend that Sabrina had been buying him underwear. When asked if he was having a romantic relationship with his foster daughter, Kevin didn't deny it, which alarmed his friend.

RELATIONSHIP BETWEEN KEVIN AND SABRINA

Kevin and Sabrina got very close in the spring of 2012, as

he often drove her to school when he wasn't on the road. They started touching each other during those rides and Sabrina performed oral sex on Kevin. Sabrina allegedly wanted to become a massage therapist and practiced with Kevin, who experienced leg pain. By the summer of 2012, their relationship included sexual intercourse.

Sabrina's school friends confirmed later that she asked them in October 2012 if they knew "a hitman" who could murder her foster mother.

Meanwhile, Kevin called Sabrina's social worker, told them he was getting divorced, and asked if Sabrina could stay with him. The social worker told Kevin that it was a possibility.

Several months before the murder, Kevin took Sabrina to the bank, and they opened up a joint checking account.

Sabrina turned 18 at the end of October 2012. Meanwhile, Lisa had a feeling something was happening between Kevin and Sabrina. But when her foster daughter started arguing with Megan and attacked her with a knife, Lisa decided that Sabrina needed to leave the house by January 1, 2013.

On November 15, 2012, Kevin cried while driving Sabrina to school. He was distraught, saying he would take his life because the fighting with Lisa couldn't continue and he needed her to die. Sabrina was easily manipulated by Kevin. The teen said she would kill Lisa herself because she loved him. Kevin didn't dissuade her, and he went home, packed a suitcase, and left for Michigan that day.

THE MURDER OF LISA KNOEFEL

Lisa's 13-year-old daughter Megan woke up sometime after midnight on November 12, 2012. The dogs were barking, and screams were coming from her mother's bedroom. She got up to see what was happening and found Sabrina on top of Lisa. She was stabbing her with a knife. Megan tried to drag Sabrina off Lisa but failed.

She then ran from the room and dialed 911. The police rushed to the scene and found Sabrina still holding the bloody knife. Randy Mullenax, one of the police officers who responded to the 911 call, ordered her to drop the knife and kneel on the ground. According to him, Sabrina was just standing there with blood all over her clothes.

They discovered the lifeless body of Lisa Knoefel in the bedroom. There was nothing the paramedics could do to save her. She was covered in cuts and deep wounds. Her little daughter Hailey was hiding in the closet. Sabrina Zunich was taken into custody. The arresting officers confirmed she was in shock.

The autopsy revealed the brutality of this crime. Lisa was stabbed 178 times and had many defensive wounds on her hands. The knife was twisted inside her body, and the blade almost broke during the attack.

Investigators wanted to know the motive behind this crime, so they began questioning everyone connected to Lisa or Sabrina, hoping they would give them more information on what happened between them. One person stood out immediately —Lisa's husband, Kevin.

KEVIN'S BEHAVIOR

He returned from Michigan and found out his wife was dead. The officers noticed he was very calm and insisted on looking at the crime scene against the officer's advice. He started asking more questions about the attack and wanted to know all the details.

The family friends who came over to check on the Knoefels also said Kevin was almost happy Lisa was gone. He asked his friend to shut down all of Lisa's social media accounts and her email because he didn't want to reply to any messages.

Kevin drove down to the Lake County Jail and requested to see Sabrina but was denied. He slammed his hands down on the desk and yelled, "I am her father!" The officer arranged for him to be added to Sabrina's visitor list.

Furthermore, Kevin started asking about Lisa's life insurance before her funeral. He collected $785,000 in the Spring of 2013 and purchased a property in Florida and several vehicles.

For six months, Sabrina claimed she acted alone. The

teenager said she felt betrayed by Lisa. But her story completely changed in August 2013.

Sabrina Zunich agreed to talk to the investigators and tell them the whole story. According to the teen, Kevin was the one who came up with the idea to murder Lisa. She was manipulated by a much older man to think he would harm himself over the divorce.

He allegedly promised Sabrina they would buy a new house from Lisa's insurance money and live together as a family. Kevin guaranteed Sabrina would attend college and take care of little Hailey. Sabrina knew she was responsible for the murder but wanted to ensure the police knew Kevin actually planned it.

He even wanted to stage the scene to look like a robbery. But it all fell apart on the night of the stabbing because Megan woke up. While the police didn't have any physical evidence to confirm Sabrina and Kevin were in a relationship, her story was believable.

Kevin Knoefel was arrested on August 9th and charged with conspiracy to commit aggravated murder, complicity to aggravated murder, and sexual battery. Sabrina Zunich pleaded guilty to aggravated murder and became the main witness in the trial of Kevin Knoefel.

Kevin's trial started in May 2014, and the majority of the case relied on Sabrina's testimony. Other witnesses confirmed that the two had a relationship, which solidified her story.

Sabrina testified that Kevin showed her how to kill Lisa and where to stab her depending on how Lisa was lying in the bed. According to Sabrina, Kevin told her to stab Lisa between the shoulder blades if she was on her side and stab her in the throat if she was on her back. He told her to rotate the knife after stabbing Lisa. He also advised her to make it look like a burglary by emptying out drawers and the jewelry box. She said she was instructed by Kevin to use an insanity defense if she was caught.

After hearing Sabrina's lengthy testimony, the jury deliberated for nine hours and reached a verdict on June 11, 2014. Kevin Knoefel was found guilty of three counts of complicity to commit aggravated murder and two counts of conspiracy to commit aggravated murder, as well as six counts of sexual battery.

After Kevin Knoefel's conviction, Lake County Sheriff Daniel A. Dunlap issued a statement saying,

> "This was a senseless and violent act, and our condolences go out to Lisa Knoefel's family and friends. The Lake County Sheriff's Office is dedicated to bringing justice to the victims of these heinous crimes, and we are pleased that the perpetrator has been held accountable for his actions."

On August 6, 2014, he was sentenced to life in prison with a possibility of parole after serving 30 years. Then on September 29, 2014, Sabrina Zunich received the same sentence. She was very emotional and remorseful during the sentencing and apologized to Lisa's loved ones. Sabrina is serving her sentence in Dayton Correctional Institution and will be eligible for parole in 2042. She will be 47 years old.

THE BUFFALO RIPPER

"As I saw this tall, gaunt, decidedly odd-looking character coming toward me from the rear of the cell, I heard a clank. The goodly sheriff had locked me into a cell with a man who had killed four people for no apparent reason, two with his bare hands! I decided to be extremely gentle in my approach to George..."

ATTORNEY FOR THE DEFENSE, F. LEE BAILEY

NOVEMBER 18TH, 1973

Thirty-six-year-old George Fitzsimmons decided not to run this time. He sat outside on the curb in front of a

Buffalo sandwich shop and waited for the police to pick him up.

A few minutes earlier, he'd called his attorney and confessed to murdering his aunt and uncle with a hunting knife at their home in Roulette, Pennsylvania. They were trying to poison him, or at least that's what he later told the police. He said Euphresia and DeAlton Nichols, both 80 years old at the time of their deaths, were spiking his food with arsenic, and it was a "kill or be killed" situation.

His attorney, Herb Siegel, was the same one George used four years earlier when he murdered his parents because they wanted him to go to church.

George Fitzsimmons was born on May 7th, 1937, in Buffalo, New York, to parents William and Pearl Fitzsimmons. He grew up to be a tall and athletic teen.

George attended Canisius High School, a private college prep school for young men, but dropped out before graduation. He enlisted in the Army and was stationed in South Korea.

While in Asia, George became interested in karate and quickly mastered this martial art. He also spent hours weightlifting, which made him even stronger and more muscular. George became addicted to amphetamines while serving overseas and was dishonorably discharged from the US Army in 1961. He promptly moved back to New York and into his parent's apartment in Eggertsville.

It was clear that George was unwell because he experienced hallucinations after his return from Korea. His use of amphetamines led to violent and unpredictable behavior. To help him, William and Pearl sent their son to the Buffalo State Hospital, where he spent several months detoxing from drugs and receiving psychiatric treatment.

After his release, George tried to live a normal life. He got an apartment and was hired as a lifeguard at a YMCA. The job and the independent lifestyle didn't last long, and soon he was back with his parents again.

The neighbors often saw George outside, exercising and lifting weights. But they didn't know their active and sporty neighbor often cried uncontrollably and would scream at his parents.

George's traumatic experiences during the war and his drug abuse had had a profound impact on his mental health. Despite undergoing treatment at the psychiatric hospital, he continued to be tormented by hallucinations and explosive outbursts of anger and violence.

His relationship with his parents deteriorated quickly after his release from the hospital. George started frequent arguments over petty matters, leaving William, age 64, and Pearl, age 60, helpless in their attempts to calm him down.

SUNDAY MORNING

On January 12th, 1969, a peaceful Sunday morning ended in a deadly family feud. George refused an invitation to join his parents for church, and a heated argument erupted between George and his father. George grabbed a souvenir tomahawk and started swinging it at his father. Then he used his karate skills on William, leaving him dead on the ground with a bloody head wound. In a frenzy, he turned his rage on his mother and subjected Pearl to a brutal beating, leaving her dead on the floor next to her husband.

George fled the scene and drove his father's car to a remote motel in Attleboro, Massachusetts. He decided to stay there until he could make a plan to leave.

Neighbors in Eggerstville grew concerned about the Fitzsimmons family because no one had seen them for over a week. The police were called, and the lifeless and decomposed bodies of William and Pearl were discovered in the hallway of the house on January 21st. The authorities went on the hunt for their prime suspect—George Fitzsimmons.

George decided to head West to Arizona but quickly ran out of money. Unaware that the bodies of his parents had been found, he sent a telegram to his local bank requesting a money transfer to a bank in Illinois where he had stopped. Since the police were actively investigating the case, the bank employees were warned about George's account, and they reported him to law enforcement as soon as he called. He was apprehended in Altamont, Illinois.

George was dubbed the *Karate Chop Killer* and a "physical culture faddist" once the media learned about the murder of his parents and his obsession with Karate and exercise.

He was extradited back to New York and charged with two counts of first-degree murder. He pleaded not guilty but then confessed to the murder of his parents, which confused investigators. The judge ordered George to talk to a psychiatrist, and he was diagnosed with paranoid schizophrenia soon after. The psychiatrist also mentioned that George didn't feel remorse for killing his parents. He also couldn't offer any motive to explain what happened in the Fitzsimmons' house.

George was sentenced to treatment in the Buffalo State Hospital because of his diagnosis, and the murder charges against him were dropped.

According to psychiatrists who worked with him, George showed fast improvement right away. He attended therapy regularly and did his best to get better. He spent less than three years in the Buffalo State Hospital, and in 1970, since the murder charges against him were dropped, George inherited his parents' estate, which was worth $123,000.

During his stay at the hospital, George met a woman named Beverly, who was also a patient. She was released two months before George, and once he was released, they married and started their life together in Coudersport, Pennsylvania, near George's aunt and uncle.

ALL IS NOT WELL

George snapped a few weeks later and physically assaulted his wife. Her injuries were so severe that she needed to stay in the hospital. He was arrested and charged with assault, but Beverly refused to testify against her husband, and the case was dropped.

George's lawyer went to Pennsylvania to convince him to return to Buffalo State Hospital for treatment. But George was certain he wasn't mentally ill and refused to go back. Instead, he briefly moved in with his aunt and uncle, Euphresia and DeAlton Nichols, who lived in Roulette, Pennsylvania.

Even though George murdered her brother, Euphresia still wanted to support her nephew. She claimed he grew up in an abusive household, which caused his mental illness.

The residents of Roulette weren't very welcoming to George. They knew he'd murdered his parents, and the news about beating his wife spread quickly.

On November 18th, 1973, George worked out in the morning and then watched a football game with his uncle. He couldn't focus on the TV and tried to do something else. When he started reading the newspaper, he saw that the lines of text were moving around. It led him to believe his aunt and uncle were poisoning him.

George stood in front of the mirror and saw his pale complexion. He was now sure his food was spiked with arsenic. George rushed into the living room, screaming and arguing with his uncle about poisoning him. After a couple of minutes, he grabbed a hunting knife and stabbed his uncle twice in the heart. He then went to find his aunt and stabbed Euphresia twenty-two times. The elderly couple didn't survive their nephew's attack.

After George called his attorney and was picked up by police at the Buffalo sandwich shop, he confessed on video to the murders of his aunt and uncle. George said,

> "It was kill or be killed. I know damned well they did (poison me) because I looked in the mirror, and I was all drawn out. And my head thumped . . . I could feel it going through my system."

He was arrested and charged with two counts of first-degree murder. His wife Beverly filed for a divorce two days later and sued him for battery.

The media now labeled George the "Buffalo Ripper."

Since he had access to his inheritance, George hired F. Lee Bailey, a well-known defense attorney who had represented several high-profile clients charged with murder.

Bailey immediately requested a change of venue due to the pre-trial publicity, and the trial was moved to Greensburg.

George appeared in court in July 1974, and Bailey entered an insanity defense, citing his client's medical history. Bailey collected several important pieces of evidence that confirmed George had a mental illness. One was his video-taped confession, in which he mumbled and was almost incoherent.

Against his attorney's advice, George took the stand and claimed he wasn't home at all during the murders and that he had no mental health issues.

Bailey tried but failed to prove his client had a mental disorder and was experiencing an "episode" when he murdered his aunt and uncle.

George had opted for a non-jury trial and was found guilty on December 19th, 1976. He was sentenced to life in prison by Judge Earl S. Keim.

JUDGE KEIM

Judge Keim was very vocal about his decision and openly discussed the reasons why he sent George Fitzsimmons to prison. According to Keim, he didn't believe that mental health institutions could do anything for people like George. He simply couldn't allow him to walk out once again after murdering four people.

He said to the media,

> "Quite frankly, I do not have a great deal of confidence in our system of mental health treatment. I don't like the procedures now in effect for the release of potentially dangerous people such as Mr. Fitzsimmons from this state's mental institutions. And I certainly would not want it on my conscience if Mr. Fitzsimmons were ever permitted to go free and to kill again."

Bailey didn't waste any time and filed an appeal to the Pennsylvania Supreme Court, saying,

> "George Fitzsimmons is the sickest man I have ever seen in 26 years of practice. I do not advocate that Mr. Fitzsimmons be released to prey upon society, but it seems to me that from the outset we have failed to protect the public from George Fitzsimmons. The question now is whether we will permit that failure to be buried in a conviction which is highly suspect."

The appeal was rejected.

George served his time at the State Correctional Institute

in Dallas, Pennsylvania. At first, he would often pick fights with guards and other inmates, but over time he became withdrawn and was seen talking to himself and avoiding contact with others.

George received a cancer diagnosis in 1999. The last two months of his were difficult. He was in severe pain and was unable to leave his bed. He died at the State Correctional Institute in Dallas, Pennsylvania, in 1999.

Pearl and William Fitzsimmons and Euphresia and DeAlto Nichols were all buried in Saint Gabriel's Cemetery in McKean County, Pennsylvania.

SCHOOL ABDUCTION

> "If they shouldn't hang me, then they never should hang another man. My crime was one of the most gruesome in history."
>
> WILLIAM HICKMAN, CONVICTED MURDERER

On December 15th, 1927, Marion and Marjorie Parker, 12-year-old twins, left home for their school day at Mount Vernon Junior High School in Los Angeles.

Marion was a tomboy and played sports with the boys during recess, a rarity for girls in 1927. Marjorie loved to dress up and was a very feminine girl. However different they were, the Parker twins got along and were best friends as well as sisters. Their mother, Geraldine Parker, was a homemaker, and their father, Perry, worked at First National Trust and Savings Bank in Los Angeles.

On that particular Wednesday, the usual routine at Mount Vernon Junior High was disrupted when the principal, Cora Freedman, was out of the office. The substitute teacher, Mary Holt, was managing the office when a man who called himself 'Mr. Cooper" appeared in the doorway. Cooper said he was a coworker of Perry Parker and told Mary that Perry had been in an accident and was in the hospital. He was there to pick up Perry's daughter on his behalf. Mary asked the man which daughter he was picking up, and the man simply stated he was there for the younger daughter.

Marjorie and Marion were identical twins, but Mary had overheard the girls talking about who was born first. She knew that Marion was born a few minutes after Marjorie, making Marion the younger sister. She retrieved Marion from her class and brought her to the office.

Mr. Cooper explained to the young girl that her father was ok but needed her to visit the hospital. Marion Parker was upset but didn't ask any questions, believing Mr. Cooper was telling her the truth, and so she left with him.

When principal Freeman returned to the school later that afternoon, Mary Holt told her that Marion had left the school early with her father's coworker. Cora Freeman noted it and carried on with her day.

MISSING

After school, Marjorie waited outside for Marion like she always did. Marion failed to walk out of school with her classmates, so Marjorie walked to their streetcar stop, expecting Marion to be waiting there. The stop was empty, and when the streetcar arrived, Marjorie got on. She was afraid she would miss her ride home and end up stranded in the city. When she got home, she told her parents that Marion never arrived at the streetcar stop.

Perry and Geraldine assumed Marion had stayed late after school for Christmas festivities however, when it was time for dinner and Marion still hadn't returned home, Perry called the school. Still in the office, Mary Holt answered the phone and was surprised to hear Perry's voice. Mary was confused and explained to Perry how his coworker, Mr. Cooper, had come to the school that afternoon to pick up Marion.

Perry knew no “Mr. Cooper” and hung up the phone, intending to immediately call the police, but as he was dialing the operator, he heard a knock at the door. A telegram from Western Union had arrived at his home. The telegram read, "Do positively nothing until you receive a special delivery letter.” It was signed by his daughter, Marion Parker.

The Parkers decided not to alert the authorities and followed the instructions in the telegram. Several hours later, another telegram arrived at their home saying,

"Marion is secure. Use good judgment. Interfering with my plan is dangerous." This telegram was signed by Marion Parker and by *George Fox*.

After receiving the second telegram, the Parkers called the Los Angeles Police Department. A third telegram showed up just after the LAPD arrived at the Parker house. It read,

---

> "PM Parker, use good judgment. You are the loser. Do this, secure 75 $20.00 gold certificates in United States currency...keep them on your person, and go about your daily business as usual. Leave out the police and detectives. Make no public notice. Keep this affair private. Make no search. Fulfilling the terms with the transfer of currency will secure the return of the girl. Failure to comply with these requests means no one will ever see the girl again, except the angels in heaven. The affair must end one way or another in three days, 72 hours."

A letter written by Marion accompanied the telegram. Marion's message said,

---

> "Dear Daddy and Mother, I wish I could come home. I think I'll die if I have to be like this much longer. Won't someone tell me why this had to happen to me? Daddy, please do what this man tells you, or he'll kill me if you don't."

Detectives asked the Parkers to keep Marion's abduction out of the newspapers. They needed the kidnapper to think that Perry had followed his instructions. The next day, Perry reported to work at the bank and tried to stay calm so his colleagues wouldn't notice his distress.

The police questioned Mary Holt at Mount Vernon Junior High School. They wanted to know more about the man who called himself Mr. Cooper. She estimated Cooper to be between 25 and 30 years old and said he was approximately 5' 8" tall and weighed 150 pounds. He was clean-shaven with dark brown wavy hair.

Around 8 pm the following day, a phone call was received at the Parker home. "Mr. Parker, do you have the money?" the caller asked. Perry replied that he did, and the caller said he would call back shortly. Thirty minutes later, the phone rang again, and Perry was given instructions to take the ransom money, put it in his car, and park it at Gramercy and Tenth.

Perry put the money in his car and drove to the location of the meeting. He didn't tell the police about his plans to meet Marion's kidnapper, fearing the police presence would spook the kidnapper. When Perry got to Gramercy and Tenth, he parked his car, sat there until almost midnight, and finally returned home when the kidnapper didn't show.

When he got home, he discovered LAPD officers had followed him to the meeting place. Angry at the officers,

Perry presumed that the kidnapper saw the police cars, got frightened, and left.

ANOTHER LETTER

A letter arrived at the Parker home the day after Perry's botched meeting with the kidnapper. Marion's abductor wrote that he drove away when he saw police cars circling the night before. He wrote, "I am so ashamed of you." The kidnapper told Perry he would give him one final chance to exchange the ransom money for his daughter.

Inside the letter from the kidnapper was another note from Marion. Marion's message read,

---

> "Dear Daddy and Mommy, please don't bring anyone with you today. I'm sorry for what happened last night. We drove right past the house, and I cried the entire time. If you don't meet us, you'll never see me again. Love to all, Marion Parker. PS Please, Daddy, I want to come home. Please come by yourself, or you won't see me again.

Perry begged the lead detective on Marion's case to let him meet alone with the kidnapper. The detective reluctantly agreed. Before trying to meet with the kidnapper again, Perry received two more letters warning him that Marion's life was at risk if he went against his instructions.

THE FINAL MEETING PLACE

On December 17th, 1927, Perry drove to a new meeting place. He sat in his car for some time until a Chrysler Coupe approached him. As the car pulled alongside Perry, the driver, whose face was covered by a bandanna, pulled out a gun and pointed it at Perry. He could also see his daughter sitting slumped over in the front seat, but her eyes appeared open.

Perry handed over the ransom money to the kidnapper. After telling him to remain where he was, the kidnapper accelerated forward 100 feet, and as Perry watched, the kidnapper stopped, pushed something out of the car, and sped off. Perry drove ahead as soon as the kidnapper's car was out of sight, toward what he presumed to be his daughter's body.

Perry stopped his car and jumped out to pick up his daughter, who appeared to be wrapped in a blanket. When he saw her face, he knew she was dead. Her body felt suspiciously light and when he unwrapped her from the blanket, he discovered her body had been severed below the navel. Marion was also missing both arms. They had been removed just below the elbow.

Several people heard Perry screaming in the street, and soon the police arrived.

THE AUTOPSY

The medical examiner revealed the details of Marion's death, and it painted a gruesome picture. Her killer went to great lengths to make her appear alive by sewing her eyelids open and applying makeup to her face.

There was no evidence of strangulation and no bruises on the body. Despite the challenge of working with partial remains, the medical examiner determined that Marion did not suffer a sexual assault. He also stated that she'd been dead for about 12 hours, meaning she was still alive during the initial failed meeting. Her cause of death was listed as exhaustion and fright.

GRUESOME DISCOVERIES

A man strolling in a park in LA stumbled upon several packages wrapped in newspaper. He opened one package and discovered a human arm. The other packages contained Marion's other limbs, including her legs.

Later that day, two boys hiking in a nearby wooded area made a horrifying discovery. They found the remaining parts of Marion's torso and thighs. The medical examiner conducted an autopsy on the remains and concluded that Marion may have been alive at the time of her dismemberment.

A BREAK IN THE CASE

The Chrysler Coupe driven by Marion's murderer was found in a parking lot in downtown Los Angeles. According to the lot attendant, the driver had dark brown wavy hair and planned to pick up his car the day after dropping it off.

In the vehicle, fingerprints found by officers matched those of 19-year-old William Edward Hickman. Hickman already had a criminal record for forgery and robbery. Residents of the Bellevue Apartments where he lived said William Hickman was known to them as Donald Evans.

When detectives investigated William Hickman, they found he once worked as a messenger in the same bank as Perry Parker. After Hickman forged over $400.00 in checks while working at the bank, he was terminated and arrested. As a result, William Hickman was sentenced to probation.

Hickman moved to Los Angeles from Kansas to become an actor in Hollywood. As a child, William excelled in school and was considered a bright, popular student. Debating was one of Hickman's favorite pastimes, and he was an excellent speaker.

Perry Parker recognized William Hickman as his former coworker once he saw a picture of him. Having never interacted with Hickman, Perry couldn't understand why he would target his family in such a horrific manner.

Within a week of Marion's abduction, LAPD officers received reports that Hickman was driving a stolen vehicle in Oregon. Hickman paid for gas in Washington with one of the gold certificates he received in the ransom exchange. Its serial number corresponded to the one Perry Parker gave Marion's kidnapper.

In Oregon, police officers spotted the stolen vehicle and pulled it over. They discovered two passengers in the car with Hickman. When they searched inside, they found a sawed-off shotgun, a pistol, and the ransom money. The passengers claimed they were only hitchhikers with no connection to the murder. Hickman was arrested and extradited back to California.

Hickman readily confessed to the kidnapping and killing of Marion Parker, and soon after, a grand jury in Los Angeles indicted him for murder. According to Hickman, he robbed people because he wanted money to return to college, but he decided he needed larger amounts, and kidnapping was the only way to accomplish that.

Hickman said he chose Marion because Perry always brought her into the bank with him. He figured an older child would be easier to take than a baby. Hickman had Parker's address from his time working at the bank, and he staked out the residence. After he picked Marion up from school, Hickman rode around with Marion. He took her to the movies and watched "Figures Don't Lie." He and Marion continued driving around after the film, and William said he would periodically stop and send telegrams.

When they went to his apartment, Hickman said he restrained Marion with bandages so she couldn't escape, but sometimes, she was free to roam around. Due to the press attention given to Marion's kidnapping, William became nervous once the kidnapping made headlines. He was upset and felt that his plan wasn't working. He felt he had to kill Marion to get his money and escape the crime. She was dead before the last telegram was sent to Perry.

According to Hickman, he strangled the 12-year-old with a towel until she was unconscious, even though the autopsy report said there was no evidence of strangulation. When she was knocked out, he carried her to the bathtub, where he dismembered her. He said Marion didn't wake up when he began cutting her, but blood squirted from her body, indicating her heart was beating when he started the dismemberment.

Newspapers debated whether Hickman's love of films inspired him to commit such a depraved crime. The public demanded his execution.

William Hickman's trial began in January 1928, and a jury found him guilty one month later. He was sentenced to hang and awaited his execution in San Quentin Prison.

OCTOBER 29TH, 1928

William Hickman climbed the creaky, white steps of the gallows in San Quentin and fainted as the executioner put the black hood over his head. The rope placed around his neck was too loose and didn't snap William's neck when the floor opened beneath him. William fell and suffocated for 14 minutes before the doctor declared him dead.

THE PARKER FAMILY

The Parker family encouraged forgiveness and asked the public to forgive Mary Holt and others at the school for allowing Marion to go with a stranger.

Marion Parker was laid to rest in Forest Lawn Memorial Park in Glendale, California.

Marion's sister Marjorie Parker Holmes lived her adult life in San Diego, California, and died in 1987.

DEATH DECIDED

"He had planned this for a long time. I don't think he was going to let her suffer. He always said he would see to it. She would never know when. He had spiritual beliefs, and he wanted to go on that journey with her."

MARY-ANN, SISTER OF RICHARD HORNE, TO *THE SCOTSMAN* NEWSPAPER 2007

The passing of legendary political cartoonist and children's author Richard Horne, also known as Harry Horse, shocked the UK public in 2007.

Horne was a skilled artist and a beloved figure in Edinburgh, Scotland. However, his final years were marred by immense stress and heartache as he struggled with the debilitating illness of his wife. What was initially reported as a tragic suicide pact was later uncovered to be a horrific murder-suicide.

Richard George Anthony Horne was born on May 9th, 1960, in Coventry, UK. He grew up surrounded by the stunning natural beauty of Brandon, a village outside the city. His vivid imagination was shaped by the stories his mother told him and his siblings. Those details from his childhood would later come to life in his work as a children's author, illustrator, and political cartoonist. At Bilton Grange Preparatory School, Horne got the idea for his pseudonym, "Harry Horse," after a schoolmaster made a mistake with his surname.

While at Wrekin College, he discovered his love for cricket and art. But it wasn't until he took a job as a notetaker in a lawyer's office that he realized he didn't want to spend his life behind a desk taking notes. Horne packed his bags and boarded a train to Edinburgh to pursue his passion for art.

LIFE IN SCOTLAND

Despite his lack of formal art education, Horne's raw talent as an illustrator was undeniable. Undeterred by his setbacks, he would go to great lengths to hone his skills, even sneaking into art lectures at the University of Edinburgh. Despite repeated rejections, Horne refused to give up on his dreams. With quick thinking and resourcefulness, he convinced the owner of Canongate, an independent book publisher, to give him a chance by posing as an agent calling about a fantastic illustrator named "Richard Horne." The bold move paid off and Horne eventually found himself working for Canongate in 1981. Over the years, he left his mark on the publishing world with his iconic illustrations for famous titles such as Dr. Jekyll and Mr. Hyde.

The newlyweds moved into a tiny apartment in Edinburgh, where they lived with their dog Roo. The pet became one of the main characters of Horne's books. Horne continued to work as a freelancer, but financial difficulties forced them to relocate to a cottage in Warwickshire owned by his parents.

In the late 1980s, Horne's artistic pursuits took a musical turn as he joined the eclectic band Swamptrash. The band's fusion of punk, bluegrass, and psychobilly earned them a dedicated following and the chance to tour in the Shetlands, where Horne would meet his future wife, Mandy Williamson. The couple's love story bloomed, leading to their marriage in 1990.

They started their lives together in a tiny apartment in Edinburgh, but the newlyweds faced financial struggles while Horne worked as a freelance illustrator. They eventually moved to a less expensive cottage in Warwickshire, near Horne's parents. The couple tried unsuccessfully to conceive a child during this time period.

Horne used his dog Roo as a frequent subject of his illustrations, and Roo would eventually play a starring role in his books.

The couple stabilized their finances and returned to Edinburgh in 2001, and everything seemed fine until Many started feeling unwell. She was diagnosed with an aggressive form of multiple sclerosis in 2004, and the news turned their lives upside down. Knowing Mandy's nervous system was deteriorating quickly, the couple moved back to the Shetlands so that she could be closer to her parents.

Mandy's mother and father did everything they could to help, but the disease's progression couldn't be stopped. The young woman lost her ability to walk and required a wheelchair to get around. Soon after, she started losing her ability to speak.

The changes in Mandy's health and the stress of caring for his wife unlocked a dark side of Horne. He would get enraged quickly, and it terrified everyone around the couple.

Horne even got into a fight with Mandy's social worker. They denied Mandy the right to disability benefits, which made Horne mad. Instead of discussing different options with the social worker, Horne punched a hole in the wall of their home which scared Mandy and the social worker.

THE SUICIDE PACT

On January 9, 2007, two of Mandy's friends from New

Zealand came to see the couple at their house. They spent the evening talking to Mandy and comforting their friend, but they noticed Horne was acting strange. He was pacing around the house and even said, "It's a wonderful night for a killing." When her friends decided to leave, Mandy motioned that she didn't want them to go and managed to ask them to stay.

The friends had to go but returned in the morning to pick up a jacket they had forgotten. They discovered Horne and his wife, Mandy, on the bed. They both had died during the night. Richard was 46 and his wife Mandy was 39.

Rumors started circulating that the illustrator and his terminally ill wife had made a suicide pact and committed suicide by overdosing on painkillers. While the public was sympathetic to the couple's plight, the truth of what really happened to Richard and Mandy was hidden by law enforcement.

A GRUESOME MURDER

Months had gone by, and the details regarding the death of the famous illustrator and his wife started to emerge.

Mandy's parents, Grace and George Williamson, were silent for months and unable or unwilling to speak publicly about the death of their daughter.

A journalist named Peter Gillman started researching the story, thinking he would write a romantic piece about eternal love. Instead, he discovered a horrifying murder-suicide.

When interviewed, Mandy's friends from New Zealand, who found the bodies, said the walls of the house were covered in blood when they arrived. They were surprised that the initial story was that of a suicide pact and drug overdose. Later reports revealed that the forensic team spent days inside the Horne home, collecting evidence.

The pathologist released a report which said that Mandy was stabbed more than 30 times. It was clear Horne attacked her in a frenzy because a knife broke during the attack, and he grabbed another one to continue stabbing his wife. There were clear signs of defensive wounds on Mandy's arms, suggesting this wasn't a suicide pact but a senseless murder.

None of the stab wounds killed Mandy. Instead, she bled to death over a period of hours.

Horne then moved on to kill the couple's chihuahua and cat before stabbing himself 47 times. Again, none of the wounds were fatal, and Horne bled to death. Horne had shallow cuts on his arms, and he mutilated his genitals.

ONCE THE TRUTH WAS OUT

Those who knew the couple confirmed that Horne wasn't acting like himself in the months leading up to the murder-suicide. Watching Mandy deteriorate had had a profound effect on Horne's mental health.

Horne's mother, Jo, didn't have anything nice to say about Mandy, which was unnecessary considering the situation. She went public with claims that the Williamson family was strange and rude. Jo criticized Mandy for always being negative and unsupportive of Horne's hobbies, namely his love of cricket. She claimed Mandy hated washing Horne's dirty clothes, which was unacceptable to his mother.

Jo mentioned her son's drug use and, again, blamed it on Mandy. According to her, the couple was taking ecstasy to help Mandy with her multiple sclerosis symptoms. The rest of the Horne family adored Mandy and disagreed with Jo's public statements.

The media criticized the work of the Northern Constabulary and accused them of covering up a crime. Some even urged the police to reopen the case because they couldn't believe a single man could stab himself 47 times, suggesting there was a third person involved in the attacks. But the police never suspected anyone else besides Richard Horne.

George Williamson, Mandy's father, said his daughter wasn't thinking about suicide no matter how difficult her MS symptoms got. He said Mandy had made plans with her mother to go for a dentist appointment on January 10, 2007, the day the bodies were found.

Horne's sisters said in an interview with *The Scotsman* newspaper said their brother had distanced himself from the family over the years of his wife's illness. One by one, he cut his own family out of his life which his sisters believe he did to maintain his resolve to end his life and Mandy's at the same time. They also believe Mandy agreed to the suicide pact but didn't want to know when it would happen.

Kay, Horne's sister, told *The Scotsman* her last visit with her brother ended with him saying, "My beautiful wife is dying, and there is nothing I can do about it, and I'm in hell."

We might never know what happened to Horne in the days before the murder-suicide. He was likely depressed for quite a while and was experiencing a mental breakdown due to the stress of his wife's condition in combination with his drug use.

Online communities that focus on mysterious deaths continue to theorize there was a third person involved in the deaths of Richard and Mandy Horne. But the investigators are adamant Richard Horne murdered his sick wife in a fit of rage.

The couple was buried in the same grave on the Isle of Burra with Richard being lowered into the grave first. Together in life and in death.

SWEDISH SHOCKER

"Sometimes he said sick things that I just pushed away. He talked about causing children harm so that someone would know how bad he felt, how tough he had had it."

WORK COLLEAGUE

TWO SEPARATE MURDERS committed months apart involved a young child and an adult sex worker. They were unrelated in every way except for dog hair and plastic bags. For nearly two decades, the police tried to find the guilty party and were even taunted by a letter and a phone call from the killer confessing to the crime.

THE ABDUCTION

Helén Nilsson was ten years old in 1989 and lived with her parents and two older siblings in Hörby, Sweden. On March 20th, 1989, Helén made plans to meet with two friends in front of a grocery store at 7 pm. She asked her parents if she could go out, and they said yes. When Helén arrived, the girls weren't there yet, so she took a quick walk. Two other friends noticed her and said she better hurry to the grocery store because the girls were waiting for her. They watched Helén walk away and after that she disappeared.

She was supposed to be back home at 8 pm, but her parents thought she was probably playing with her friends and not paying attention to the time. A few minutes later the two girls Helén was supposed to meet dropped by to ask if she was at the house. Realizing something could've happened to Helén, her parents went searching for her.

The family covered the usual route to the grocery store and checked her favorite places in the neighborhood. By 10 pm, the Nilsson family knew they needed to contact law enforcement. An investigation started immediately after, and the police asked the public for help. People who were near the grocery store at the time of the disappearance said they saw a man in his twenties in the area. While he didn't look suspicious, most of them remembered him.

The best witness the police found was someone who knew Helén. A neighbor saw the girl walk past her window right after 7 pm. According to the woman, she saw a man with a dog walking right behind Helén. After several minutes, she heard a scream. The police struggled to find the exact place of the abduction. They weren't sure if she had disappeared from the parking lot in front of the store or if someone had grabbed Helén while she was walking home.

THE DISCOVERY OF HELÉN'S BODY

On March 26, less than a week after Helén's disappearance, a mother and daughter were picking mushrooms in the woods near Hörby. They saw a black plastic bag with brown tape around it. The woman called her husband to come and take a look at it because there was a smell, and she was scared of what might be inside. Her husband cut a small hole in the bag and saw a human leg. They called the police right away.

The body was identified as Helén Nilsson. The autopsy confirmed the girl was murdered on March 25th, so she had been held captive for five days. She had been sexually assaulted, and bruises around her neck suggested her attacker tried to strangle her. However, the cause of death was trauma to the head. Whoever committed this gruesome crime hit her more than 20 times with various objects. Helén was also starved during her time in captivity.

The forensic examination discovered dog hair on the black plastic bag and human hair other than Helén's on the body itself. Foreign bodily fluids were recovered and stored, hoping they might lead to the killer one day. Months went by without any good leads regarding the murder. The police worked around the clock and even made one arrest. A man living close to the Nilsson family was a prime suspect, but he was cleared and released.

THE MURDER OF JANNICA EKBLAD

Jannica Ekblad was a 26-year-old woman who lived in the city of Malmö, less than an hour away from Hörby. She was addicted to drugs and often resorted to sex work to support her habit. But in the Summer of 1989, Jannica met a new boyfriend who motivated her to get healthy. But, she had a difficult road ahead of her because she was in debt. Eager to close that chapter of her life, Jannica decided to engage in sex work a few more times to earn the money she needed.

On August 3, 1989, Jannica confirmed a meeting with a client well-known among the sex workers in Malmö as unpredictable. Some of them avoided him, but Jannica needed the money. She told her friend where she was going and asked her to contact the police if she failed to return home. Neither Jannica nor her friend knew the man's real name.

The next day Jannica's lifeless body was discovered at a rest stop next to a road leading out of Malmö. The autopsy revealed she'd been dead for six to ten hours. Her body was cleaned postmortem, but the killer didn't wash her hair. While Jannica had a lot of bruises on her body and signs of strangulation, she died from blunt force trauma. The pathologist found 18 wounds to her skull. Jannica was sexually assaulted too.

The forensic team discovered a black plastic bag close to Jannica's body and confirmed the killer used it to cover the woman. Both the body and the bag had potential DNA traces, such as dog hair, human hair, and foreign bodily fluids. These were all collected and processed by the forensics team.

A CONNECTION BETWEEN THE MURDERS

The investigators were confused by the profiles of the victims because the age difference was unusual. However, those working on the cases made a connection quickly. Both Helén and Jannica were sexually assaulted, strangled, beaten, and killed with blows to their heads. Then there was dog hair and identical black plastic bags.

While the police had the killer's DNA, they had nothing to compare it to in 1989. And so the second biggest investigation in Sweden's history began. The biggest was the assassination of Olof Palme, the Swedish Prime Minister in 1986.

A CALL FROM THE KILLER

Law enforcement did their best to identify the killer, and he even communicated with them. In December 1989, the police received a letter from a person claiming to be the murderer. He said the killings were an act of revenge. Two years later, on April 6th, 1991, the lead investigator did a radio interview, prompting someone to call him on his private line.

The unknown caller said he murdered Jannica because he hated drug addicts and described the areas where he left the two bodies. The man also showed remorse for taking Helén's life. Unfortunately, the police could not trace the caller, and the case slowly started to get cold.

REOPENING THE CASE

By the end of the 1990s, the police stopped actively investigating the murder of Helén Nilsson. However, the evidence and witness statements were reviewed in 2002, and two arrests were made in November of that year. A man who lived in Helén's neighborhood was a known sex offender, and it was confirmed he was with his cousin on the day of the kidnapping.

During the initial interviews, the man and his cousin told completely different stories of their activities on March 20th, 1989. Eyewitnesses recognized the duo and remembered they acted strangely in the parking lot in front of the grocery store on the evening of Helén's disappearance.

The investigators found girls who were Helén's age in the 1980s and lived in the same area. Most confirmed that the two men sometimes harassed them on the street. But there was no link between them and the physical evidence collected from Helén's body, and they were eventually released.

THE DNA PROFILE

Reopening the case allowed the investigators to get the killer's DNA profile but it took two years once they started the process. A semen sample collected from Helén's body had been frozen at a laboratory in Linköping since 1989. In 2002, that sample traveled to the Forensic Science Service in Birmingham, United Kingdom. By August 2003, the Swedish police had a complete DNA profile.

The investigators working on the case reviewed all available transcripts, witness reports, and tips to assemble a list of 29 names. These were all potential suspects, and the detectives hoped to talk to each of them again. They decided they would ask for a voluntary DNA sample at the end of the interview.

The interviews began in April 2004, and the police received a DNA match on June 23rd, 2004. They arrested a man named Ulf Olsson that same evening.

ULF OLSSON

Ulf Olsson was born on December 19, 1951, in Höör, Sweden. He grew up with four siblings and both parents. Ulf's father was an alcoholic who regularly abused his children and wife. Ulf ran away from home several times before joining the Swedish Army after high school graduation.

In the late 1970s, Ulf married a young woman he met when she was only 16. The marriage didn't last long, and she asked for a divorce, claiming he assaulted her numerous times. Wanting to start fresh, Ulf found a new job. But all his female colleagues steered clear of him, thanks to his inappropriate comments and jokes about harming women and children.

By the end of 1989, Ulf was dating another woman who became pregnant and gave birth to a baby boy in 1990. Again, Ulf was verbally abusive towards her and threatened her. She eventually left him.

During one of the office parties, Ulf talked with his female colleague and bragged about going to brothels when he served in the military. He recounted paying for an 8-year-old girl and spending a night with her. The colleague was disgusted and recalled the story years later when talking to her friend, a former police officer. She was urged to contact the police and tell them about Ulf. This is how he ended up on the list of 29 potential suspects in 2002.

WHAT REALLY HAPPENED

Ulf Olsson maintained his innocence after the arrest, but the police managed to come up with likely series of events that happened in 1989. Ulf owned a remote cabin, so the investigators went there with a forensic team to search for clues. They knew Jannica Ekblad was killed indoors, and a large amount of blood was discovered underneath the floorboards of the cabin in the living room.

The investigators suspected that Ulf Olsson happened to see Helén Nilsson on her way home while walking his dog. He abducted her and took her to the cabin. After sexually assaulting her, Ulf realized he couldn't let Helén go. He first attempted to starve her by locking her in a shed and denying her food and water. Days later, Ulf tried to strangle Helén and finally killed her by beating her with a pipe.

The phone calls Ulf made to the police confirmed the motive behind the murder of Jannica Ekblad. Ulf did hate drugs – he even forbade his girlfriend to smoke cigarettes. He picked Jannica up, and the two went to his cabin. There, Jannica started talking about drugs, which enraged Ulf, who then hit her multiple times with a blunt object.

~

Ulf Olsson continued to claim that his DNA was planted by the police, who were trying to pin the two murders on him. He rarely spoke when questioned in court, saying he had no idea how or why the girls were killed.

Judge Jan Alvå said to Olsson in court, "If it is you who did this, I ask you to tell the court. Whoever did this cannot expect to be forgiven, nor can he demand to be understood. One can perhaps attain a certain sympathy but it requires courage to talk about such a thing."

Ulf continued to maintain his innocence throughout the proceedings. Lund District Court found him guilty and sentenced him to life in prison.

In July 2005, the Court of Appeal in Malmö sent Ulf to a secure mental institution because the defense managed to prove he needed psychiatric care.

At the time, there was much speculation in the media about why Ulf murdered the girls. After a more in-depth look at his childhood, the consensus was that he took revenge on his victims to get back at his parents for their abuse. His mother claimed his father would beat him so severely that she decided to take over the beatings to protect Ulf because she knew when to stop. Ulf developed a strange and hateful dependency on his mother because of this dysfunction, leading to his hatred of women.

On January 10, 2010, Ulf published a final post on the personal blog he started during his time at the Sundsvall Forensic Psychiatric Center. He wrote that living was pointless because he would never be free. He never confessed to the crimes and hung himself in his cell.

SECOND DEGREE PLAYMATE

"They couldn't do any restoration on his face. They told me he was green and blue. They strongly discouraged it, so I didn't go."

JUDY EARP TO ELLE MAGAZINE
REGARDING THE DEATH OF HER
PARTNER DR. THOMAS BURCHARD

JUDY EARP'S worst fears were confirmed when she received the news that her partner of 17 years, Dr. Thomas Burchard, had been brutally murdered and left in the trunk of a car in the Las Vegas desert. She had tried multiple times to reach out to authorities to let them know something was wrong. Burchard wasn't returning her calls, and that never happened. She even gave authorities three names of people she thought could be involved in his disappearance, but it took a week before she received a confirmation of his death.

~

A body was discovered in the trunk of a Mercedes on a dirt road east of Las Vegas. The car belonged to a well-known child psychiatrist from Salinas, California. Unfortunately, the doctor himself was identified as the body.

Thomas Burchard was born in Boston, Massachusetts on February 16, 1948. His father taught architecture at Harvard University at that time. The Burchard family then moved to Virginia because Thomas' father became the dean of Virginia Tech's College of Architecture. Thomas studied medicine and decided to become a child psychiatrist.

After working at Cincinnati Children's Hospital and Massachusetts General, Dr. Burchard moved to California and spent some time at UCLA. He was employed by the Community Hospital of the Monterey Peninsula and stayed there for 40 years. Dr. Burchard was loved by his young patients because he was caring and truly wanted to help people in need.

Dr. Burchard was divorced by the 2000s when he met his future girlfriend, Judy Earp. The two were on a group trip to Las Vegas with mutual friends and had a lot of free time because neither one drank alcohol or liked to gamble. Judy was also married before and was 12 years younger than the doctor. She had four children from the previous marriage.

Judy moved from Orange County to Salinas and began living with Dr. Burchard. Her three children, who still went to school, became a part of the Burchard family. The doctor officially retired in the 2010s. However, he continued working a few days week because he wished to be there for his long-time patients.

MEETING KELSEY TURNER

Even though he had a long-time girlfriend, Dr. Burchard liked to talk to women online. His first wife filed for divorce in 2001 because she suspected he was cheating. But Judy was different and more understanding. She knew Dr. Burchard wasn't planning on meeting these women even though he sent them money. She said he was just trying to help because many of them struggled financially.

Chatting with women online boosted Dr. Burchard's confidence, and he also received explicit photos. But again, Judy wasn't jealous. Then in 2017, Dr. Burchard met Kelsey Turner, a mother of two and a lingerie model who was down on her luck.

Kelsey Nichole Turner was born on May 5th, 1993, in Norfolk, Virginia, to parents Samantha and Christopher. The couple divorced when Turner was just a girl, and she moved with her mother to Jonesboro, Arkansas. As a teen, Turner was striking because of her natural beauty. Encouraged by the attention she was getting, she started her modeling career.

She was booking lingerie and swimsuit photoshoots and appeared on the cover of Maxim and Playboy Italia in her early twenties. Even though these were major publications, Turner failed to make an impact. By 2017, she was a single mother of two sons and still lived with her mother, Samantha.

Turner didn't want to leave California because she still hoped to launch her modeling career. But rent was expensive, so she made money by selling online photos. She was barely paying the bills when she met Dr. Burchard. After learning about Turner's life, the doctor wanted to help her get back on her feet.

THE RELATIONSHIP BETWEEN TURNER AND DR. BURCHARD

According to his girlfriend Judy, she was informed about Turner and Dr. Burchard's plan to help her financially. In the fall of 2017, he paid rent for a house in Salinas for a year, and Turner moved in with her mother and two sons. The doctor also provided her with money and bought her various things, hoping she would start working soon. It was later discovered that he gave her more than $300,000.

But one year later, Turner was still using the doctor as her prime source of income. That's when Dr. Burchard decided to stop supporting her financially. She was evicted, but the doctor felt terrible because of the whole situation. After talking to Turner, the two decided she should relocate to Las Vegas and try to launch her modeling career there.

Dr. Burchard helped her find a house in Las Vegas, and she moved to a four-bedroom house in the suburbs. Turner also lost custody of one of her boys in 2018. She searched for roommates because her house was enormous. Plus, the doctor was paying for it, and she could make some money along the way.

Diana Pena and Jeremy Escherich moved in, and things were going great. The trio was throwing parties at the house and had fun. In early 2019, Turner met her future boyfriend, Jon Kennison. Dr. Burchard had no idea what was happening in Las Vegas, even though he kept in touch with Turner. She knew how to manipulate the doctor, and he continued sending her money.

But in February 2019, he was determined to cut her off again. Turner did everything to keep the cash flowing. She invited Dr. Burchard to Las Vegas on March 1st, 2019, and he went to check on her.

His girlfriend Judy later said he was determined to end the financial support. He'd paid the rent until June, and Kelsey would need to find work and pay her bills after that.

Judy also said that Burchard was starting to show signs of early dementia. He occasionally would lose his way in a parking lot and didn't always recognize people he knew, including one of her daughters.

MISSING IN LAS VEGAS

Dr. Burchard didn't tell his girlfriend Judy about his trip, but he called her when the plane landed in Las Vegas. She was informed that he would be staying at Turner's place.

One day later, Dr. Burchard stopped responding to Judy's calls and messages. She knew something was wrong because the two of them talked daily. Judy contacted the

Las Vegas Metropolitan Police on March 3rd, but they didn't take her seriously. After all, Dr. Burchard was in Las Vegas and might not be answering his phone on purpose.

But on March 5th, the police agreed to do a welfare check. Judy gave them Turner's address, and a patrol found the house empty. No one was answering the door, but officers noticed that the windows were open and the front door was unlocked. They could see a lot of cleaning products inside the house.

Sensing that Judy might be right, detectives called her back to ask more questions about Dr. Burchard. Judy said she received some odd messages on March 4th from Burchard's number. The two had been together for so long that she knew someone else was using his phone. The person posing as the doctor was asking about her financial information. Judy found it strange because Dr. Burchard knew her bank account information by heart.

On March 7th, 2019, the police were contacted by a man driving toward Lake Mead, east of Las Vegas. He reported seeing an abandoned blue Mercedes with a shattered window on a dirt road. Officers went out to check the vehicle and discovered a body in the trunk. They found Dr. Thomas Burchard.

He was badly beaten with a blunt object. The forensic unit processed the Mercedes and found a bloody baseball bat beside the doctor, as well as his jacket and house keys. The investigators found fingerprints in the car and sent them for testing alongside several DNA swabs discovered on the back seat.

The registration was checked, and the investigators knew the owner of the blue Mercedes was Dr. Burchard. But they found a contract that said the car was sub-leased to Kelsey Turner in November 2018. Since they knew Dr. Burchard was staying with Turner, the police obtained a search warrant for her house.

COLLECTING THE EVIDENCE

There were visible signs of a struggle inside the house. The police immediately noticed a bedroom door that was broken in half. Even though it was clear that someone had attempted to clean up the bedroom and living room, the investigators still found traces of blood on the floor and blood spatter inside the bedroom with the broken door.

The detectives then received the results of the DNA swabs from the abandoned vehicle and confirmed that the blood on the back seat belonged to Dr. Burchard. The fingerprints on the steering wheel belonged to Turner. There were two sets of unidentified fingerprints inside the Mercedes too.

Meanwhile, the coroner was working on Dr. Burchard's autopsy. It was confirmed he died of blunt-force trauma to the head. Defensive wounds on his hands were present. The doctor was bludgeoned to death, and his face caved in by his murderer.

The police were sure Turner was the killer, but they couldn't locate her or her roommates. Suspecting she might run to California, the Las Vegas police contacted the FBI, and she was found hiding in her friend's house in

Stockton, California, on March 21, 2019. Kelsey Turner was sent back to Nevada a couple of days later.

The fingerprints and the DNA from the blue Mercedes identified two other people who might be involved in the murder of Dr. Burchard. The police issued two arrest warrants for Diana Pena and Jon Kennison. Pena, a 31-year-old bartender and Turner's roommate turned herself in, and it was determined she was an accomplice. Kennison, Turner's 27-year-old boyfriend, was arrested in April and refused to cooperate with the police.

Pena, on the other hand, was willing to accept a plea deal for a reduced sentence. She agreed to testify against Turner in court and tell the investigators what exactly happened to Dr. Thomas Burchard in Las Vegas.

PENA'S TESTIMONY

Diana Pena appeared in court in June 2019, and her testimony was crucial for the prosecution because it confirmed to the judge that they had a solid case. According to Pena, she was working a night shift on March 1, 2019. She was back home at 1 am, and the doctor was at the house. He was shocked to see that Turner had two roommates but went along with it.

Jeremy Escherich, Turner's second roommate, arrived at the house with his girlfriend. The girlfriend started flirting with Dr. Burchard, and Turner didn't like that. Turner screamed at Escherich and his girlfriend and accused them of trying to take Dr. Burchard from her.

The following day, Turner used Dr. Burchard's phone to check the GPS and saw nude photos on his phone of another woman. She got upset again, this time with Burchard. Dr. Burchard had had enough and slammed the door to his bedroom in her face.

Kennison, Turner's boyfriend, saw this and got mad. He kicked down the door, grabbed a baseball bat, and started hitting Dr. Burchard. According to Pena, Turner was encouraging the attack. The doctor was badly injured, with a large bruise on the side of his head, but he was still alive and begging them to drive him to the hospital.

After a while, Turner agreed to take him to the emergency room if he said he was mugged. The doctor agreed and went inside Turner's Mercedes. However, she changed her mind and suggested they clean the house first because of all the blood.

Pena went to her bedroom upstairs but could hear loud noises from the ground floor. Once she came back down to see what was going on, Kennison exited the garage covered in blood. It was clear that he had just murdered Dr. Burchard.

Kennison waited for the morning to drive the blue Mercedes with the body to a remote location. He used Turner's phone for navigation, and it was later confirmed that it connected to a tower near Lake Mead.

Turner was in charge of removing the evidence from the house. She turned off Dr. Burchard's phone and called a cleaning service. According to them, Turner said they had a party last night and that someone had spilled a lot of wine.

She then drove her son to stay with a friend and rented a hotel room for Pena, Kennison, and herself to hide in.

Diana Pena was arrested first and agreed to a plea deal in return for building a case against Turner and Kennison. Turner and Kennison fled Nevada and went to Stockton, California where they were arrested by the FBI.

SENTENCING

Kennison and Turner pleaded not guilty to second-degree murder and conspiracy to commit murder. Their trial was scheduled for September 2020. It was delayed because of the COVID-19 pandemic. Then Kennison had second thoughts and changed his plea to guilty in July 2022. He was sentenced to 18 to 45 years behind bars.

On November 11th, 2022, Turner entered an Alford plea. She admitted that there was enough evidence to prove that she committed a crime but maintained her innocence. She would be eligible for parole in 10 years. On January 2023, Kelsey Turner was sentenced to 10 to 25 years in prison.

Judy Earp chooses to remember her partner as a generous, giving man. She told Elle Magazine in 2019,

"He was extremely generous. If he saw somebody in need, he would literally give them the shirt off his back. Which, in the end, you know, that's...."

GRAVE DECISIONS

"The Burke and Hare story has it all: murder, greed, exploitation, and a quest for scientific knowledge."

RUTH RICHARDSON, *DEATH, DISSECTION AND THE DESTITUTE,* 1987

In the early 19th century, Edinburgh, Scotland, was the center of anatomical science studies. Experts worldwide who wanted to learn more about human anatomy came to the city and stayed there. While anatomical studies were incredibly interesting to professors and students, they faced one major challenge: having fresh human corpses at their disposal.

The law in Scotland allowed the University of Edinburgh

to use the bodies of executed prisoners, people who committed suicide, and unclaimed corpses. However, everything changed in 1823 when the government passed an act that reduced the number of death penalties. With fewer cadavers available, the anatomists were willing to bend the rules and accept bodies from other sources.

It created a brand new trend in criminal circles —grave robbing. Corpses were sold for profit, and body snatchers could earn up to £10 per cadaver, a small treasure for that time period. As years passed, grave robbing became increasingly difficult, with people placing cages on graves to prevent a grave robber from reaching a casket.

Two Irish immigrants who weren't graverobbers quickly found a more sinister way to deliver corpses to the University of Edinburgh and earn money. The bodies they delivered were fresh and never made it into the ground.

WILLIAM BURKE

William Burke was born in 1792 in Urney, Ireland, and grew up in a loving family alongside his brother Constantine. The two boys even joined the British Army together as teens.

Burke left the Donegal militia after marrying his first wife. The couple separated in 1818 after Burke had an argument with his father-in-law. He moved to Scotland and became a laborer. Burke lived in Maddiston, where he met Helen McDougal, his second wife.

McDougal and Burke relocated to Edinburgh in November 1827, and he started working as a cobbler. McDougal enjoyed finding and selling second-hand clothes. According to his friends and clients, Burke was a cheerful man who would often sing while working.

WILLIAM HARE

William Hare's background is still a mystery, but it is known he was either born in Armagh or Newry, Northern Ireland, sometime between 1792 and 1804. He arrived in Edinburgh in the mid-1820s and rented a room from Logue and Margaret Laird. Logue passed away in 1826, and Hare started a relationship with Margaret.

Hare and Burke met in 1827 in Penicuik while harvesting the crops in the area. Burke was there with McDougal, and all three became friends. Once they were back in Edinburgh, Hare invited the couple to live at his Tanner's Close lodging house.

DEATH OF A LODGER

On November 29, 1827, a man named Donald, who rented a room in Hare's lodging house, passed away before paying £4 for rent. Hare complained to his friend Burke, and the two men figured out they could reduce the financial loss by selling Donald's body to one of the anatomists at the University of Edinburgh.

The local parish paid for a coffin, and a carpenter delivered it to Tanner's Close lodging house. Burke and Hare removed Donald's body from the coffin, hid him under the bed, and filled the casket with wood. The two men waited for nightfall to take Donald's corpse to the university and into Surgeon's Square, where they asked a student for the famous anatomist Alexander Monroe. The student gave them directions to Robert Knox, a different anatomist.

Knox paid them £7 for the cadaver and didn't ask too many questions. After all, he had two classes a day and needed human bodies. As Burke and Hare left the Surgeon's Square, Knox's assistant said that the anatomist would be happy to pay for more corpses in the future. It gave the men a horrible idea, and the killing spree began.

THE MURDERS

The exact details of the murders that followed the natural death of Hare's tenant are unknown because of the different stories told by those involved. Burke and Hare admitted they brainstormed the idea to start killing people and selling the corpses as soon as they returned home from the Surgeon's Square.

In January 1828, Hare complained about a lodger named Joseph, who was constantly sick and couldn't care for himself. Hare was turning away potential tenants and losing money.

JOSEPH THE LODGER

Burke and Hare agreed they should murder Joseph for their financial gain. Aware that Joseph was an alcoholic, the two gave him a bottle of whiskey and got him drunk. The man started losing balance, and once he was on the ground, Burke lay on top of him, preventing Joseph from taking deep breaths. Meanwhile, Hare suffocated him with a pillow.

Their go-to man was Knox, who was sure the man dropped dead without any foul play. After all, there were no marks or wounds on the body which would suggest otherwise. By the time Knox paid the men £10 for Joseph's body, Burke and Hare were already planning their next murder.

UNKNOWN ENGLISHMAN

This time it was an unnamed Englishman from Cheshire who stayed at the lodging house. He worked as a traveling salesman and became ill with a cough while in Edinburgh. Hare thought he would make potential guests run away from the lodging house with his coughing, so he suggested they could repeat what they had done to Joseph, and the other man agreed. Burke stopped him from making noise and breathing by using his body weight, and Hare suffocated the salesman with a pillow.

ABAGAIL SIMPSON

The next victim was Abigail Simpson from Gilmerton, a village near Edinburgh. She often traveled to the city to sell salt for some extra income. On February 12, 1828, she was invited to the lodge house, where she got drunk with Burke and Hare. Simpson was suffocated, placed in a large wooden box, and transported to the Surgeon's Square alongside the unnamed English salesman. Not asking any questions, Knox gave £10 for each corpse.

UNNAMED SCOTTISH WOMAN

The same month, Margaret Hare lured an older woman to the lodge house and served her a lot of alcohol. She passed out soon after. When her husband returned home, Margaret told him about the woman, and he covered her face with a heavy mattress cover. Unable to breathe, the woman died a couple of hours later. Burke and Hare got £10 for her body too.

MARY PATERSON

In April 1828, Burke was at a tavern and struck up a conversation with Mary Paterson and Janet Brown. He bought them alcohol, and the group continued to chat. After some time, Burke suggested they should all go to the lodging house to grab something to eat. Instead, they arrived at Constantine Burke's house with two bottles of whisky. Constantine headed to work and left the group to drink in the living room.

Mary Paterson passed out while sitting at the table, and Burke and Brown continued to talk. McDougal, Burke's wife, burst into the room, accusing her husband of cheating. The two had a very loud fight in front of Brown. Shocked and worried McDougal might attack her, Brown said she had no idea Burke was a married man and left the apartment.

Paterson slept through the fight, and McDougal left to get the Hares. The men then suffocated Paterson and brought her corpse to Knox, who paid £8 this time. Burke claimed that the girl died from alcohol poisoning. Knox was thrilled with Paterson's corpse and kept her preserved in whiskey for three months.

Meanwhile, McDougal took Paterson's clothes and kept them for herself. Janet Brown came looking for her friend two days later, but Burke told her Paterson was probably in Glasgow now with a traveling salesman she had met.

MRS. HALDANE

The next victim was Mrs. Haldane, who often stayed at the lodging house. Again, the woman drank too much alcohol, fell asleep, and was suffocated by the duo. Her daughter came to the lodging house several weeks later, and Burke offered her a drink. The two got drunk together, and he suffocated her without Hare's help.

EFFY

Their next victim was a woman named Effy, an acquaintance of Burke, who sometimes sold him supplies when he worked as a cobbler. Burke himself invited the woman to the stable, promising her alcohol. Once inside, she got drunk, and the two men suffocated her. Burke brought yet another woman to the lodging house, but this time there was no need to offer her alcohol – she was already too drunk to stand on her own. She was killed by Burke and Hare soon after.

OLDER WOMAN AND BOY

In June, the duo killed two more people —an older woman and her grandson. According to Burke, the murder of the young boy stayed in his memory and continued to haunt him. At the end of that month, Burke and McDougal left for Falkirk. Meanwhile, Hare remained in Edinburgh and was short on money. Hare sold the body to Knox without informing Burke, which enraged the other man. Burke and McDougal moved out of the lodging house.

UNKNOWN WOMAN AND MCDOUGAL'S COUSIN

Then in September, the two made up and killed another woman the same night. Two weeks later, they targeted McDougal's cousin Ann, who came to Edinburgh from Falkirk. Thinking McDougal might go to the police and report them to the authorities, Hare's wife Margaret suggested they get rid of her, but Burke wouldn't even consider it.

JAMES WILSON

At the beginning of October 1828, Burke and Hare noticed a young man named James Wilson. He was homeless, and many residents of Edinburgh had seen him begging on the streets. Most people helped him as much as they could. But instead of giving him some change, Hare invited him to the lodging house. Burke arrived minutes later, and the duo tried to get Wilson drunk. Since he didn't like alcohol, Wilson kept his drinking to a minimum. Burke and Hare attacked him, but he didn't go down easily. In the end, they suffocated the poor man.

Wilson's body was delivered to Knox the following day, and the anatomy students recognized him. Knox denied it was Wilson, but a few days later, everyone in Edinburgh knew that the young man had disappeared. Before the police could do anything, Knox used the corpse in a class.

MARGARET DOCHERTY

October 31, 1928 marked the end of the killings. Burke befriended a woman from Ireland named Margaret Docherty by saying they were related. She believed him and agreed to come to the Broggan lodging house where Burke was staying at that time. Burke asked Ann and James Gray, a couple living with them, to spend the night at

Tanner's Close lodging house, because Docherty was family.

As they drank whiskey, McDougal went to get Hare. The group was tipsy at around 9 pm when the Gray family dropped by to collect some extra clothes. Burke and Hare killed Margaret and hid her body under a pile of straw.

THE DISCOVERY OF THE CRIME

On November 1, 1828, the Gray family returned to the Broggan lodging house. Ann noticed that Burke was acting weird and didn't allow her to approach the straw near the bed. It bothered her, so when Burke went out, Ann dug into the straw and found Margaret Docherty's body. Without hesitation, the Grays went to the police.

Since McDougal saw the Grays on their way to the station, Burke and Hare took the body straight to Knox. The police officers who searched the Broggan lodging house didn't find the corpse but did locate Margaret's clothes, which had blood all over them. Burke and McDougal claimed Margaret left but couldn't provide the exact time. They were both taken into custody.

James Gray accompanied the police during the visit to Knox's classroom on November 2 and confirmed that the body delivered by Burke and Hare the previous day was indeed the woman he saw drinking with them. Soon after, William Hare and his wife were arrested too.

A surgeon and two forensic specialists were brought in to examine Margaret Docherty's body, and all three concluded that she was suffocated. However, they were unable to provide the police with concrete evidence. Law enforcement didn't hesitate and charged all four of them with murder. Robert Christison, one of the forensic specialists, talked to Knox, who was adamant Burke and Hare purchased the bodies from lodging houses around Edinburgh and then sold them to him.

Considering the nature of the crime, the police were sure more victims were connected to Burke and Hare. It caused a frenzy among the citizens of Edinburgh, and the pair were blamed for almost every disappearance in 1828. But some missing people could be connected to the killers.

A rhyme circulating around Edinburgh at the time:

"Up the close and doon the stair,
But and ben' wi' Burke and Hare.
Burke's the butcher, Hare's the thief,
Knox the boy that buys the beef."

Janet Brown went to the police station to identify clothes that belonged to her missing friend, Mary Paterson. A baker also saw Burke's nephew wearing James Wilson's trousers.

That was enough to secure two more murder charges. But none of the four suspects was talking, so Hare was offered immunity in exchange for information about the murders.

Knowing this was the only way to avoid the death penalty, Hare began to talk.

On December 4, Burke and McDougal were charged with the murders of Margaret Docherty, Mary Paterson, and James Wilson.

While he didn't commit any crimes, Knox became the talk of the town. His reputation and career were severely damaged by his association with the killers. The public was sure he was partially guilty of the crimes because the anatomist didn't question why the two men delivered so many bodies.

He was widely criticized for his involvement in the scandal and faced a backlash from the public and his colleagues. He was ostracized by many in the medical community and his reputation never fully recovered.

The trial began on December 24, 1828, in Edinburgh's Parliament House. A crowd of curious citizens gathered in front of the courtroom, trying to get inside. But all the seats had been filled out right after 9 am. Burke and McDougal were tried together for three murders, and the defense lawyers asked the judge to separate the charges.

The prosecution decided to proceed with the murder of Margaret Docherty because they had examined her body and the eyewitnesses placed her in Burke's and McDougal's company on the day of the murder. Both McDougal and Burke pleaded not guilty.

Hare and his wife Margaret were among the first witnesses who appeared on the stand. But some, such as Knox, avoided testifying in court. But that didn't stop his assistant from confirming that Burke and Hare brought more than three corpses to the doctor. It was later determined the duo killed sixteen people. The defense didn't call any witnesses to the stand.

The trial lasted the whole night, with the prosecution and defense giving their final statements at 3 am and 5 am, respectively. The jury began the deliberation at 8:30 am on December 25th. They returned to the courtroom less than one hour later. William Burke was found guilty of the murder of Margaret Docherty. He received a death sentence. The charges against McDougal couldn't be proven in court.

THE EXECUTION OF WILLIAM BURKE

On January 3, 1829, Burke talked to law enforcement again and completely changed his story. This time he blamed all sixteen murders on William Hare. The execution was a large event. Those with windows overlooking the scaffold sold spots to watch the execution for 5-20 shillings each.

On January 28, 1829, Burke was hanged in front of 25,000 viewers, one of those being Sir Walter Scott, who said later in his book, *Letters on Demonology and Witchcraft*, 1830, "It is a strange fact that Burke, who could not write his name, and Hare, who was equally illiterate, should have left behind them a name infamous throughout the world."

His body was taken to Professor Monro's anatomy theatre and was scheduled for dissection on February 1, as ordered by the judge during the sentencing. A crowd of people showed up at the Old College demanding to see the dissection. The police were called to calm down the situation.

Professor Monro publicly dissected Burke's body at the Anatomy Theatre located in the Old College building. The procedure lasted for two hours, during which Monro dipped a quill into Burke's blood and wrote the sentence, "This is written with the blood of Wm Burke, who was hanged at Edinburgh. This blood was taken from his head."

Burke's skeleton was given to the Anatomical Museum, where it remains on display today. In addition to the skeleton, visitors can also see Burke's death mask and a book that is bound with his skin at the Surgeons' Hall Museum.

Burke's death mask can be seen in the Surgeons' Hall Museum.

McDougal went home at the end of the trial but was attacked by a group of angry citizens on December 26. She was taken to a police station for protection, but the mob gathered at the front door, not allowing her to exit. She escaped through a window and left Edinburgh as soon as possible. What happened to her after that is unknown.

Margaret Hare was released from custody on January 19, and she made plans to return to Ireland. Her ship was scheduled to sail from Glasgow, but she was recognized while waiting at the docks. An angry mob attacked her, and

Margaret fled to the police station. She then boarded a ship to Belfast.

William Hare was released on February 5, 1829 and managed to get to Dumfries with the help of law enforcement. The public soon learned about his location and gathered in front of Hare's hostel. A riot began soon after, and Hare had to escape in a decoy carriage while the mob threw stones at the building. He reached England, but Hare's fate after that is still a mystery.

BROKEN GLASS

"He was charming and irritating and smart and annoying. He was a good man."

AMBER HILBERLING DISCUSSING HER HUSBAND JOSH

They were arguing, and Josh's wife Amber shoved him. He teetered, losing his balance, and he crashed through the glass window. It took three seconds for Josh to make impact with the ground after falling face-first from the 25th floor. 23-year-old Josh Hilberling died on impact.

A paramedic later said it just looked like a pile of clothes on the ground, but there was a body there. And Amber Hilberling was screaming at him, "Please fix him! He can't die!"

Joshua Hilberling, also known as Josh, was born in Tulsa, Oklahoma, on May 30th, 1988, to parents Patrick and Jeanne Hilberling. He grew up in a large family with three brothers and two sisters. A star on his high school football team, Josh was quite athletic, thanks to his height and strength. Soon after graduation, he enrolled in the United States Air Force.

JOSH AND AMBER

Amber Fields was born on October 1st, 1991, in Joplin, Missouri, and her family moved to Tulsa soon after. Her parents were divorced, and her mother, Rhonda, remarried. Her stepdad was a well-known plastic surgeon in Tulsa, and Rhonda worked as a nurse.

Just like Josh, Amber was athletic and enjoyed team sports like soccer and volleyball. She attended Wheaton High School and Jenks High School and was an excellent student.

Josh met Amber at a Halloween party in 2008. The pair started spending time together in January 2010 and quickly fell in love.

Josh was leaving for Lackland Air Force Base in San Antonio, Texas, to begin his basic training, and Amber followed him there. As soon as his training was over, he was scheduled to report to Eielson Air Force Base in Alaska, outside Fairbanks. Unfortunately, Amber couldn't live with Josh in on-base housing unless the two were married. So they tied the knot in August 2010 in Wichita Falls, Texas, and were on their way to Alaska one month later.

ALASKA AND THE RETURN TO OKLAHOMA

Winter months can be tough in Alaska. Amber struggled because she spent so much time alone. She had no friends and usually spent her days waiting for Josh to come home. Things changed when Amber found out she was pregnant.

In May 2011, Josh was honorably discharged from Air Force, and the couple decided to return to Tulsa where Amber thought she'd be more comfortable giving birth. They temporarily moved in with Amber's mother, Rhonda.

Rhonda caught Josh using drugs in the house, which made her angry. She ordered Amber and Josh to pack their things and move to an apartment in the University Club Tower, a 32-floor building. Amber's stepdad owned the unit, and his plastic surgery patients sometimes stayed there.

FIRST SIGNS OF TROUBLE

On June 6th, Josh and Amber started arguing. According to Amber, Josh promised to go with her to her father's wedding but then made different plans. He wanted to go to a concert in Tennessee with his friends instead. Amber thought he was going to the concert to sell drugs. The argument got heated, and Josh threw a laundry basket at the window in the bedroom. The glass cracked, and Amber called the building manager to report the damage.

THE DAY OF THE INCIDENT

The pair continued bickering on June 7th, 2011. Two repairmen were fixing another window in the apartment building, so the manager also sent them to the Hilberling unit. When the two repairmen arrived, both noticed that the couple seemed tense.

One of the men went down to the van to grab the supplies while the other stayed in the unit. Amber and Josh were arguing in the living room, and the repairman later confirmed he was scared for Amber. Not wanting to meddle, the repairman started repairing the window. That's when he heard a loud crash. Scared that Josh might have done something to Amber, he entered the living room. There he found Amber screaming. The other repairman called up to say he just saw someone fall from the building.

Josh landed on the roof of a parking garage, and Amber ran into the elevator. When she reached Josh's body, she realized he was beyond help, but she couldn't accept he was gone and screamed for someone to help her. Josh fell for 25 stories and was declared dead at the scene. Unwilling to accept he was gone, Amber continued screaming for help.

Amber was in shock, and an officer took her to the police station to get her away from the apartment building. She was unwell, so Amber's grandmother sat with her in an interview room.

Unaware the camera was on, Amber started talking to her grandmother about the events that happened that morning.

> "I didn't mean to push him. Josh hates me. I'm not even gonna be able to meet him in Heaven anymore because he hates me. I killed him."

She blamed herself for Josh's accident, saying she pushed him. Her grandmother tried to tell her it wasn't her fault, but Amber didn't want to hear about it. She asked Amber if she wanted to kill Josh, and Amber said no.

A VIOLENT RELATIONSHIP

The police initially thought Josh's fall was an accident, but Amber became the prime suspect after police reviewed the audio and video tapes from the interview room.

The families shared details of the couple's relationship, revealing they were both abusive to each other. It was unclear when the violence started, but the police uncovered domestic dispute records from January 2011 while they were living in Alaska.

Amber called the police to report an incident with Josh.

According to her, Josh knocked a plate out of her hand, started hitting her, and then attempted to pop her breast implant. The young woman was taken to the emergency room, where the nurses noted visible bruising on her body. Josh was in custody but was released after Amber refused to file any charges.

The violence continued after their return to Oklahoma, and Josh filed a restraining order on Amber. She allegedly attacked him with a lamp, and he needed 21 stitches. But according to Amber's mother, neither took the restraining order seriously and acted as if nothing had happened, so it was dismissed.

Josh's family confirmed the abuse allegations, and his father, Patrick, mentioned he often heard from his son while the couple was in Alaska. Josh would cry over the phone while describing everything he went through with Amber. Patrick advised his son to leave Amber and even confirmed that it was Josh's plan to leave Amber on the day of the accident.

AMBER'S STORY

On June 7th, 2011, Amber Hilberling was arrested and charged with first-degree murder. The only proof the police had against her was the recording from the interview room. Since she hadn't been officially interrogated, it was unclear if the tapes could be presented in court. But it was later decided Amber made those statements herself, and the footage can be shown as evidence. The charge was later changed to second-degree murder.

Amber talked to the police while in custody and shared her version of the events. After the repairmen arrived at the unit, the couple continued their argument in the living room. What started as a yelling match soon turned physical. Josh lunged towards Amber, grabbing her by the shoulders and shaking her.

She was seven months pregnant and scared for the baby, so she pushed him away. Josh lost his balance and stumbled towards the window. He went through the glass and fell to the garage roof. The neighbor in the unit below confirmed he heard the argument and Amber's screams.

Amber was released on a bond on June 9th, 2011, and ordered to wear an ankle monitor. She gave birth to a baby boy named Levi in August 2011. However, her bail was revoked several times before the trial because she failed the mandatory drug tests. Amber used marijuana recreationally and often forgot to charge her ankle monitor.

Her trial was scheduled for the beginning of 2013, and the prosecution offered her a plea deal. Amber could avoid the court case and get a sentence of five years in prison if she pleaded guilty. She refused and opted for the trial.

THE TRIAL

Despite the heavy media coverage of the case, the trial

began in March 2013 in Tulsa, Oklahoma. Amber's defense relied on her claims that she wasn't strong enough to push a man of Josh's size out of the window. Furthermore, her lawyers found a window expert who took the stand and confirmed that the unit where the Hilberlings stayed had the original windows, meaning they were 46 years old.

On the other hand, the prosecution presented their version of the events that included Amber planning the murder after seeing first-hand how weak the glass was. According to them, she ran towards Josh when he was looking out of the window. The topic of Josh's drug addiction wasn't mentioned in the court, but Amber talked about it influencing the relationship dynamics. According to her, the couple always argued in Alaska, and the photos of her bruises were shown in court.

Josh's father testified his son called him on June 7th, 2011. Allegedly, Josh wanted to leave Amber, file for divorce, and try to get full custody of their unborn baby. The reason was Amber's drug use that continued throughout her pregnancy. His bags were packed, and he needed someone to pick him up.

Amber offered a different explanation for the packed bags. The defense presented messages exchanged between their client and Josh, which confirmed she wanted to kick him out because of the fight on June 6. She put his stuff in bags herself and asked for a divorce.

After a week-long trial, the jury deliberated for three hours and found Amber Hilberling guilty of second-degree murder. She received a sentence of 25 years behind bars.

THE AFTERMATH

Amber Hilberling was sent to Mabel Bassett Correctional Center near McLoud in Oklahoma. She continued to proclaim her innocence, and the case was covered by well-known crime shows such as *Women Who Kill* and *The First 48.*

Dr. Phil interviewed her in February 2016, and Amber admitted she acted in self-defense but wouldn't have hurt Josh intentionally if she knew what would happen.

On October 24, 2016, Amber was discovered dead in her cell. She allegedly committed suicide by hanging.

Josh's brother Zach Hilberling posted on Facebook, "Muhahahahaha ding dong the witch is dead!! Muahaha," when he heard that Amber had killed herself. He added that with her death, his family can now have some closure.

The Hilberling family have custody of Levi Hilberling, Amber and Josh's son.

Amber's family openly criticized the Mabel Bassett Correctional Center, saying they were likely hiding details of Amber's suicide. Amber's mother, Rhonda, said her daughter felt unsafe in prison.

Rhonda sued the Oklahoma Department of Corrections in 2018. The wrongful death lawsuit stated that the ODOC failed to protect Amber from well-known predators within the correctional center, didn't provide her with proper medication and therapy, and used faulty surveillance equipment. The lawsuit was dropped in 2019.

TWIN CRIMES

"Look, I don't want to stereotype here...but has there ever been a set of twins that weren't evil?"

THE CAVE, VIDEO GAME

Everyone in Pulaski, Tennessee, knew the Bondurant twins because of their imposing size and their bad reputation. The two felt invincible when they were together, which led them to commit some of the most gruesome crimes recorded in Giles County, Tennessee.

Hugh "Pete" Bondurant Jr. and Kenneth Patterson "Pat" Bondurant were born on April 4th, 1955, in Memphis, Tennessee, to parents Pete Sr. and Polly Bondurant. Pete Sr. was a military contractor, and Polly worked at Redstone Arsenal, an army base in Huntsville, Alabama.

According to those who knew them, both parents were very strict. The boys were known for their bad behavior at a young age, and family members reported that they started harming animals when they were around 12 years old. They would bury cats in their yard up to their heads and then run them over with a lawnmower.

The twins were exceptionally large for their age, and they were bullied at school because of this. Pete and Pat weighed about 250 pounds each by the time they were in the seventh grade.

In high school, they liked reading books and wore similar clothes, which made them easy targets for teasing from other kids. But once the twins realized they were more imposing together, they became bullies themselves. In high school, they made up stories about themselves and spread rumors about their exploits to make them appear more dangerous.

Pete was the dominant twin and was usually seen as more of a troublemaker. Pat, on the other hand, was quieter and calm but always went along with his brother's plans. They protected each other in high school and rarely spent time apart.

AFTER HIGH SCHOOL

The twins graduated high school in 1973, and Pete immediately enlisted in the Army. He returned home one month later, confessing that he didn't like to be given orders.

Still wanting to leave Elkton, Pete packed his bags and moved constantly. He was unable to keep a job. Pat stayed in Elkton and was employed at the Pulaski Rubber Company. He soon married a woman named Denise.

THE MURDER IN CINCINNATI

In 1975, nineteen-year-old Pete was in Cincinnati, Ohio. He lived in an apartment complex with two other men. Two female friends often stayed at their place too. One evening, the women went out to buy cigarettes and food at a nearby store, leaving Pete alone with his two roommates. When they returned, the door was locked.

Pete then came outside, holding a bloody knife, and said: "*You're next.*" Thinking this was a prank, the women entered the apartment to find a gruesome scene. Roger Mills, one of the roommates, was on the bed, covered in blood. The other man was unconscious on the floor. Terrified, they called an ambulance.

Pete calmly walked out of the apartment. The police found him standing in the parking lot, where he approached them and said he had attacked his roommates. Mills was taken to a hospital but didn't survive the attack. The other roommate was alive. An autopsy showed Mills was stabbed more than 40 times with a thin instrument, probably a screwdriver.

Pete was arrested and told several versions of what happened in the apartment. The first was that the two men tried to sexually assault him, and he was protecting himself.

Then he said that his roommates were doing drugs and didn't want anyone to find out, so they attacked him and tried to shut him up. The police didn't believe him because both women said Mills had just taken a shower and gone to sleep when they left the apartment. It was unlikely he threatened Pete in any way.

Pete was found guilty of murdering Roger Mills and sentenced to 25 years in state prison. But in the 1970s, Ohio was struggling with overcrowding, and Pete saw this as an opportunity to get out earlier. Since he was from Tennessee, his parole was granted after serving only five years. In 1980, Pete was back in Elkton, ready to reunite with his brother Pat.

DRUG DEALING TWINS

Pete moved in with Pat, who lived with his wife Denise and their child. But almost instantly, things started to change. Pat always deferring to Pete changed his behavior. Even though he had a high-paying job at the Pulaski Rubber Company, Pat started dealing drugs with his brother.

The twins were in their twenties and became very popular in the area. Young people started gathering at their house and partied around the clock. Pete and Pat could get their hands on any type of drug imaginable. The locals knew they were allowed to do narcotics in the Bondurant home.

THE DISAPPEARANCE OF GWEN DUGGER

On May 30th, 1986, Gwen Dugger went to the Bondurant house with her brother and his friend to retrieve a car. She knew the Bondurant twins and considered them to be their friends. Gwen was a friendly person who had a young son. She frequently participated in drug parties with the twins.

Once Gwen's brother managed to start his car, she told him to go back home without her. Gwen wanted to stay at the Bondurant house a bit longer. Pat was there and promised Gwen's brother that he would give her a ride later. That was the last time Gwen was seen alive. She simply disappeared. Suspecting the Bondurant twins were behind her disappearance, the Dugger family confronted them several times, asking for information.

People in Elkton started talking about what could've happened to Gwen, and all theories led straight to the brothers. Weeks later, the Dugger family pressured the police to conduct a proper investigation. The detective assigned to the case did his best to connect the twins to Gwen's disappearance, but no one was willing to talk. The case was slowly going cold when another person disappeared.

THE DISAPPEARANCE OF RONNIE GAINES

Ronnie Gaines was another Elkton resident who often hung out with Pat Bondurant. The two of them worked together at the Pulaski Rubber Company. Co-workers didn't consider them very close, but the two sometimes went out and drank. Ronnie was outgoing, cheerful, and generally well-liked, but it was known that he had financial problems.

On October 23rd, 1986, Ronnie was with Pat. According to Pat, he spent a couple of hours at Ronnie's house, and the two were playing cards. One day later, Ronnie's friends and family reported him missing. Mysteriously, Ronnie's house burned down too. After the investigation, the fire marshal concluded the cause of the fire was arson.

The police talked to those closest to Ronnie but focused on Pat Bondurant because his story kept changing. Finally, Pat named a woman called Terrie Lynn Clark as his alibi. Allegedly, they went to Westpoint, Tennessee on October 23rd. Terry agreed to come to the station on November 18 for an interview regarding Pat's alibi but she never made it.

THE OVERDOSE OF TERRY LYNN CLARK

The police were called to the Bondurant home on November 17th, 1986. The officers were told a woman died in her sleep. When they arrived on the scene, officers realized it was Terry Lynn Clark. According to the twins and other guests at the house, she was doing drugs all evening.

Since she died in bed next to Pete, he was supposed to go to the police station and give a statement. But instead of speaking to law enforcement, Pete saw his lawyer. After that, he drove to his doctor because he was too upset to deal with anything at that moment.

Days after Terry's death, Denise Bondurant, Pat's wife, moved out of the house. Denise and Pat had one child together who had cerebral palsy, and Denise was pregnant with a second child. On more than one occasion, Pat had beaten her and even put a gun to her head. She filed for divorce.

NEW INVESTIGATOR

In 1989, a new investigator named Michael Chapman decided to have a fresh look at the evidence collected in the disappearance of Gwen Dugger. He noticed that Pat's wife, Denise was allegedly at the house on May 30th, 1986.

Chapman had an entire network of informants, and he asked if any knew Denise. It turned out that one of the informants was dating her at that time. The new investigator on the case encouraged him to bring up Gwen Dugger's disappearance. He did, and Denise shared enough information to get the police on the case again.

Hoping she could be their main witness, the detectives visited her. They reminded Denise that twins were dangerous and aware that she knew all their secrets. Denise knew Pat and Pete might harm her. She was initially reluctant to talk but then asked for immunity and made an official statement to the police.

DENISE'S STORY

Once Denise started talking, the police learned what had happened to Gwen Dugger in 1986. According to her, Pete, Pat, Gwen, and two unnamed men were doing drugs in the living room. Pete saw it as an opportunity to sexually assault Gwen, so he gave her pain pills. Denise walked in while Pat was forcing himself on Gwen.

Furious at her, Denise slapped Gwen and then proceeded to shout at her husband, thinking he was cheating on her. Only then did she see that Gwen was high to the point that she had no idea what was happening around her. Denise ordered everyone to leave, but Gwen didn't understand and just wandered around.

Pat suddenly appeared with an axe, telling Denise to use it on Gwen. When she refused, Pat approached Gwen from behind and struck her in her head several times until she fell to the ground. Pete then came into the room with a gun and shot Gwen. Denise also described how Pete and Pat disposed of Gwen and the evidence. They took her to the backyard, placed the body in a 55-gallon drum, and set it on fire. They did this several nights in a row until nothing was left. They dumped the ashes near a creek on Pat's property.

While Denise wasn't present for the murder of Ronnie Gaines, the twins shared most of it with her. Pat's wallet went missing in October 1986, and he suspected Ronnie was the thief. The twin continued acting like nothing was wrong while at work, but inside, Pat was furious.

The wallet contained the money Pat and Denise received each month from the government for their son's care. On October 23rd, he arrived at Ronnie's house to play cards and have a few beers. Things went south once Pat confronted Ronnie about the wallet and the money inside. Ronnie denied he stole anything from Pat, which infuriated Pat. Unable to control his rage, Pat grabbed a small rocking chair and beat Ronnie with it. He beat him until nothing was left of the rocking chair. Ronnie was dead within minutes. Knowing he needed help covering the crime, Pat called Pete, who drove to Ronnie's house to help him.

The twins cut Ronnie's body in the tub, placed the parts inside garbage bags, and loaded everything into Pete's truck. The Bondurants lived on a large property, so they burned Ronnie's remains in several fire pits. Pete then returned to Ronnie's house and left a candle in the bedroom, underneath the curtains.

THE INVESTIGATION AND ARRESTS

Denise gave the investigators enough information to get a search warrant for the Bondurant property. She accompanied the police and showed them where the twins said they disposed of Ronnie Gaines' body. After digging up several locations, the forensic pathologist identified a piece of a human skull. Following an examination, they determined it belonged to Ronnie.

Two days later, the investigators were back on the Bondurant property. This time they were inside the house. Gwen Dugger was killed indoors, so the police focused on DNA and blood spatter. The luminol testing confirmed Denise's version of the events. Unfortunately, the DNA from the blood couldn't be matched with Gwen's because that technology wasn't widely available back then.

While the investigators knew Gwen's body was burned for three days, they weren't ready to give up. Denise showed them where the ashes were dumped, and they started digging. After several hours one of the investigators found a burnt shoe with a diaper pin on it. Gwen was known to wear it as a reminder of her son. That pin was the only piece of physical evidence that could be connected to her murder.

Even though the twins knew about the investigation, they still acted like everything was fine. Pat showed up at work and was apprehended at the rubber factory. Pete Bondurant was arrested while driving in town when a police officer recognized him.

THE TRIAL AND AFTERMATH

The prosecution worked tirelessly on preparing a solid case against the Bondurant twins. The trial began in March of 1991 in Pulaski, Tennessee, but neither Pat nor Pete were too concerned about the outcome. For some reason, the brothers were sure they would be free soon.

Denise was the star witness for the prosecution. She shared all the details she knew regarding the murders. The defense tried to blame her for Gwen's murder because, according to them, Denise bashed Gwen's head in a fit of jealousy.

On March 30th, 1991, the jury found both Pete and Pat guilty of the second-degree murder of Gwen Dugger. Each received a sentence of 25 years in prison.

Pete was tried for the death of Terry Lynn Clark and received 15 additional years. He was also found guilty of arson.

In December 1991, Pat was on trial for the murder of Ronnie Gaines. He was found guilty and sentenced to life in prison.

Pete Bondurant was released from prison on December 26th, 2016, after serving 25 years. His whereabouts are unknown to the public.

Pat Bondurant is in Northeast Correctional Complex in Mountain City, Tennessee. He was eligible for parole in 2012 and his next parole hearing is in 2025.

THE DEATH AND THE LIFE

"I'm going to have a boy! I'm going to have a boy!"

MATTHEW LEE ON FINDING OUT THE GENDER OF HIS CHILD

Not all murders are the same in the eyes of the law. Sometimes killing another person isn't even considered murder. Take the case of a Korean immigrant wife and soon-to-be mother. Did she kill her husband in cold blood? Or was it in self-defense?

Matthew Lee was thrilled to have a child. He told anyone who would listen about the imminent birth of his son.

Lee was trying to get healthy. He'd started jogging, and he was trying to give up smoking. A local grocery store employee said he'd buy a pack of cigarettes but leave them at the store so he would have fewer during the day.

Despite doing very well in his IT career, Matthew gave up his computer job in Connecticut to look after his ailing father in New Jersey. His mother also lived with him and his wife. For Matthew, his family was everything.

Matthew had recently decided to become an officer with the NYPD and was preparing to enter the police academy when he was murdered.

THE CALL

June 2004, Sung-Ann Choi-Lee called 911 from her Staten Island home and told the dispatcher that she had just killed her husband, Matthew Lee.

Officers of the New York Police Department arrived at the home on Bay Street to find the 29-year-old pregnant woman bleeding. She had slit her wrists.

The body of her husband, 30-year-old Matthew Lee, was discovered in their bedroom. There were multiple stab wounds on his chest, and it looked like he'd been hit in the head. Nearby on the floor was a bloody hammer and a kitchen knife.

First responders transported Sung-Ann to the hospital to treat her for the wounds from her suicide attempt, and while at the hospital, she went into labor. Sung-Ann gave birth to a healthy baby boy within an hour of arriving at the hospital. Investigators, however, had to wait until Sung-Ann recovered before questioning her because she delivered her baby via C-section.

As Sung-Ann recovered at the hospital, news of Matthew's murder spread. The couple's neighbor, Rosary Pabey, described the murder as shocking. She had never heard the couple fight.

Another neighbor told the media he often saw Sung-Ann and Matthew exercising together. According to him, the couple seemed to be in love. However, the local police had logged several 911 calls from the residence, which they classified as domestic disputes.

Matthew Lee's mother, a nurse, was shocked by his murder. A friend told the New York Post that his mother was so stunned she couldn't even cry, and when she finally did start crying, she couldn't stop.

As soon as Sung-Ann was well enough, she was charged with the second-degree murder of her husband and criminal possession of a weapon. Sung-Ann entered a plea of not guilty.

The couple had been married for eleven months. Sung-Ann was born in Korea and struggled to learn English and American customs. During Sung-Ann's trial, her psychiatrist argued that she suffered from depression and psychotic episodes. According to her doctors, Sung-Ann also suffered from post-traumatic stress disorder from domestic abuse.

Psychiatrists who evaluated Sung Ann for the defense and the prosecution both said she'd been subjected to multiple "rapes and beatings" throughout her two-year relationship with Matthew Lee.

She once went to a Korean priest for advice on escaping the abusive marriage but received no help to do so. Her defense team claimed she had nowhere to turn to for help, and she snapped.

It was ultimately determined that Sung-Ann was not guilty of murder in the second degree, but instead of manslaughter.

Sung-Ann apologized before receiving her sentence from the judge of five years in prison. Additionally, the judge ordered continued medical attention and psychiatric evaluation for Sung-Ann and five years of psychiatric evaluation after her release from prison. The judge also mentioned deportation as a possibility.

At the time of the trial, the child, who was two years old, was living with Matthew Lee's grandparents.

Sung-Ann's defense attorney told the media, "She's never going to see her child again. She'll have to live with that."

COP KILLER

"Chief Adams was a dedicated and respected law enforcement officer who was loved by his community. His murder was a tragedy that still haunts us today."

DAN ROBBINS, FORMER CHIEF OF POLICE IN SAXONBURG, PENNSYLVANIA

Before 1980, the small town of Saxonburg, Pennsylvania was known as a quiet community and a nice place to live. Saxonburg had only one murder in its 150-year history. On December 4th, they logged a second.

Chief Adams was on Water Street, two blocks away from the police station, when he saw a driver run a stop sign.

The driver pulled into the Agway Feed Store, intending to turn his car around in the parking lot, but Chief Adams blocked the exit, forcing the vehicle to a halt.

Expecting a routine traffic stop, Adams approached the car from the driver's side and asked the male occupant for his license. The driver followed the instructions and handed over his license but immediately after, pulled a gun on the officer and shot him twice in the chest. The men fought and the Chief returned fire and hit the man. His attacker grabbed his revolver and pistol-whipped the officer in the head. The man took the keys to the police car, got in, and ripped out the radio microphone hoping to buy himself some time. He then sped away in his own car, a white Mercury Cougar.

A young boy across living across the street heard the *pops* from the man's pistol followed by a *boom* from the chief's revolver. He got scared and went to tell his mother. She was sure it was just local hunters but went outside to investigate. That's when she found Chief Adams in the bushes, still alive. He was bleeding and his face was barely recognizable from the beating. The woman screamed for the boy to call 911.

Chief Adams managed to tell the woman he didn't recognize his attacker and was sure he wasn't a resident of Saxonburg. The paramedics arrived quickly, but the chief lost consciousness on his way to the hospital and died soon after.

Earlier that day, Chief Adams had lent his bullet-proof vest to another officer. An autopsy showed that one bullet hit his arm, went into his chest, and collapsed his lung. The second bullet tore through the bottom of the officer's heart.

Adams, survived by his wife and two young sons was 31 years old at the time of his death. He was a Marine Corps Veteran who had served in the Saxonburg police department for seven years.

IDENTIFYING THE SHOOTER

It got dark early, and the official investigation of the crime scene began the day after the shooting. The police quickly found the driver's license that was handed to the Chief before the shootout. It was issued in New Jersey to a man named Stanley John Portas. The killer's .25-caliber Colt pistol was at the scene, and technicians collected traces of blood that were later tested, revealing the shooter had O-type blood.

The Chief's revolver was missing, but it was found on the side of the road in Winfield Township, Pennsylvania. An abandoned Mercury Cougar was discovered in front of a motel in Warwick, Rhode Island, and there were traces of O-type blood on the interior of the vehicle. After contacting the state police and various police departments in the area, investigators discovered that the license was fake. Stanley John Portas was an alias of a criminal named Donald Eugene Webb.

DONALD EUGENE WEBB

Donald Eugene Webb was born Donald Eugene Perkins on July 14, 1931, in Oklahoma. He spent his childhood with his grandfather and later enlisted in the US Navy. Webb then worked various jobs and was associated with criminals from Taunton and Fall River in Massachusetts. Those groups were connected with the New England Mafia, also known as the Patriarca Family.

Webb married a woman named Lillian, who had a son from a previous marriage. Her first husband, Stanley John Portas, had heart disease and died in his early twenties. Webb decided to use his name as an alias for his criminal activities.

Since Webb was associated with criminals who specialized in jewelry store robberies, it is believed he was in Saxonburg doing reconnaissance on a family-run jewelry shop. The police discovered that Webb was wanted in New York because of skipping bail after an arrest.

A POSSIBLE ACCOMPLICE

The Mercury Cougar had been rented and contained so much blood that investigators immediately thought Webb had an accomplice or someone who helped him drive to Rhode Island. Frank Joseph Lach, another criminal, was associated with Webb, and the two were often seen together. Lach was also from Rhode Island and had connections with the same criminal groups.

While Webb could've been alone in the vehicle during the murder, Lach was perhaps in the area, scoping out the jewelry store too. However, Lach never confirmed he was in Saxonburg in December 1980. He was in and out of prison for decades and passed away in November 2017 in Cranston, Rhode Island.

THE SEARCH FOR WEBB

The FBI office in Pennsylvania contacted the field office in New Bedford, and agents then called the state police. A sketch of a suspect was shared with them, and the officers immediately recognized Webb since he was a well-known criminal in the area. A state police officer who was close with Lillian, Webb's wife, called their home and asked about her husband, saying he was wanted by the FBI.

Even though it is later confirmed that the officer didn't mean to tip Webb off, the man immediately went into hiding. He knew the police suspected him for the murder of Chief Adams in Saxonburg. On December 31, 1980, a federal arrest warrant was issued for Donald Eugene Webb for the murder of Chief Adams. Webb was charged with murder, attempted burglary, and unlawful flight to avoid prosecution. In May 1981, he was placed on the FBI's Ten Most Wanted list.

One of the main problems investigators faced was that the case didn't get a lot of publicity from the local media. People from the New Bedford area had no idea Webb was a wanted man. But law enforcement wasn't ready to give up.

They firmly believed his wife Lillian knew where her husband was.

They knocked on her door regularly, asking for Webb. She was under constant surveillance, and a patrol car would follow her frequently. She sometimes tried to lose the cops. Coincidentally, Webb's stepson —Stanley Webb, became a New Bedford police officer, and his colleagues talked to him about the case, trying to find out more information.

Since not many people knew about the crime, Webb allegedly stayed in the New Bedford area and even continued to do jobs with the Fall River Gang in the years after the murder of Chief Adams. It was confirmed he was in New Bedford in July 1981 after the police received an anonymous call. The tips from other parts of the country came in too, but those were never confirmed.

In September 1999, Webb became the fugitive who spent the most time on the FBI's Ten Most Wanted list. His name was removed from it in March 2007 because of the lack of tips. Most FBI investigators considered him to be deceased at this point. His record was surpassed by Víctor Manuel Gerena in 2010.

NEW INFORMATION

In December 2015, the FBI announced a $100,000 reward for any information about Webb's whereabouts or the location of his remains. On June 1, 2017, Mary Ann Adams Jones, Chief Adams' widow, filed a lawsuit against the

Webb family. It led to the discovery of many new details regarding the case.

A few days later, the FBI announced that in 2016 they found a secret room in the basement of Lillian's house in North Dartmouth, Massachusetts. The agents informed Mary Ann, and she started preparing the lawsuit.

The room itself was behind a wall. It was tiny, with just enough room for a small chair. The investigators found a cane inside and assumed it was used by Webb after the fight with the police chief. His leg was shattered, and it took a while for his bones to heal. The FBI published new photos of Webb, taken in 1979.

SECRETS UNCOVERED

Wanting to avoid the civil lawsuit, Lillian Webb agreed to a deal with the prosecution. After 27 years of silence, she was ready to share all her family secrets. In July 2017, Lillian told the investigators that Webb died on December 30, 1999. He spent 19 years living in the basements of their two houses. One was in Dartmouth, and the other was in New Bedford.

Both residences featured secret rooms where Webb would sit while guests were upstairs. Webb had a stroke in 1999 while staying in their home in Dartmouth. Since he was a fugitive, Webb knew he couldn't just walk into a hospital. Sensing his end was near, he told Lillian to bury his body in the backyard.

Then he instructed her to dig a grave behind a shed, which she did despite the difficulties of breaking the ground in December. Webb had another stroke on December 30, and Lillian wrapped his lifeless body up in plastic. She placed her husband in the grave.

After 37 years of not knowing where he was, the authorities and the family of Chief Adams finally had answers.

The backyard of Webb's house in Dartmouth was excavated, and human remains were located.

When career criminal Donald Eugene Webb became a cop killer, it forced him into living in a prison of his own making and while it wasn't the federal prison he should have been in, many would agree there is some justice in his self-imposed incarceration.

A LONELY HEART

"Raymond Fernandez, complete with toupee, was no bargain, but Martha Beck was not without certain physical disadvantages too, and when she met him she latched on to him for good —you might even say for better or for worse, especially worse. Raymond's chosen career was not an easy one, but Martha was a wonderful help-meet."

NEW YORK DAILY NEWS, SUNDAY
FEBRUARY 11TH, 1951, PAGE 302

A handsome lothario who cheats women out of their life savings finds a woman so desperate for love that she abandons her own children to join him in crime. Their joint malice escalates into multiple murders, but she still professes her love for him on the day she goes to the electric chair.

Meeting new people is easy in the age of the internet. Various dating apps are available. Just fill out a profile. However, things were very different in the 20th century. People looking for soulmates would place ads in romance magazines, and they could also sign up for a lonely hearts club. Unfortunately, these options were quite dangerous, and many assaults weren't reported because victims felt ashamed.

RAYMOND MARTINEZ FERNANDEZ

Raymond Martinez Fernandez was born on December 17th, 1914, in Hawaii. His Spanish parents then relocated the family to Bridgeport, Connecticut. Wanting to learn about his roots, Fernandez traveled to Spain to help his uncle on a farm. There he met a local woman, and the two fell in love. The couple had four children.

World War II disrupted Fernandez's plans, and in 1939, he began his career as a merchant marine. He then became involved with British Intelligence and ran an ice cream stand in Gibraltar while gathering information for the British.

When World War II ended, Fernandez needed to find work. He left his wife and children in Spain and boarded a ship headed to the United States. During this trip, he had an accident. A steel hatch fell on him, resulting in a fractured skull and a brain injury.

He was hospitalized for three months, and his family immediately noticed a change in his behavior. He was erratic, couldn't control his impulses, and became addicted to sex. He was caught trying to move stolen clothing through customs, something he would never do. This theft resulted in one year behind bars in Tallahassee, Florida.

His cellmate was from Haiti, and he believed in Voodoo and black magic. The mysterious man was open to sharing his religion with Fernandez, so he became a practitioner as well. According to Fernandez, it made him more attractive to women. While serving time, Fernandez made a plan to scam women out of their fortunes using his Voodoo practice.

NEW YORK LONELY HEARTS

When he was out of prison, Fernandez rented an apartment in New York and began going through personal ads in magazines and newspapers. He also bought a list of names of widowed women for $2 and he joined a lonely hearts club called *Mother Dinene's Family Club for Lonely Hearts*. He was looking for women who seemed desperate to find love.

Fernandez wrote beautiful letters, and women started responding to him. He embellished a lot about his achievements but often mentioned his service to the British during the war.

Fernandez said in his letters that he wished to settle down and find a wife. Once he gained someone's trust, he would empty their bank accounts and steal their jewelry. The women who were scammed by Fernandez felt ashamed, and no one reported him to the police.

THE MYSTERIOUS DEATH OF JANE LUCILLA THOMPSON

In 1947, Fernandez started dating a newly divorced woman named Jane Lucilla Thompson. She was disappointed after her first marriage failed and was excited about this second chance. The two exchanged many letters, and Jane desired to meet Fernandez. She paid for a romantic getaway to Spain, and the two booked a hotel room as newlyweds.

Jane didn't know that Fernandez's first wife was in Spain with their four children. He was still legally married to his first wife. He decided to introduce the two women, and they somehow became friends. However, the two women argued on November 7th, 1947. Jane then argued and attacked Fernandez in their hotel room, and Fernandez was seen exiting the hotel room by the staff.

Jane was found dead in her hotel room bed the next day. The medical examiner didn't discover any bruises on her body, leading them to the conclusion she died of natural causes. An autopsy wasn't performed, but investigators later suggested she was poisoned.

Fernandez returned to the United States and got Jane's apartment in New York by creating a fake will. Jane's elderly mother was living in the apartment at the time and received the news of her daughter's death and her summons to vacate the home simultaneously.

Now with a permanent place to live in New York City, Fernandez started up his lonely heart letter writing once again. At the end of 1947, he'd found a new target —a young woman from Florida named Martha Beck.

MARTHA JULE BECK (NÉE SEABROOK)

Martha Jule Seabrook was born on May 6, 1920, in Milton, Florida. She gained extra weight as a girl because of a glandular issue and entered puberty before her peers. Always an outcast, Martha was bullied in school almost daily. As a teen, she ran away from home and became a part of a traveling circus. She would later claim that she disappeared because of physical and sexual abuse by her older brother, which happened when she was 13. After telling her mother about it, the woman scolded the girl and refused to believe her story.

Martha wanted to finish school and create a better life for herself. As soon as she graduated from high school, she began studying nursing. Being a hard-working student didn't pay off. Nobody wanted to employ her because of her weight. But she did find employment at a funeral home where she worked on female bodies.

Believing she might have better luck in the west, Martha packed her bags and moved to California. It turned out she was right because she was employed by an Army hospital almost immediately. At night Martha would go out to the local bars and have sexual encounters with Army men on leave. She got pregnant, and the man she'd been sleeping with refused to marry her, so Martha returned to Florida to have the child.

Embarrassed about the situation, she bought a wedding ring and sent herself a telegram informing her about the death of her "husband" in the Pacific Campaign. The community consoled her for her "loss."

She gave birth to a girl, Willa, and started dating a new man – a bus driver named Alfred Beck. The two married after she became pregnant but divorced after six months. This union resulted in the birth of Martha's second child – a baby boy.

Certain she would never find love, Martha was depressed. She spent her free time reading romance novels and *True Confession* magazine. After months of unemployment, she got a job at Pensacola Hospital for Children. Thinking her luck was changing, she placed an ad in *Mother Dinene's Family Club for Lonely Hearts,* and Raymond Martinez Fernandez answered.

A TWISTED RELATIONSHIP

Just like many women before her, Martha was attracted to Fernandez. She could tell from his letters that he was ambitious and might be a good father. Fernandez had a receding hairline but had a special toupee he wore for his pictures. After seeing his photos, Martha knew she was in love. Martha sent him photos in which she positioned herself behind other people to obscure her size. Fernandez asked for a lock of her hair, and she happily sent it to him in the mail, not realizing that Fernandez wanted it for a Voodoo ritual.

Then in December of 1947, Fernandez appeared on her doorstep. He came to Florida to meet her, and she invited the still-unfamiliar man into her home.

Strangely, Fernandez changed his routine and didn't steal anything from Martha or try to kill her. They started an affair which was meant to distract Martha and it gave Fernandez the time he needed to evaluate her assets.

She wasn't a wealthy woman and she had two children to care for. After several days, he told her that he had to return to New York, but he would send her money to come and stay with him.

He returned to New York and sent her a letter telling her it wouldn't work out. Martha was devastated and attempted suicide. After that, Fernandez let her visit him in New York. She spent two weeks with him but when she returned to Florida, she'd lost her job. She and the children packed their bags and headed to New York to live with Fernandez.

When Fernandez saw the whole family, he balked. He told Martha the kids couldn't stay, and she needed to abandon her children if she wanted to be with him, so she did. She took them to the Salvation Army and left them there.

Fernandez never had a partner in his cons and was used to working alone. But since neither of them had a job at the beginning of 1948, he decided to tell Martha everything, hoping she would support him. She wanted to join him after learning about the scams. Allegedly, she didn't have anything against him flirting with other women.

THE SCAMMING

After becoming a duo, Esther Henne was selected to be their first victim. Esther was a schoolteacher from Pennsylvania who started exchanging letters with Fernandez in February of 1948. Things moved fast, and Fernandez met Esther just one week later. The two were married soon after, and he took her to his apartment in New York. There Esther met Fernandez's "sister" Martha.

Esther would later say that Fernandez was polite to her until she refused to sign over her pension and insurance policies. He then started screaming at her, which alarmed her. When she overheard Fernandez and Martha talking about the death of Jane Lucilla Thompson, Esther decided to return to Pennsylvania. Fernandez did take her car and some of her money.

Fernandez and Beck continued scamming unsuspecting women through lonely hearts ads, and after several months, they zeroed in on Myrtle Young, who lived in Greene Forest, Arkansas. Martha once again played the role of Fernandez's sister, but it was clear she was very jealous of Myrtle. Fernandez and Myrtle were married in August 1948. However, Martha made sure the two were never alone with each other.

Myrtle was becoming suspicious and angry at Martha, so Fernandez drugged the poor woman, stole her money, and placed her on a bus that would take her back to Arkansas. But once the bus arrived at its last station, Myrtle wasn't moving. The emergency services were called, and Myrtle Young died in a hospital from a brain hemorrhage.

THE MURDERS

Janet Fay was a widow from Albany, New York, who, at 66, had almost given up on finding a husband. She was very religious and was thrilled to learn that a man who responded to her lonely hearts ad was Catholic. He assured her of his intentions and even promised to bring his sister with him to Albany, New York.

On December 30, 1948, Fernandez and Beck arrived to meet Janet. The women liked each other, and the trio spent the next few days sightseeing. After Janet learned the two were staying in a hotel, she invited them to her house. Fernandez did his usual scheme and proposed to Janet, who said yes.

He insisted she should leave Albany and rent an apartment in Long Island where they could live together. Once again, Janet agreed, and all three moved to their new place on January 4, 1949. Janet also emptied her bank account and had $6,000 with her. But jealousy was bubbling up in Martha, who lost her temper after seeing Fernandez and Janet in bed together.

Martha had her version of the story, which included Janet throwing her out of the apartment. But one thing is sure – Martha went out of the bedroom to get a hammer. She came back in and hit Janet several times in the head. Fernandez then strangled the woman with a scarf. Without missing a beat, the killers placed Janet's body in a closet and cleaned up the entire bedroom.

The following day, they purchased a trunk large enough for a body. They rented a house using Janet's money and buried her in the basement. As an attempt to hide the crime, they typed out letters and sent them to Janet's family. There were several versions, but the content was nearly the same: Janet was going to Florida with her much younger husband and was excited about the future.

Janet usually wrote letters by hand since she didn't own a typewriter. Her family contacted the authorities right away, and officers went to check on Janet.

Meanwhile, the murderous couple were already on the road to Grand Rapids, Michigan. They were about to meet Delphine Downing, yet another woman Fernandez met via personal ads.

Delphine was a 41-year-old widow who lived in a large house with her two-year-old daughter, Rainell. Again, Martha introduced herself as Fernandez's sister, and Delphine generously invited them to stay at her place. But the situation looked strange to Delphine from the very start. Her suspicions were confirmed when she saw Fernandez in the bathroom without his toupée. He used it to hide his receding hairline and the scars from the accident on the ship. She accused him of fraud.

Fernandez tried to charm his way out of this situation, but it didn't work. Delphine was very upset, and Fernandez was able to give her some sleeping pills to calm her down. Little Rainell got upset and started crying, asking for her mother. Martha was already agitated and started choking the little girl leaving visible marks on her neck.

Fernandez was sure that once Delphine woke up and saw the bruises, she would contact the police. He found a gun from Delphine's late husband, placed a towel around it to muffle the sound, and shot Delphine in the head. Beck helped him carry Delphine to the basement, where Fernandez buried her in a grave.

With Delphine out of the picture, Fernandez and Beck weren't in a hurry to leave. They took two days to go through the house and collect the valuables. Rainell wouldn't eat and the couple had no idea what to do with her. After a long discussion, Fernandez told Martha to get rid of the girl. They took her down to the basement and put some water that had accumulated down there into a metal tub. Martha held the child's head under the water until she stopped breathing. They buried Rainell next to her mother.

The neighbors noticed the strange couple in the Downing house, and they hadn't seen Delphine or her daughter for days. One neighbor called the police.

Fernandez and Martha drove to town to see a movie after they murdered Delphine and Rainell. When they returned to the house, they started packing up to leave. The police knocked on the door and searched the house for the mother and child. They found two freshly dug graves in the basement. It was the end of the Lonely Hearts Killers, and they were arrested on March 1, 1949.

THE TRIAL

Fernandez and Beck were willing to talk to the police as long as they were tried in Michigan because the state didn't have the death penalty then. They were told by police officials that Martha would only get six years in prison at most.

The couple wrote a 78-page confession which they signed without a lawyer. They confessed to murdering Delphine Downing, Rainell Downing, and Janet Fay.

The case became a media sensation across the United States overnight. The governor of New York spoke to Michigan prosecutors, and they cut a deal. There would be no charges filed in the deaths of the Downings, and Raymond Fernandez and Martha Beck would be extradited to New York to stand trial for the death of Janet Fay.

The newspaper media discussed Martha Beck's weight as much as they discussed the murder victims. They estimated her to be between 200-300 pounds. This made Martha upset, and she wrote open letters from prison to the media.

> "I'm still a human, feeling every blow inside, even though I have the ability to hide my feelings and laugh. But that doesn't say my heart isn't breaking from the insults and humiliation of being talked about as I am. O yes, I wear a cloak of laughter."

The trial began in June 1949, and Raymond Fernandez and Martha Beck took the stand. Beck tried explaining her actions by mentioning the past abuse, suicide attempts, and her horrible experience with men. When asked about the murder of Janet Fay, Martha claimed she blacked out and couldn't remember hitting the woman with a hammer.

The trial lasted over a month, with multiple witnesses discussing Janet Fay and what they remembered about her relationship with Raymond Fernandez.

Martha and Fernandez supported each other throughout the trial, trying to give testimony they knew would help the other person. They exchanged loving looks, and Martha would get upset when the prosecutor would yell at Fernandez.

They both gave lurid details of their sexual escapades and murders, reliving it again for a live audience. The courtroom was packed daily, and attendees skipped lunch to avoid losing their seats.

The trial lasted 44 days, and finally, the jury deliberated overnight. There were ten men and two women, and one juror was hesitant to convict. After more discussion, the juror changed their mind, and all twelve returned a guilty verdict.

On August 22nd, they were sentenced to death by electric chair and sent to Sing Sing Prison.

Both Fernandez and Beck tried appealing the decision but were rejected.

March 8, 1951 was set as the date for both executions. Beck managed to send Raymond a note, saying she still loved him.

Fernandez had to be carried to the chair as he was too distraught to walk to it. Martha, on the other hand, went into the chamber, and sat down while the matrons strapped her in. She mouthed the words, “So long,” to those who were watching.

UNIVERSITY KILLING SPREE

"He was a predator, a hunter, and he enjoyed the thrill of the hunt."

DETECTIVE KEVIN ALLEN, ALACHUA COUNTY SHERIFF'S OFFICE

The movie *Scream* was released in the Summer of 1996. Written by Kevin Williamson and directed by Wes Craven, the movie was panned by critics before it debuted. They thought general movie-goers wouldn't see a horror flick in the Summer. Those types of films were usually reserved for Fall releases, but they were wrong.

The film's killer *Ghostface* wore a mask of perpetual horror, the same look the audience had as they watched the film. Moviegoers fainted and they walked out, but most were enthralled, and a new movie franchise was born. This simple Summer flick revived an entire genre of slasher films grossing over 100 million dollars.

Moviegoers didn't know that screenwriter Kevin Williamson was inspired to write the screenplay after watching a documentary about a series of murders that frightened him. These murders occurred on the University of Florida campus in Gainesville and happened only six years prior to the release of the film.

Each August, the city of Gainesville, Florida, wakes up after a long, sleepy summer. There are always a few students who stay on the University of Florida Campus to take Summer classes, but August is the month when the students return before the Fall semester starts.

AUGUST 1990

First-year students were moving into their dormitories and off-campus apartments while returning students were reconnecting with old friends and professors. The university had a new president and football coach this year, and there was excitement among students, staff, and the Gainesville locals. As the end of August drew near, Gainesville's streets were so crowded that anyone could slip into the crowd and blend in, even someone with murderous intentions.

On August 24th, 1990, Sonja Larson and Christina Powell moved into apartment 113 at the Williamsburg Apartment Complex. Both of them were incoming freshmen at the University of Florida.

Christina Powell, known as "Christy," was born on November 30th, 1972. Christy hoped to become an architect. Being the youngest of seven children and the first in her family to attend college, she was thrilled to begin the semester.

Sonja Larson wanted a degree where she could work with children. One of Sonja's old supervisors at her job in high school said she had a way with kids and always had one on her lap.

Without a doubt, the two 17-year-olds would have achieved remarkable things if a serial killer hadn't brutally murdered them in their apartment on August 24th.

An intruder entered their apartment around 3 am through the rear door. The killer stood over Christy, who was asleep downstairs on the couch and watched her. He then went upstairs, crept into Sonja's room, and wrapped duct tape around her mouth, muffling her cries. He brutally stabbed Sonja and then made his way back down to Christy. The killer placed duct tape over her mouth, cut off her clothes, and sexually assaulted her. He then flipped her over and stabbed her five times in the back with a knife. He then posed both of the dead girls in sexually suggestive positions. The killer was covered in blood, and he took a shower in the apartment before he left.

Christy Powell's sister drove to Gainesville the following day to help Christy move the rest of her belongings into her apartment. Neither Christy nor Sonja answered the door when her sister knocked. The girls had yet to start classes, so Christy's sister couldn't figure out where they were.

Christy's sister called her parents who drove over to the Williamsburg Apartments. Upon pulling up to Christy's building, her parents saw both of the girls' cars parked in their spots. Despite the family's repeated knocks on the door, no one answered.

Seeing a maintenance worker pass by, the family asked him to open the door to their daughter's apartment. They explained that Christy and her roommate hadn't been in contact for several hours, which was unusual. He was uncomfortable opening the door, but he agreed to contact the police for guidance. Christy's parents contacted Sonja's parents, and they were all anxious about the girls' safety.

An officer arrived at the apartment complex shortly after the maintenance worker hung up the phone with 911. Using his copy of the key to apartment 113, the maintenance man let the police officer into the apartment. The officer found the bodies of the teenage girls and called for backup.

~

There was a fear among police officers that this killer would strike again, and he did. They had barely processed the first murders when on Monday, August 27th, another body was discovered.

Christa Hoyt was born on November 20, 1971. Unlike the Gainesville Ripper's first two victims, Christa Hoyt did not attend the University of Florida. Having a passion for safety and criminal justice, Christa studied crime scene investigation at Santa Fe Community College nearby. She held a position in the sheriff's department's Explorer program. The Explorer program recruited young people interested in a law enforcement career. Christa also worked for the Alachua County Sheriff's Department. Christa was a hard-working employee who never missed work.

On Monday, August 27th, 1990, the sheriff sent an officer to check on Christa Powell at her apartment after she failed to show up for work. The Alachua County Sheriff's Department officers knew all about the campus murders, and they were concerned.

The officer knocked hard on Christa's door, but no one answered. While walking around the apartment complex grounds, the officer spotted a maintenance worker. He asked him to open Christa's door. When the police officer used his flashlight to shine into the darkened apartment, he saw her body sitting up, headless, at the end of her bed. There was a bookcase in Christa's bedroom, and her head was sitting on one of the shelves.

According to investigators, the killer broke in and waited for Christa to return from work. Christa's killer choked her before covering her mouth with duct tape. He cut her clothes from her body and then sexually assaulted her in the bedroom. He then forced her to lie on her stomach and stabbed her several times in the back, rupturing her aorta. He flipped her back over and cut her from her pubic bone up to her breastbone.

In Gainesville, officers were stunned. The police now had three young female victims, and they had no idea when he would kill again.

On Sunday evening, **Tracy Paules** spoke on the phone with her friend, who had heard about the murders in Gainesville. Her friend was concerned about Tracy. Despite her concerns, Tracy said she felt safe. One of her close friends, Manuel "Manny" Taboada, the star player on their high school football team, lived with her. They both acknowledged Manny wasn't about to be beaten by anyone. He was 24 years old, strong, six-foot-two, and weighed over two-hundred pounds.

Manny Taboada was born on September 14th, 1966. He was a handsome young man who was a member of the National Honor Society during high school. Manny was also a talented performer who landed the lead role in *Grease* at American High School in South Florida. Manny was accepted into the University of Florida's College of Architecture. It was an exciting time for him. He and Tracy Paules shared an apartment in Gatorwood Apartments.

The killer broke into Manny and Tracy's Gatorwood apartment at 3 am on August 27th. Investigators believe the killer was startled when he found Manny asleep in the apartment and did not expect him to be there. Using a K-bar knife, the killer struck Manny in the chest, waking him up. Manny managed to stand up, and he fought back. During the assault, he was stabbed 31 times. When Tracy opened her bedroom door, she saw Manny being stabbed. Running back into her bedroom, Tracy locked the door, but the killer followed her and kicked it open. Tracy asked the man, "You're the one, aren't you?" He replied, "Yes, I am."

The killer taped her mouth and wrists and cut off her clothes with his knife. He sexually assaulted her, turned her over, and stabbed her three times in the back. He posed her body in a sexual way, left Manny's body on the floor, and left the apartment.

THE NEXT DAY

Tracy's friends kept calling and leaving messages on her answering machine. As a result of what was happening around the university, one friend drove to Tracy's apartment. When he pulled up outside Tracy and Manny's apartment, he noticed their vehicles were parked there. The friend was too afraid to peer through their apartment windows for fear of appearing suspicious. He tracked down an employee of the Gatorwood Apartments and begged him to open the apartment's door. The man did, and inside, they found the bodies of Manny and Tracy.

A COMMUNITY AFRAID

The Gainesville Ripper, a name given to him by the media, was bold enough to attack Manny, and the entire community of Gainesville was frightened. Anxiety and panic were on the rise. People called 911 when they heard the tiniest noise, and stores closed before dark. No one wanted to be on the streets at night.

Students began arming themselves with guns. Male students carried baseball bats and knives on the streets. Police warned residents of Gainesville not to let their guard down. Many parents pulled their children out of school.

The police determined early on that the same person committed the five murders. Over 600 officers and FBI agents formed a task force. Each day, investigators released updates on the case. Investigators told the media that the killer spent time in the apartment with the dead bodies. He didn't just murder them and leave. The killer was meticulous in his work. He poured dish detergent and liquid solvents on the lower portion of his victims' bodies to clean off any fluids that may have been left behind.

As thousands of leads came in, people named their ex-partners and neighbors as suspects. Despite police telling the public they had several suspects, only Edward Humphrey, 18, was publicly announced. A former part-time University of Florida student, Edward Humphrey, had pulled a knife on students days before the murders of Christy and Sonja.

He remained incarcerated throughout the investigation. Witnesses approached the police and reported seeing Edward Humphrey walking through the woods behind campus with a knife.

Edward had even assaulted his grandmother with a knife, but his family said he wasn't capable of murdering five college students. Even so, investigators believed Edward Humphrey was the Gainesville Ripper until an arrest on September 7th, 1990, changed everything.

DANIEL HAROLD ROLLING

Daniel Harold Rolling, 36, was arrested on September 7th after holding a gun to the head of a grocery store employee. After his arrest, Danny Rolling appeared very remorseful during his interview. Investigators reported that he acted like a child caught with his hand in the cookie jar before dinner.

During a competency evaluation with a psychiatrist for his burglary trial, Danny confessed to killing five college students in Gainesville. In his confession to the doctor, Danny explained that he had left his wallet at Christa Hoyt's apartment. He went back to her apartment and then decided to decapitate her.

The doctor chose not to disclose anything to investigators due to patient confidentiality. With Danny Rolling behind bars, he felt confident that no more killings would occur.

The doctor remained silent, and he believed investigators would get there independently.

The murders stopped after Danny Rolling was arrested.

Investigators back in Gainesville had Edward Humphrey as a suspect, but they decided to use VICAP, the Violent Crime Apprehension Program computer system, to cross-check. They entered everything they knew about the five Gainesville murders, and VICAP came back with an unsolved homicide from Shreveport, Louisiana as a match.

There were striking similarities between Gainesville's five murders and the Shreveport crime scene. Julie Grissom had been murdered, assaulted, and posed in a grossly inappropriate manner after her death. During the killing, the girl's father and seven-year-old nephew walked in. The killer then brutally murdered them both.

Two Gainesville Ripper task force officers visited Shreveport to speak with investigators about the Grissom homicide. Detectives from Shreveport told the task force that Daniel Harold Rolling's name frequently appeared in their investigation. When they checked Danny Rolling's background, they discovered he also had an arrest warrant for attempted murder in Louisiana. The victim was Danny's father, a former Shreveport police officer. Danny allegedly shot him after years of abuse.

BACKGROUND ON DANNY ROLLING

Danny was born on May 26, 1954, in Shreveport, Louisiana. He had a troubled childhood due to the physical abuse from his father, James Rolling, which started at the age of one when his father thought he was crawling improperly. Rolling also endured emotional abuse from his mother, Claudia. Danny also witnessed his father's disturbing and abusive behavior towards his mother, which may have contributed to his own violent tendencies.

Danny was expelled from school in the eighth grade for fighting and had a criminal record as a young adult. His childhood experiences and early exposure to violence likely played a role in his later criminal behavior, which included multiple murders and acts of sexual violence.

Danny Rolling was now an adult career criminal with several convictions for armed robbery across three states. When officers from the task force investigated Danny Rolling's whereabouts, they discovered he had already been in custody in Florida since September. The task force was intrigued by robbery during the killing spree on August 27, 1990. They decided to take a closer look at it.

The robbery occurred at First Union Bank of Gainesville. Following the robbery, the suspect ran into the wooded area behind the bank, leading to the University of Florida. Police officers and tracking dogs searched the woods for the bank robber and found a campsite. They found a dye-stained money bag, a screwdriver, an audio tape, and a knit ski cap. Because the evidence was not linked to homicides occurring in Gainesville, police officers placed the tent and other items in the evidence room.

An officer listened to the audio tape they found at the campsite. A voice rambled on, singing and saying things like, "I love my mother. I love my father. I love my brother." Eventually, the voice identified itself as Danny Harold Rolling.

Of the five Gainesville Ripper victims, three were sexually assaulted. The killer left DNA at the crime scene and the police had preserved it. In 1990, it took several weeks to develop a DNA profile. As soon as the lab created the profile, investigators got a search warrant for Danny Rolling's blood and sent it to a lab for comparison. The lab made a match. Danny Rolling was the Gainesville Ripper.

A grand jury indicted Danny Rolling on November 15, 1991 for the murders of Sonja Larson, Christy Powell, Christa Hoyt, Tracy Paules, and Manny Taboada. Edward Humphrey was officially cleared of all suspicions concerning the murders.

At his pretrial hearing, Danny Rolling's attorney pleaded not guilty on his behalf. Later, Danny and his attorney would change that plea to not guilty by reason of insanity.

According to his attorneys, Danny Rolling saw demons and heard voices. However, the prosecution said Danny Rolling was very competent and knew what he was doing during the murders. He said Danny Rolling aspired to become a world-famous serial killer. He was narcissistic and blamed the five murders on a demon named *Ynnad*. Ynnad is Danny reversed.

Eventually, Danny confessed, but bizarrely. He told the prosecution he would talk only through Bobby Lewis, a death row inmate. Bobby Lewis, who escaped death row and was captured days later, dictated Danny's answers to the prosecutor.

Danny Rolling eventually pleaded guilty to all five murders in February 1994, which surprised everyone.

According to Danny's attorneys, he confessed because it was the right thing to do. Prosecutors believe Danny was trying to avoid the death penalty. It didn't work. The judge sentenced Danny Rolling to death. It was a long road to his execution, as Danny Rolling appealed, desperately trying to save his life.

The Florida State Prison finally executed Danny Rolling on October 25th, 2006, sixteen years after the murders. As a final statement, Danny Rolling performed a song three minutes before he died.

FAMILY IMPACT STATEMENTS

Initially, Tracy Paules's sister, who witnessed the execution, said it was a relief; however, she later admitted it wasn't. The emptiness was still there.

Friends remember Christy Powell for her beautiful smile whenever they think of her. In an interview, Sonja Larson's mother said that she was looking forward to being with her daughter in eternity.

Because of her bright smile, Christa Hoyt was known as a "glow-worm." She got along with everyone.

Manny Taboada's brother still bumps into people who say Manny had an impact on their life. To him, Manny will forever be 24 years old.

Tracy Paules's sister often talks to her children about their aunt.

Gainesville still honors the five victims with a painting on the main thoroughfare.

A FULL YEAR OF MURDER

> "Please do not blame the guy I was with last night, we only had sex then I left. He knows nothing of what I have done."
>
> FAKE SUICIDE NOTE LEFT NEXT TO THE BODY OF DANIEL WHITWORTH

An East London gay man used dating apps to entice one victim after another. What began as sexual assaults escalated into serial murder. And despite repeatedly being a suspect and even being convicted of lesser crimes, he was always quickly released to commit more and worse crimes. To this day, nobody knows how many people he murdered.

Stephen Port was born in 1975 to a working-class family. Because Stephen was disengaged and distant in elementary school, many of his classmates assumed he was deaf. After graduating high school, he attended an art university. His family couldn't afford the college tuition, so Stephen quit his studies and decided to train to become a chef.

In his 30s, Stephen moved to Cooke Street in Barking, East London. Ryan Edwards, his neighbor, met him in 2005. Like Stephen, Ryan Edwards was gay, although they were never more than friends. Stephen was a tall, silent man. Also, he seldom made eye contact and answered in one or two words when conversing with others.

Due to his awkward demeanor, Stephen had difficulty meeting men in person, so he turned to social media and dating apps. Stephen could take all the time he needed to formulate the proper response to someone's question behind a screen. To impress his potential suitors, he created a fantasy world that he claimed was filled with military experience, Oxford University graduation, and special education training. He presented himself however he wished.

Stephen tricked the men he spoke to by using photos of himself from ten years ago on his profile. When the men met Stephen, they would be shocked to find a potbellied, cross-eyed, balding man, not the military hero he portrayed himself as online. Using dating apps such as Sleepyboy, Badoo, and Grindr, Stephen lured young men he never felt comfortable flirting with in person.

Stephen Port was attracted to men in their early and mid-twenties. He enjoyed the control he could have over these vulnerable young men. Ryan Edwards, Stephen's neighbor in Barking, said he sometimes chatted with Stephen's dates when he visited with Stephen and witnessed Stephen's verbal abuse of the men he brought home.

Stephen started using dating apps about the same time he started experimenting with drugs. He began to develop an unhealthy penchant for drugs and violent sex. Despite consuming hours of violent pornography online, Stephen's appetite for control was never satisfied.

ANTHONY WALGATE

Through a male escort website, Stephen met 23-year-old fashion student Anthony Walgate in June 2014. Anthony told Stephen that spending the night together would cost him 300 pounds, and Stephen readily agreed. Two days later, on June 17, Anthony and Stephen met. Within minutes of entering Stephen Port's apartment, Anthony was subdued, drugged, and sexually assaulted.

Anthony died during the assault, either because Stephen accidentally gave him too many drugs or because he deliberately killed him. Stephen didn't have a plan for getting rid of Anthony's body, so he left it on nearby Cooke Street. He then called 999 and told them he had found the body on his way home from work.

Sarah Sak was on a trip and promised her son Anthony she'd call him when she got home. Sarah last contacted Anthony on June 15. The morning before she returned home, she woke to several hundred text messages and missed phone calls. That's how Sarah learned her son had died.

Sarah was devastated. She now tells her friends to take as many pictures as possible because you never know what could happen. Sarah said Anthony loved being in the spotlight and taking photos. He'd recently made a book full of photos called, "All About Me."

When Sarah Sak returned to London, she headed to the police station to learn more about Anthony's death. Officers informed Sarah that Anthony had been found dead in the street, and she wanted to know how he died: was he shot, stabbed, or beaten? The detective investigating her son's death told Sarah they weren't sure what caused Anthony's death.

Anthony's friend told the detective that Anthony had planned to meet with a man the night he passed away. Upon some investigation, the detective found that the person Anthony was supposed to meet on the night he died was the same person who called 999 to report Anthony's body, Stephen Port.

Within days of Anthony Walgate's death, Stephen Port was arrested. Investigators seized his computer and took a DNA sample. During his interrogation, Stephen reported Anthony had come over, done drugs, and fallen asleep. Stephen said he left the 23-year-old alone in his apartment, and Anthony was dead when he returned the next day. He carried his body outside in a panic. Astonishingly, detectives believed Stephen and charged him with perverting the course of justice. He was released on bail and was scheduled to appear in court in March 2015.

GABRIEL KOVARI

Two months later, Stephen Port was back on dating apps and met 22-year-old Gabriel Kovari on Grindr. Ryan Edwards, Stephen's neighbor, said Gabriel was a smart, nice guy. Gabriel was passionate about art and wanted to become an artist. Gabriel moved into Stephen's apartment within days of meeting him. According to Ryan Edwards, while hanging out with Gabriel, Gabriel confided that Stephen was not the man most people thought he was. He called Stephen Port a "bad man."

Ryan Edwards and Gabriel were frequently in contact, and Ryan became concerned when Gabriel stopped responding to his messages. When Ryan asked Stephen what had happened to Gabriel, Stephen told him that Gabriel had met a soldier and left with him. However, Ryan became very concerned when Stephen told him he had news about Gabriel a few days later. Stephen said he received a text message from a friend of Gabriel's who informed him Gabriel had returned home, contracted a mysterious illness, and died as a result.

An East London woman was walking her dog in St Margaret's Church graveyard on August 28th, 2014, when she came upon a body slumped against a brick wall. The body belonged to Gabriel Kovari. Initially, investigators believed Gabriel died of a drug overdose and never suspected he was the victim of a serial killer, so Stephen Port was free to kill again.

DANIEL WHITWORTH

Next on Stephen Port's list of victims was Daniel Whitworth. They connected through a dating app, and two days later, Daniel's body was found in the same graveyard by the same woman walking her dog. After learning of Daniel Whitworth's death, his stepmother Mandy Pearson was heartbroken. Investigators told Daniel's family that the cause of death was an overdose of GHB, a popular party drug. The same drug caused the deaths of Gabriel Kovari and Anthony Walgate.

To evade capture, Stephen Port left a suicide note next to Daniel Whitworth's body in the graveyard. In the letter, "Daniel" claimed he was responsible for the death of Gabriel Kovari in the same spot days earlier. Daniel's stepmother didn't believe it belonged to her stepson. The handwriting didn't match, and there was no information about his personal life in the letter. Daniel didn't address the letter to his mother or father either. One line in the alleged suicide note concerned Daniel's family and friends: "Don't blame the guy I was with last night. It was only sex."

In March 2015, Stephen Port finally had his court date regarding Anthony Walgate. He pleaded guilty to perverting the course of justice and was sentenced to serve eight months in prison. Stephen Port was released on June

4, 2015, after serving only two months of his sentence. He was free to kill one final time.

JACK TAYLOR

A year after Stephen Port's last murder, 25-year-old Jack Taylor was found dead in the graveyard of St Margaret's Church. He worked as a forklift driver, and his death devastated his sisters, Jen and Donna. Jen and Donna were concerned when they discovered a vial of GHB next to Jack's body because Jack wasn't a drug user. Two weeks later, investigators contacted Jack Taylor's family and asked them to review CCTV footage of Jack on the day he went missing.

In the footage, Jack was seen with a tall blonde man. Investigators released the footage to the public and urged anyone with information to come forward. Eventually, a tip revealed that the man in the video was Stephen Port. During the investigation of Stephen Port, the investigators found disturbing evidence that led them to arrest Port on October 15, 2015.

After being arrested, Stephen Port confessed that he knew Daniel Whitworth. He said the two met at a party some time ago, but he did not know how he ended up dead. Although Stephen Port denied drugging or killing any of the four men, investigators were able to see past his words and charged him with their murders.

Stephen Port was dubbed the "Grindr Killer" following the

shocking murders of the four men. When Ryan Edwards saw the name Gabriel Kovari on the victim list, he was devastated. After the news of the Grindr Killer was released, several men accused Stephen Port of assaulting them. Stephen Port faced charges in July 2016 of eight more sexual assaults.

Despite pleading not guilty to the charges against him on October 5th, 2016, Stephen Port was convicted of 22 offenses after a four-week trial. He has been sentenced to a whole life tariff, meaning he will never be eligible for parole.

Since the Grindr Killer has been taken off the streets, Barking, East London police are investigating over sixty mysterious deaths. Investigators believe Stephen Port may have left many more victims in his wake, and they are thankful he is now off the streets.

SATAN IN THE CITY

"We knew he was a little nuts, but we never thought he would do anything like this."

NEIGHBOR OF ROBIN GECHT

As the Satanic panic swept through the nation in the 1980s, the Windy City dealt with a hellish group of killers. They targeted women who were out walking alone at night but would also kidnap victims in broad daylight. This murderous group evaded law enforcement for nearly two years, during which they brutally murdered more than 18 victims. Sadly, some of them were never identified.

THE LEADER: ROBIN GECHT

Every group needs a leader, and the Chicago Ripper Crew had Robin Gecht. He was born on November 30th, 1953, in Menard, Illinois. Gecht grew up with six siblings and didn't get along with his parents. He clashed with his mother and developed a deep hatred toward her. His parents sent him to a school for troubled children, but it clearly didn't help because Gecht was kicked out of the school and sent to live with his grandparents.

When he was 16, Gecht dropped out of high school and found a job. By the age of 19, he was an electrical contractor in the construction industry. He met a young woman named Rose Marie, a waitress, and the two began dating. They got married, and the newlyweds settled in a Chicago suburb.

THE DARK SIDE

The Gecht family had three children. During that time, the neighbors thought Gecht was a polite and hard-working young man. But he had a dark side – Gecht was obsessed with Satanism. He would devour satanic literature and obsess over descriptions of torture. Over time, he created a secret room in the attic of his house, where he put together a satanic temple.

The walls were painted red and had black inverted crosses on them. Gecht even made a sacrificial altar in the middle of the room. While reading about different rituals and torture methods, Gecht became fixated on a particular text that described hunting down a woman and removing her breasts. This type of torture sexually aroused him.

Gecht already had a fetish for large breasts, and his wife, Rose Marie, knew about it. After learning about the specific ritual, Gecht asked her to place needles in her nipples and leave them in as she cleaned around the house or went to work. Rose Marie did it for a while because it made her husband happy. But their bliss didn't last long, and Gecht began cheating on her.

Gecht was well-spoken and was becoming a Manson-like figure in his neighborhood. Teenage girls would hang out in Gecht's basement when Rose Marie was at work, and he would somehow talk them into putting needles in their nipples willingly. When Rose Marie found out her husband was having affairs in their house, she immediately requested a divorce. But Gecht wouldn't hear about it.

PUTTING TOGETHER A GROUP

By 1980, Robin Gecht knew he wanted to make his dark fantasies a reality. While it's unclear what made him start killing, some suggest that the discovery of John Wayne Gacy's crimes was the catalyst. Gecht had a connection with the notorious serial killer from Chicago. Gacy owned a construction business and hired Gecht to be a part of his crew when he was 20. When Gacy got caught, Gecht followed the case carefully in newspapers and on TV.

ANDREW KOKORALEIS

Curiously, Gecht didn't want to kill alone, which was unusual. He met Andrew Kokoraleis when the young man was working part-time at a donut shop. Gecht would often come in late at night, and on one occasion, Gecht offered to help Andrew out by getting him a hotel room because his car wouldn't start.

At that time, Gecht launched his own small construction business and needed workers. Andrew brought along his brother Thomas Kokoraleis, and another young man named Edward Spreitzer. All three were between 19 and 20 years old when they met Gecht, and all struggled financially. Gecht became their employer and friend. They sometimes stayed in his house and even babysat Gecht's children.

The Kokoraleis brothers and Spreitzer felt like they owed a lot to Gecht. After all, he was there for them when no one else was. All three were loyal to him, and Gecht knew it. Knowing they wouldn't tell on him, Gecht showed the group his improvised satanic temple in the attic. It's still unknown how Gecht introduced the subject of murder to the three men, but months later, the group would start terrorizing the citizens of Chicago.

THE FIRST MURDER

On May 23rd, 1981, Gecht, the Kokoraleis brothers, and Spreitzer got into the reddish-orange Dodge utility van owned by Gecht. As evening approached, they cruised Chicago, looking for their first victim. Gecht spotted 28-year-old **Linda Sutton** near Wrigley Field. He jumped out of the van and grabbed her. Linda was put in the van, handcuffed, and taken to an unknown location, where all four men sexually assaulted and tortured her.

She was stabbed in the chest, and Gecht amputated her left breast. The group then left Linda's body in a field in Villa Park near the Rip Van Winkle Motel. The group thought she was dead, but Linda was just unconscious and slowly bled to death. Meanwhile, her four attackers retreated to Gecht's attic temple, where they masturbated on her amputated breast and then ate it raw.

On June 1st, 1981, Linda's body was discovered. It was heavily decomposed, and the authorities had trouble identifying her. But one detail stood out right away —the amputated breast. The investigators knew this wouldn't be a typical murder case. Even after they identified the body, the police had no clues that could point them in the right direction. And so the case went cold.

THE KILLINGS CONTINUED

On May 15, 1982, 21-year-old **Lorraine Borowski** was abducted in front of her office. She worked at a real estate office in Elmhurst and loved to walk to work in the morning. Her boss arrived before 9 am expecting to see Lorraine inside. However, the door to the office was locked, and he noticed personal items on the ground scattered near the entrance.

Suspecting something had happened to Lorraine, her boss called the police and reported her missing. The officers talked to people who worked in the area and found their first witness, a business owner who saw a reddish-orange van on the morning of Lorraine's kidnapping.

Lorraine was found on October 10th, 1982. Her body was left on a cemetery side road in Darien and was identified through dental records. The examination of the remains confirmed Lorraine was tortured and stabbed multiple times in her chest and back. Her left breast was amputated, which was a clear connection to the murder of Linda Sutton.

On May 29th, 1982, 30-year-old **Shui Mak** was in a car with her brother. The two were going back home from the family restaurant in Streamwood. They fought, and Shui's brother left her by the side of the road without money to wait for her parents to pick her up. Once Shui's brother got home, he told his parents to drive back and bring her home.

They got in the car and drove to the spot where her brother had left her, but they couldn't find her and reported her missing. Her remains were found three months later in Cook County. She had been hit in the head with a blunt object several times, sexually assaulted, and stabbed in the chest.

On June 13th, 1982, **Angel York** was snatched from a street. She was pulled inside a van, handcuffed, and tortured. Gecht forced her to perform oral sex and demanded that she cut her left breast. He slashed her several times in the chest area and masturbated on her. Angel's wounds were closed up with duct tape, and she was thrown out of the van. Angel survived and reported the assault to the police. Even with this first-hand information from the victim, no arrests were made.

On August 28th, 1982, 18-year-old **Sandra Delaware** was found dead on the bank of the Chicago River. Her hands were bound, and her left breast was missing. She was stabbed and strangled. Sandra was a young sex worker, and the police suspected she was picked off the street. The autopsy confirmed she was killed six hours earlier.

Two weeks later, 31-year-old **Rose Davis** was found dead near a North Lake Shore apartment building. She had been strangled, stabbed, and sexually assaulted. Rose's face was unrecognizable because the killer used a hatchet.

On October 6, 1982, the group abducted 18-year-old **Beverly Washington**. She was tortured, sexually abused, and dumped by the railroad tracks. The men thought she was dead, but Beverly survived. Her left breast had been amputated, and she was rushed to the hospital. Beverly couldn't speak, but she wrote down everything she could remember.

THE DETAILS OF HER ATTACK

She provided the police with crucial details that finally led to arrests. After getting inside the van, her hands were tied behind her back, and she was forced to take tranquilizers. The Ripper Crew then took Beverly to a room and tied her to a bed, where she was sexually assaulted and tortured. She was able to describe the van interiors and the man who lured her in. Beverly even remembered that there were feathers hanging on the van's rearview mirror.

THE ARRESTS

The police knew the description of the van driven by their suspects and were on the lookout in the weeks after the attack on Beverly Washington. On October 20th, officers pulled over a reddish Dodge utility van that matched the information they had. The driver didn't match the description of Beverly's attacker. The driver, Edward Spreitzer, told police the vehicle belonged to his boss, Robin Gecht.

Spreitzer was on his way to meet Gecht, so the police followed him there. As soon as the officers laid eyes on Gecht, they realized he was the man described by Beverly. Gecht denied being involved in the crimes and appeared very confident, almost cocky. But the police knew he was their guy.

Gecht was linked to Rip Van Winkle Motel in Villa Park. After speaking to the manager, the investigators found out

Gecht rented rooms there all the time. But he was always accompanied by three men. One of them was Spreitzer.

The police knew they wouldn't get a confession out of Gecht, so they focused on Spreitzer. Even though he was scared of Gecht, Spreitzer started sharing all the gory details of the crimes and even mentioned unnamed victims that were never found.

When faced with these accusations, Gecht maintained his innocence and called a lawyer. Meanwhile, Spreitzer was taken to a location where one of their victims was discovered. Detectives trailed behind with Gecht, hoping he would figure out that Spreitzer was collaborating with the investigation. But when Spreitzer saw Gecht, he changed his story. This time, the killer was Andrew Kokoraleis.

Not wanting loose ends, the police interviewed Kokoraleis, who confessed to everything. He described the torture and abuse in detail and admitted he killed 18 women. Kokoraleis mentioned that Gecht had a breast fetish, and the investigators got yet another proof that he was involved in the murders. But Gecht kept denying he knew anything about the torture and abduction of women in Chicago.

Then, Andrew Kokoraleis' older brother Thomas was brought in for questioning. He finally started talking about Gecht's satanic temple in the attic and the rituals the group did up there. The police found out about the cannibalism and the reason for severing the breasts from the victims. The older Kokoraleis brother said the group had 15 breasts stored in the box at one point.

Edward Spreitzer and the Kokoraleis brothers accepted the responsibility for the crimes, but Gecht still maintained his innocence. However, Beverly Washingon identified him as her attacker from the photo lineup, and Gecht was scheduled to appear in court.

THE SENTENCING

Since Robin Gecht kept his mouth shut during the interviews, the police had no physical evidence connecting him to the murders in 1983. But he was found guilty of attempted murder, aggravated kidnapping, and sexual assault of Beverly Washington. He was sentenced to 120 years in prison. Gecht could be released from Menard Correctional Center on parole on October 10th, 2042. He will be 88 years old.

In 1984, Edward Spreitzer pleaded guilty to four murders, attempted murder, aggravated kidnapping, and sexual assault. He was sentenced to life in prison without the possibility of parole. Two years later, Spreitzer was found guilty of the murder and aggravated kidnapping of Linda Sutton. He received a death sentence. In 2003, Governor George H. Ryan commuted the sentences of all death row prisoners in Illinois, including Spreitzer.

In 1985, Andrew Kokoraleis appeared in court and was found guilty of murder, aggravated kidnapping, and the rape of Rose Davis. The defense argued he was following Gecht's orders and shouldn't be sent to death row. The judge sentenced him to life in prison without the possibility of parole. Then in March 1987, he was found guilty of the aggravated kidnapping and murder of Lorraine Borowski and was sentenced to death.

Andrew and his brother Thomas Kokoraleis belonged to a Greek Orthodox Church, which tried to prevent Andrew's execution. The death penalty was carried out on March 17th, 1999, and Andrew Kokoraleis was executed by lethal injection. As a result, the future bishop of the Greek Orthodox Metropolis of Chicago became an activist and helped end the death penalty in Illinois. Andrew Kokoraleis was the last executed prisoner in this state.

Since Thomas Kokoraleis' confession was the most useful one, he was sentenced to life in prison without parole for the murder and sexual assault of Lorraine Borowski, thus avoiding the death sentence. After several years, Kokoraleis filed an appeal and was granted a new trial for the murder of Borowski. He pleaded guilty and got his sentence reduced to 70 years. He was paroled on March 29, 2019, and now resides in Aurora, Illinois.

A NOVEL MURDER

> "From that moment on, I don't remember much. She hit my hand, we wrestled and came to the back door. That's where it happened. She was yelling, screaming —never stopped screaming...It's haunting me still."
>
> RICHARD KLINKHAMER AT TRIAL, 2000

IN 1992, a Dutch crime writer presented his new manuscript to his publisher. The story was gruesome and chilling, but it was rejected. The writer's wife had gone missing one year prior and hadn't been found, and the crime writer's book detailed seven ways he could have killed his wife.

Richard Klinkhamer was born in 1937, in Ermelo, Netherlands. His mother, Maria, was from Austria, and she met Jacob Klinkhamer in the Netherlands, and the two got married. Richard was their third child. Maria had had several affairs over the years, and Jacob finally filed for divorce shortly after Richard was born.

Maria got custody of the children but wasn't ready to be a single mother and Richard was put into foster care.

Meanwhile, Maria was living in Amsterdam and earned money as a sex worker. Her clients were often German soldiers, which led her to be shamed after the war ended. Her hair was chopped off, and she was forced to participate in an *ugly carnival* alongside other women who collaborated with the Nazis in any way.

Richard had spent some time with his uncle in Austria but returned to Amsterdam when his uncle was murdered. He was soon sent to live with his dad Jacob. During this time, Jacob opened up to Richard and revealed he wasn't his father but loved and cared for the boy regardless.

A GROWN MAN

When he turned 18, Richard enlisted in the French Foreign Legion and was sent to Algeria.

Four years later, he was back in Amsterdam and struggling to find employment. He took a risk and opened a butcher shop with his brothers. The business was an absolute success, and around that time, Richard met a woman named Leontine von Emmerik, who would become his first wife.

Their relationship was slightly toxic from the beginning, but Leontine got pregnant, and Richard felt like he didn't have a choice, so he proposed. They got married on April 5, 1962, and six months later, Leontine gave birth to their first child. The couple had three children together.

THE RELATIONSHIP WITH HANNELORE

Richard had known Hannelore Godfrinon since she was a teenager. The girl was adopted by the von Emmerik family after going through a traumatic event at the age of 10. Her father brutally murdered Hannelore's mother, and the little girl found her mother's body at the bottom of the stairs.

Richard was already married to Leontine, but that didn't stop Hannelore from flirting with him. He kept his distance, but when Hannelore turned 18, the two began an affair. Hiding it from Leontine was impossible, and she knew about it. Richard's wife hoped he would end the relationship with her adopted sister. Three years later, Richard asked Leontine for a divorce.

In 1978, Hannelore and Richard got married and decided to leave their life in Amsterdam behind. The newlyweds moved to Ganzedijk, a small village near Finsterwolde. Hannelore worked as a pediatric nurse at a hospital while Richard explored his creative side and started writing a book about the French Foreign Legion.

The book called *Obedient as a Dog* was a success, and Richard soon began working on a collection of short stories. In his free time, Richard traded on the stock market, and as a result, the couple made a lot of money.

Their relationship looked idyllic, but Hannelore wasn't happy at all. Richard would drink alcohol when he was writing, and his temperament changed. He would sometimes hit Hannelore during their arguments. She tried to leave Richard several times but always came back.

In 1987, Richard lost all his savings after a stock market crash. It made him depressed, which led to him drinking more than usual. Hannelore experienced horrific domestic abuse during this time and would frequently seek refuge at her neighbor's house. Her friend and coworker at the hospital lived next door to the couple and confirmed she saw bruises on her.

HANNELORE IS MISSING

On February 6th, 1991, Richard showed up at the local police station and reported his wife, Hannelore, missing. He said her red bike was at the train station in Winschoten, but she didn't return home. After questioning those closest to Hannelore and finding out about the domestic abuse, the investigators were sure her husband had harmed her. Richard became the prime suspect almost immediately.

During the initial interview, Richard denied abusing Hannelore, but the police weren't convinced. They searched his house and the rest of the property, including the garden and the shed, which served as Richard's writing studio. However, there was no trace of Hannelore. Sniffer dogs canvased the land around the house to no avail. Finally, the investigators had a Royal Dutch air force F-16 fly over the entire property with an infrared scanner.

The police needed any evidence to prove Richard had murdered his wife, but there was none. Soon the case went cold, regardless of the suspicions that Hannelore's husband was guilty of the crime. There was no physical evidence that he harmed her.

THE BOOK

In 1992, one year after Hannelore's mysterious disappearance, Richard Klinkhamer was in his publisher's office. He'd brought in a manuscript of his new novel called *Woensdag Gehaktdag*, which was Wednesday, Mince Day in English. His latest work described seven ways Richard could have murdered his wife.

Willem Donker, his publisher, was well aware of Richard's private life and refused to publish this novel. Donker asked Richard directly if he had killed his wife, and the man replied it wasn't a good time to talk about it. One of the methods Richard mentioned in his book is closely related to the title and his experience in working at a butcher shop. He suggested that he could have gotten rid of her body by using a mincer and feeding the pigeons the remains of his wife.

Donker didn't want the controversy surrounding his publishing house, so he suggested that Richard could expand one part of the manuscript and do some rewriting to put him off.

Richard kept himself busy by writing manuscripts and drinking. After a couple of years, Richard's unpublished novel became the main topic in literary circles. The media picked up on the story, and the author even gave several interviews regarding the book.

By 1997, Richard was in a new relationship with a woman named Margreet de Heer and ready to leave the countryside behind. He packed up his bags and returned to Amsterdam. It seemed like Richard enjoyed being a notorious and strange author. He often created rumors himself by giving odd statements to those around him. Meanwhile, he sold his old house after pronouncing his wife, Hannelore, legally dead.

THE DISCOVERY OF THE BODY

A family moved into Richard's old home and immediately started doing renovations. They wanted to make the yard more suitable for the children, so the couple hired a digger to remove the concrete base of the garden shed. The construction workers noticed a tiny piece of plastic and pulled it out. Inside was a large chunk of clay that was buried underneath the floor. When they cracked the clay, the workers discovered a piece of a human skull.

The police were called, and the forensic team found the rest of the skeleton. The dental records confirmed it was Hannelore Klinkhamer. Richard was located and arrested in Amsterdam, and the author confessed to the crime the next day.

THE MURDER AND SENTENCING

According to Richard Klinkhamer, on January 31st, 1991, he got into an argument with Hannelore after she returned from shopping in Groningen. She was furious and demanded that Richard pack his things and move out right away. The two started fighting and wrestling on the floor. Struggling to get Richard off of her, Hannelore grabbed a wrench.

Richard overpowered his wife and took the wrench from her. He hit her in the head several times, and Hannelore screamed as she lay on the ground dying. Wanting to hide what he had done, the writer dug a hole in the shed, placed her body inside, covered it with compost, and filled the grave with concrete.

After the confession, Richard was sentenced to seven years in prison. However, he was released in 2003 after serving two years for good behavior.

After the arrest, Willem Donker, the publisher, asked Richard if he wanted his novel *Wednesday, Mince Day* published, and the writer refused. Eventually, the book was released and became his most infamous work. Donker was criticized for not printing the novel in 1992 because it might have led to the arrest sooner.

On January 21, 2016, Richard Klinkhamer was found dead in his apartment in Amsterdam. According to the police, he committed suicide by shooting himself in the head. He was 78 years old.

HE WILL KILL YOU

> "She started telling people she had had an incestuous relationship with her son as a way of 'curing' him of homosexuality...but I don't believe she had sex with Tony. I think she simply enjoyed shocking people."
>
> SAM GREEN, BARBARA BAEKELAND'S LOVER

Once dubbed the most beautiful woman in New York, Barbara Baekeland was a famous socialite who threw legendary parties at her apartment on Upper East Side. While she tried to make others believe her life was picture-perfect, it was everything but. Barbara dealt with a toxic marriage with her wealthy husband and even had a possessive and incestuous relationship with her son Antony. The latter probably resulted in her murder.

WHO WAS BARBARA DALY BAEKELAND?

Barbara Daly Baekeland was born in Cambridge, Massachusetts, on September 28th, 1921, to Nina and Frank Daly. They were a typical middle-class family until the Great Depression. That is when Barbara's father lost all their money. Realizing there was no way out of that situation, Frank Daly committed suicide by carbon monoxide poisoning in 1932. But he staged it to look like an accident, and the family received the insurance money.

Nina Daly had mental problems since her teens and even suffered a mental breakdown before her pregnancy. Her husband's suicide made things worse, so she decided it was time for Barbara and her to move from Cambridge. The mother was fixated on marrying Barbara to a rich husband, so the two went to New York in the late 1930s.

The Daly women lived in the famous Delmonico Hotel, and Barbara pursued a modeling career. Her beauty was noticed by the editors of the biggest fashion magazines, such as Vogue and Harper's Bazaar. Barbara became quite successful and was considered one of the most beautiful young women in New York at that time.

What people didn't know was that Barbara was unwell. She had mental health problems and was treated by Foster Kennedy, a well-known psychiatrist. Barbara allegedly had an affair with John Jacob Astor VI, a shipping businessman and the son of Colonel John Jacob Astor IV. After learning her lover wasn't planning to leave his wife, Barbara started looking for another potential match.

Since her modeling career was on the rise, Barbara thought it would be the perfect time to start a movie career. She traveled to Hollywood to do a screen test, but the producers weren't impressed. Her trip to the West Coast wasn't a complete bust because she met Cornelia "Dickie" Baekeland, another socialite who wanted to become an actress.

MEETING BROOKS BAEKELAND

Brooks Baekeland was the grandson of Leo Baekeland, an inventor who discovered Velox photographic paper in 1893 and Bakelite in 1907. He sold the Velox paper to George Eastman of the Eastman Kodak Co. for $750,000. Bakelite was the first synthetic plastic and led to the development of the plastic we all use today.

Cornelia Baekeland and Barbara Daly became fast friends and were soon inseparable. At that time, Brooks was a trainee pilot with the Royal Canadian Air Force, but his sister Cornelia invited him to his house in Connecticut for a weekend, and he managed to come. There he met Barbara Daly, and the two began a whirlwind romance.

THE MARRIAGE

Barbara knew that Brooks was everything she had been

looking for – he was both wealthy and good-looking. But it was clear from the beginning that Brooks wasn't interested in marriage. So Barbara found a way to make him marry her. She made up a pregnancy. Knowing that marriage was an honorable thing to do in that situation, Brooks proposed to Barbara.

After the wedding, Barbara said that she had lost the baby, and that was it. The newlyweds moved to the Upper East Side and continued to do what they did best – throw parties for the rich and famous. Celebrities such as Tennessee Williams, Greta Garbo, and Salvador Dali were a common sight at the Baekeland residence.

But the marriage to Brooks wasn't a happy one. He often had affairs, and it was obvious to Barbara that her husband was not planning to settle down. She also cheated on him as a form of revenge. Her mental health struggles became impossible to hide, and Barbara went through depressive episodes. Furthermore, she drank heavily, which didn't help at all. After World War II, Barbara found out she was pregnant, and this time it was for real.

THE BIRTH OF ANTONY BAEKELAND

Antony Baekeland was born on August 28th, 1946, and both Barbara and Brooks adored the little boy. They were convinced he was a child prodigy destined to do great things. Antony frequently attended dinner parties and mingled with the adults.

In 1954, When Antony was eight years old, Barbara and Brooks decided to live in Europe for a bit. They kept their New York apartment and rented luxurious places all over the Old Continent. Antony was sent to various boarding schools. The dinner parties continued, but this time they were hanging out with the European elite.

After some time, Brooks was bored with this nomadic life and wanted to return to New York. Barbara was against it but wouldn't let her husband go. Their marriage was getting more and more toxic because Barbara would either threaten or attempt suicide every time Brooks tried to leave her.

In 1960, the Baekelands were in Paris, and Brooks fell in love with a daughter of a French diplomat. The woman was 15 years younger than him, but that didn't stop them from having an affair. Brooks was determined to leave Barbara this time, but his wife attempted suicide again and demanded that Brooks end the relationship, which he did.

The family lived in Spain and Switzerland in 1967, and the 20-year-old Antony met a man named Jake Cooper, also known as Black Jake. Cooper was tall, handsome, and adventurous. Additionally, he was bisexual, and Antony fell in love with him. Brooks already suspected his son was homosexual, and Antony himself told a therapist that he had his first gay experience at a boarding school when he was 8.

Cooper was into drugs, and Antony tried hallucinogens

with him. The two even traveled from Spain to Morocco to purchase the illegal substances. When Barbara found out about this, she was furious. Believing Cooper was after Antony's money, she traveled to Spain to get her son back to Switzerland.

"CURING" ANTONY

Barbara was unable to accept that her son was homosexual and wasn't supportive at all. So when she discovered Antony was dating a girl named Sylvie, she was relieved. Hoping the two would get married, Barbara invited Sylvie to family dinners and vacations. She didn't know the girl wasn't attracted to Antony. Instead, she was with Brooks.

The affair was revealed in early 1968. Barbara attempted suicide again in hopes of keeping her husband, but that didn't stop him from leaving her this time. He filed for a divorce and left his family to live with Sylvie.

Antony and Barbara were on their own, but Brooks made sure they had money. The mother and son moved to London, United Kingdom, and rented an apartment in Chelsea. In 1969, Antony started making art, but it was terrible. He was stuck with a mentally unwell mother and was falling apart too.

Antony was treated for schizophrenia and paranoia in the past. Plagued by her own demons, Barbara believed that Antony's sexual orientation was the reason for his illness.

So she decided to "cure" him by hiring female sex workers to help him out. Barbara would frequently stay in the room with them and give suggestions.

To make things even worse, the mother started joining in. She sexually assaulted her son and even told friends about it. Barbara was confident she was helping Antony and providing him with the necessary therapy. Meanwhile, Antony continued using psychedelics after the move to London. His mental health was on a rapid decline.

His resentment toward his mother was evident. He even tried to throw her under a bus in July 1972. Antony was arrested for attempted murder, but Barbara refused to press charges, and her son was released from custody. The young man was hospitalized in the Priory, but the therapy wasn't doing much for him. After that, Antony reached out to his father. Brooks was starting a new life with his young lover Sylvie and didn't have time for his son.

Antony began physically abusing his mother and attempted to stab her in the eye with a pen after an argument. On October 30, 1972, the doctor who treated him warned Barbara that Antony was trying to kill her, but she ignored it. In the fall of 1972, the young man was frequently paranoid or completely shut off and catatonic.

THE MURDER

On November 17, 1972, Barbara was making dinner for

Antony, and he began stabbing her with a kitchen knife. As she lay dead on the kitchen floor, her son ordered Chinese food. When the police arrived to take him away, he was sitting and eating his meal.

After the arrest, Antony asked several times for his mother, which suggested that he had no idea that Barbara was dead. After a while, he confessed to murdering Barbara. His history of mental illness and the abuse he suffered made the judge go easy on him. As a result, Antony was sent to Broadmoor Hospital.

Antony spent six years in Broadmoor Hospital, and by 1980, he was doing exceptionally well. Daily therapy sessions and the right combination of meds helped stabilize his mind. His friends noticed the change and thought he shouldn't be kept in the mental hospital anymore.

They pulled some strings at the American embassy, and Antony was released on July 21, 1980. But the judge ordered that Antony go live with his 87-year-old grandmother Nina in New York. On July 27, only six days after the release, Antony asked his grandmother if he could make an overseas call. When Nina said no, Antony grabbed a kitchen knife and stabbed her eight times.

Luckily, Nina survived the attack, and Antony was arrested by the New York City Police Department. He was charged with attempted murder and sent to Rikers Island to wait for the trial. The psychiatric team at Rikers observed him for eight months, and Antony was positive he would be released on bail in March 1981.

The court hearing was held on March 20, 1981, and the case was adjourned because Antony's medical files hadn't arrived from the United Kingdom. Antony was returned to the Rikers Island prison and was found dead in his cell at 4 pm. He allegedly suffocated himself with a plastic bag.

A TIME TO HATE

"Our justice system is the laughingstock of the world. Life definitely doesn't mean life. But I choose to forgive because living a life of hate is so destructive."

DR. GEE WALKER

Every hate crime is ugly. But the case of Anthony Walker is incredibly painful because of the wonderful person he already was at eighteen. On his way to what surely would have been a fruitful and productive adult life, he was instead ambushed and killed for no other reason than his race.

Born on February 21st, 1987, Anthony Walker was brought up in a loving home. Each of Anthony's siblings was responsible because his mother, Gee Walker, raised them with strong Christian values. When Anthony was a child, his parents separated, which made things difficult for him and his siblings. Nevertheless, Anthony stepped up and was there for his mother. During this time, Gee Walker described Anthony as her rock. His love, care, and wisdom were beyond his years.

When Anthony was old enough to get a job, he applied for a job at McDonald's. Of course, Anthony was hired and gave his first paycheck to his mother. He suggested buying a new car with the money since the family's old one kept breaking down.

So, Gee and Anthony headed to a car dealership, where Anthony put down a deposit on a seven-seat passenger van that he thought would suit the family. Despite Anthony's belief that he'd "purchased" the car, Anthony didn't know his mother continued to pay for it after he made the deposit. Gee Walker had no problems with her son believing he had purchased the car. Anthony was immensely proud of himself, rightfully so.

Anthony had several hobbies, including basketball. He was a natural at the sport and played for Liverpool City Hoops. Through his love of basketball, Anthony founded a team for local children to play. He taught them how to socialize and stay out of trouble by sharing his love of the game with the children.

Anthony studied at Knowsley Hey High School in Huyton, England. Due to his diligence, he earned stellar grades.

After high school, Anthony studied media, drama, IT, and law at university.

Anthony's goal was a law degree, and he contemplated studying in America. Anthony had a level-headed quality that would have made him an excellent lawyer.

Whenever someone tried to fight him, he walked away and tried to resolve the issue without violence. Growing up in Huyton, Merseyside, Anthony's pragmatic personality would come in handy.

In Huyton, a small town near Liverpool, Afro-Caribbean families were a very small minority of the population. Many hateful residents didn't accept the Walker family as members of the community.

RACISM IN HUYTON

Residents of Huyton routinely called Gee and her children derogatory names. Gee was harassed while walking with Anthony and his siblings. It hurt Gee that her children were subjected to constant prejudice there. Despite wearing their school uniforms, some bus drivers denied boarding to Anthony and his sisters. The Walker siblings sometimes had to let buses pass them because some drivers gave them a hard time.

During a summer night in 2005, 18-year-old Anthony was out with friends in Huyton when he was attacked by a group of men armed with cricket bats. As he was being treated at the hospital for his injuries, Anthony asked Gee not to notify the police. One of Anthony's attackers was a boy with a learning disability, and Anthony feared the boy would get a criminal record.

Although Gee was angry about what happened to her son, she followed his wishes and didn't notify authorities. She raised Anthony to show forgiveness and mercy, and Gee was very proud of him for turning out the way he did. Sadly, three weeks later, there was no mercy shown to Anthony Walker when he was attacked again.

On the night of Friday, July 29th, 2005, Anthony Walker was with his cousin, 17-year-old Marcus, and girlfriend Louise. Anthony was going to attend a friend's birthday party but wanted to make sure Louise got on the bus safely before he headed to the party. At 11 pm, he and Marcus walked Louise to the bus stop.

The trio waited at the stop near the Huyton Pub. It was a windy night, and the rain had just started to come down. Amidst the howling wind, Anthony heard two men across the street hurling slurs at them. In response to the men shouting back at him, Anthony replied that they would be leaving shortly; they were only waiting for the bus to arrive.

Even though the trio tried to ignore the men, they continued to yell at them. Anthony, however, had had enough when the men started making derogatory comments about Louise.

Anthony, Marcus, and Louise decided to walk to a different bus stop and leave the situation behind. They headed toward a nearby park where they could take a shortcut to the next bus stop. The trio was walking through the park when two men emerged from the shadows and attacked them.

Louise and Marcus slipped through the men's fingers and ran for help, but Anthony couldn't escape. The attackers pinned Anthony to the ground while Marcus ran to a house and banged on the door. The homeowner was awake despite the late hour and drove Marcus back to the park to help Anthony. Anthony lay on the ground with an ice axe protruding from his head. The attackers were long gone.

STILL ALIVE

Anthony was transported to the hospital by ambulance, still alive but unresponsive. Doctors assessed Anthony's injuries and determined they were too severe for the hospital to treat. He would have to be transferred.

Gee Walker was notified of her son's condition and hurriedly drove to the neurological specialty hospital, where Anthony was sent. Nurses consoled her in a private waiting room. She was told that Anthony was undergoing emergency surgery and doctors were doing everything possible to save him.

The doctors were able to remove the ice axe during

surgery, but his brain injury was too severe and he died at 5:25 am.

Since Anthony's body was considered evidence, Gee could not say goodbye to her son. She was left in limbo while police searched for the attackers.

Huyton police said the attack on Anthony was racially motivated in a statement to the public. While many Huyton residents were devastated by Anthony's death, some racists rejoiced. In the days following Anthony's murder, racist graffiti appeared in the park where he died.

After her brother's death, Anthony's sister ventured into the Huyton pub to ask questions about who might have killed her brother. Several people mentioned two names they thought were connected to the murder, and she was shocked to learn that she knew them.

According to the group, Anthony was attacked by Paul Taylor and Michael Barton. Both boys knew Anthony and his siblings because they grew up together and attended the same schools.

Michael Barton was seventeen, and his cousin, Paul Taylor, was twenty. Huyton's St. John's Estate area, considered one of the roughest areas, is where the two boys grew up. Many teens raised on the estate felt trapped by the lack of opportunities, and they turned to crime and drugs.

Paul Taylor spent over two years in a juvenile prison for

battery and robbery. He had a reputation in Huyton for carrying a knife and using it to threaten people.

Michael Barton had a promising start to life. When he became a teenager, however, things started to change. Barton dropped out of school and failed an Army entrance exam, which devastated him. The young man longed to be a soldier, but now he had no idea what to do. He worked odd jobs around town, then worked as a roofer and forklift driver but never stayed in one position for long. Soon Barton began running around with his cousin Paul Taylor and became involved in frequent criminal activities.

Barton and Taylor were now on the run. They drove to Dover, caught the ferry to Calais, France, and then drove to Amsterdam to escape arrest.

The following day, news outlets throughout England covered Anthony's murder. A media frenzy ensued when the suspects were named. Michael Barton was the brother of Joey Barton —a famous footballer. Although Joey Barton wasn't raised with his brother Michael, he begged his brother and cousin Paul Taylor to turn themselves in on television.

He said:
"My side of the Barton family is sickened by his [Anthony] death.

Although I was not brought up with Michael, I urge him to come forward. You must do this for the Walker family, so they can mourn Anthony and because you know it is the right thing to do."

In closing, Joey Barton expressed his condolences to the Walker family. Several hours later, Michael Barton and Paul Taylor returned to England and were taken into custody.

The trial began in November 2005. Prosecutors told the jury that Barton and Taylor had attempted to steal someone's four-wheeler the morning of the murder, and once that plan fell through, the two men did cocaine before getting drunk at the Huyton pub.

Taylor pleaded guilty and expressed remorse for his role in Anthony's murder. He was found guilty and sentenced to serve a minimum of 23 years in prison.

Barton maintained his innocence the entire time and said Taylor was responsible for the crime.

Initially, Barton portrayed himself as an unwilling accomplice. After Taylor struck Anthony with the axe, Barton even claimed he attempted to help Anthony by trying to remove the axe from Anthony's head.

A jury found Barton guilty and sentenced him to eighteen years in prison.

Barton's stint behind bars at first was difficult. He received many reprimands for violent assaults and theft. According to prison officials, after his first year as an inmate, he underwent a "remarkable transformation," and his sentence was reduced by a year.

Eventually, Barton began volunteering for charities while incarcerated. He was able to leave the prison for part of the day on a work release program. Barton, now 34 years old, was paroled in October 2022 after spending 17 years behind bars.

According to the parole board, "After considering the circumstances of his offending, the progress made while in custody, and the evidence presented at the hearing, the panel was satisfied that Mr. Barton was suitable for release."

Among the conditions of his parole are living at a predetermined address, adhering to a curfew, being monitored and supervised, and not contacting victims.

~

The Anthony Walker Foundation was founded in 2006, one year after Anthony Walker's murder. As part of its mission, the foundation addresses issues such as hate crimes, discrimination, and racism.

The charity has helped over 10,000 people who have suffered racial abuse.

Anthony's mother, Gee Walker, received the Pride of Britain Award in November 2021 for her work with the foundation. In December 2022, she was awarded the

Member of the Order of the British Empire medal for services to diversity and racial injustice for her work as founder and patron of The Anthony Walker Foundation by King Charles III.

Upon receiving her MBE, she said:

> "I understand the word bittersweet now because that's exactly what it is because the sweetness is that we have got the award and the bitterness is that it should be him."

SOLVED BY SODA

"You will never breathe another free breath, and maybe that's just."

ARAPAHOE COUNTY DISTRICT
JUDGE DARREN VAHLE

Cherry Hills Village, a quiet and affluent neighborhood outside Denver, Colorado, was shocked by a gruesome crime in the Summer of 1981.

A bright young woman loved by her friends and family was found viciously murdered in her home. The police collected the DNA evidence from the scene and worked on the case for decades, hoping to catch the killer one day.

After a decades-long search for the truth, justice was

finally served in the Sylvia Quayle murder case. And it was a major breakthrough in technology that brought the killer to justice. This case serves as a reminder that even the most seemingly hopeless of cold cases can be solved, thanks to the constant advancements in science and technology.

~

Sylvia Quayle was born to parents William and Mary on September 23rd, 1946, in Englewood, Colorado. A few years later, the Quayle family welcomed another baby girl, Jo.

Sylvia was a hardworking and ambitious student who graduated from Englewood High School and quickly found a job. Since she was in love with architecture, Sylvia managed to get employed in an architecture firm working as a secretary.

In her spare time, she studied the work of her uncle, a famous architect. She loved cooking and baking, so Sylvia started her own business. She owned a small bakery where she made wedding cakes. Sylvia also dabbled in art and was very interested in pottery. Always close to her parents, she lived just two houses down from them on the 3800 block of Ogden Street in Cherry Hills Village, a suburb of Denver.

Sylvia had worked hard, and at 34 years old, she was enjoying running her wedding cake business and her beautifully decorated home.

The Quayles usually had coffee in the morning, and their older daughter would always arrive before 8 am, chat with William and Mary, and then go to work. That morning routine was broken on August 4th, 1981, when Sylvia failed to show up at her parents' house.

THE BODY IS DISCOVERED

William and Mary Quayle were worried because their daughter, Sylvia, didn't show up at their house for coffee and they couldn't reach her by phone. Her father got dressed and walked over to her house. When he arrived, William noticed that the screen door and the front door to his daughter's house were open.

Once inside, William saw a horrifying scene. He found Sylvia dead on the living room floor. Her body was naked, with a red shirt pulled over her head. Her legs were spread, and her underwear lay nearby. A white towel was covering her face. William called 911 at 7:57 am and waited for them in front of the house.

Two officers from Cherry Hills Police Department arrived on the scene, and William informed them he had taken the white towel that was on his daughter's face and covered her exposed lower body. It was an understandable act done by a parent who wanted to give their child some dignity. Officers at the scene took the towel and moved it back to the position Mr. Quayle had indicated.

EVIDENCE AND AUTOPSY

After police spoke to the Quayle family, they discovered that Sylvia's sister Jo was the last person to talk to her. The two were on the phone at 11 pm on August 4th. After that, the killer cut the phone lines using a garden hose to reach and pull down the wires outside the house.

The investigators determined the perpetrator entered the house through the bathroom window. Sylvia kept bathroom products on the windowsill, and they were neatly arranged on the floor. This meant the killer had enough time to move them and not wake up Sylvia. The killer walked around the house freely while Sylvia slept in her bedroom.

The autopsy revealed Sylvia was shot with a .22 caliber bullet in the head, but the medical examiner said it wasn't her cause of death. She died of blood loss after the killer stabbed her three times in her upper back with one of those cuts severing her aorta.

A kitchen knife was found near her body, and several large blood stains were in different parts of the house. The biggest one was in the bedroom, but the police found another near the front door. It was clear that Sylvia managed to run away from her attacker and tried to leave by the front door.

The killer sexually assaulted Sylvia. Her hands were covered in blood and most of her fingernails were broken, suggesting she fought as she was being attacked. There were clear strangulation marks on her neck, with visible bruises. She had red marks on her left inner thigh and bruising on her left hip.

The forensic team found no fingerprints at the scene but collected more than 100 pieces of evidence. The most valuable was semen left on the carpet, the white towel and on Sylvia's body.

OTTIS TOOLE CONNECTION

In 1983, two years after the murder of Sylvia Quayle, Ottis Toole, a well-known serial killer, confessed to the crime. Toole and his partner, Henry Lee Lucas, took the blame for more than 100 unsolved murders across the United States. Interestingly, law enforcement believed them and closed many cases after their confessions.

Toole is famous for confessing to the murder of Adam Walsh, the 6-year-old son of the host of America's Most Wanted, John Walsh. He described the murder in detail and claimed he cannibalized the little boy. Several years later, Toole recanted his confession, and the investigators couldn't find any physical evidence he harmed Walsh.

A large blood stain was found in Toole's vehicle, but the police didn't have the DNA testing technology in the 1980s to confirm if it was connected to the Quayle case. The piece of the carpet from the car was misplaced and was never fully examined. Toole once again confessed to the murder before his death in September 1996.

Cherry Hills Police Department reluctantly charged Toole with Sylvia's murder, but he never went on trial in Colorado. Toole was sentenced to death in 1984 for a different crime. In 1985, just one year after Toole's appearance in court, a newspaper from Texas started questioning Toole's and Lucas' murder confessions, and the investigators determined they were lying.

Ottis Toole was convicted of committing six murders. The investigators working on Sylvia's case weren't sure if he was Sylvia's killer, but in 1993 they had confirmation. DNA testing revealed that Toole wasn't Sylvia's murderer. All charges against him were dropped, and the case was immediately reopened.

THE SUSPECT

Even though DNA testing wasn't as developed back then as it is now, the investigators recognized the importance of their DNA evidence and kept it safe and secure. The carpet from the Quayle crime scene was analyzed again in 1995, but the Cherry Hills Police Department had to wait for years to get the DNA profile of the killer. They finally got the DNA profile in 2000, and they submitted it to the Combined DNA Index System (CODIS). But there was no match until 2020. The match was from a very distant DNA "cousin," so they had a lot of work to do to identify the killer.

In January 2020, Cherry Hills Police Department began working with United Data Connect, a company specializing in genetic genealogy. They uploaded the suspect's DNA to two public DNA websites and created a family tree with over 3000 people. They contacted a DNA "cousin" to do another DNA test to help them narrow the tree down even more. Five months later, in May 2020, the investigators were informed about a possible match. His name was David Dwayne Anderson.

David Dwayne Anderson was 21 years old at the time of Sylvia's murder and lived in nearby Englewood. He was arrested several times for burglaries between 1981 and 1986. Anderson usually entered the houses through windows and always wore gloves, which explained why no fingerprints were found in Sylvia's home.

In 2020, Anderson was living in Cozad, Nebraska. On January 17th, 2021, United Data Connect sent their investigator, Robert Fuller, to collect Anderson's DNA surreptitiously. The suspect lived in an apartment building, and Fuller first confirmed his address. After that, he went dumpster diving and found two trash bags that belonged to Anderson. The bags contained bills sent to the suspect and several items that could contain his DNA.

The investigator collected a Vanilla Coke can and some other bottles. Two days later, Fuller was in Sterling, Colorado, where he handed over the items to the Cherry Hills Village technician, who sent the potential evidence to the Colorado Bureau of Investigation.

On January 29th, 2021, the police got the results from the DNA collected from the trash. Anderson's DNA matched the DNA from the Quayle crime scene, namely the semen collected from the carpet, white towel, and swabs taken from Sylvia's body.

ARREST AND TRIAL

David Dwayne Anderson was arrested on February 10, 2021, and was charged with one count of first-degree murder after deliberation, and one count of first-degree felony murder.

> Former Denver District Attorney Mitch Morrissey made a statement at the press conference announcing Anderson's arrest.
>
> "Sylvia's family today means a lot to me. And when I read this case, and realized that her father found her in the condition that I know she was in. The way that she was left after being brutalized and killed — I can't imagine as a father myself of a young woman about the same age to have a morning like that. And I know he's not here. And for me, that's probably the hardest part of solving these 40-year-old cases . . . is that some of the people that want answers that need closure, they don't get it because they're gone."

The trial began in March 2022, but the judge declared a mistrial because the jury could not reach a verdict.

The second trial began in June 2022, and this time, David Dwayne Anderson was found guilty on two counts of first-degree murder of Sylvia Quayle.

In August 2022, exactly 41 years after the murder, 62-year-old David Dwayne Anderson was sentenced to life in prison.

Arapahoe County District Judge Darren Vahle said to Anderson at his sentencing, "This is the type of crime that keeps good people in any civilization awake at night. Forty-one years ago today, you snuck into these people's lives and destroyed them."

Judge Vahle said the defendant's actions were appalling, stating, "…you stalked her like prey and raped a dying or dead woman."

Anderson declined to address the court, and the judge sentenced him to life in prison.

Unfortunately, Sylvia's parents, William and Mary, died before the killer was caught, but Sylvia's sister Jo Hamit had written a statement that was read by the lead investigator during a press conference after Anderson's arrest. Below is a partial excerpt.

> "Sylvia's murder turned my family's world upside down. My father found her that morning and he would never be the same again. The crime changed

him in a way that was very hard for my mother and me to watch over the years.

For the past 41 years, Sylvia missed out on family celebrations and numerous social occasions. Mr. Anderson has lived for the last four decades without giving his crime or my sister a second thought, while my family has suffered irreparable mental and emotional anguish during this time of uncertainty.

I have found it necessary to forgive Mr. Anderson, but he needs to bear the consequences of his actions."

Thanks to a set of laws passed in Colorado in the 1980s when this crime was committed, Anderson will be eligible for parole in 2041 at the age of 81.

LUST AND MURDER

> "I was concerned that I would go to jail... because I was holding this information for so long. I told myself I can't have this burden on my shoulders. I can't live with this."
>
> PAM WYNGARDEN COURT TESTIMONY

A DISCOVERY OF TWO BODIES

Newlyweds Gail and Ricky Brink had been in their home on Ransom Street for about three weeks. They had been married a little over a year and had been working on their house for several months before their move-in.

NO CONTACT

On November 23rd, 1987, Ricky's parents, Isla and Bud Brink, became concerned when they couldn't reach Ricky, so they drove to their son's house in Holland Township, Michigan, to search for him. When they arrived, they noticed Ricky's SUV in the driveway and they went inside the house.

The television was on, as were all the lights. They called out for Ricky and Gail but got no answer. When they entered the couple's bedroom, they saw a figure under the blankets with a pillow on top of their face. Isla lifted the pillow and discovered the body of her daughter-in-law Gail Brink. She was almost unrecognizable because it looked like she had been shot in the face more than once.

Meanwhile, Ricky's boss and family friend, Don Heeringa, became worried when Ricky didn't show up to work that morning. Ricky was a dependable employee who would always call in if there was a problem. Don knew the Brink family well and decided to call Gail Brink's workplace. Gail didn't arrive that morning either, so Don and his brother Jim decided to drive to the house and check on the couple.

They had no idea that Ricky's parents were there and had discovered Gail's body. The brothers saw Ricky's Chevy Blazer parked in the driveway, but when they looked closer, they noticed something Ricky's parents hadn't seen. Twenty-eight-year-old Ricky Brink was in the car, slumped over and covered in blood. It looked like he had been shot in the head.

Inside the house, Ricky's parents were trying to use the phone to call 911, but the handset had been left off the charger, and it was dead. They all converged in the driveway, with Ricky's parents leaving the house to find a phone and the Heeringa brothers coming in to use the phone. When Ricky's parents explained that Gail was dead inside, the brothers decided to guide the couple away from the driveway so they wouldn't see the gruesome sight of their son in the SUV. Don used a neighbor's phone to alert the authorities, who responded to the Brink house, which was now a crime scene.

Police inspected the exterior and interior of the house and found no evidence of forced entry or struggle. During the search, they discovered coins and cash in jars in the bedroom and the kitchen. Gail's wedding rings were still on her hand. Clearly, burglary was not the motive for the murders.

Officers initially thought this was a murder-suicide. They suspected Ricky had murdered Gail before committing suicide in his truck. Based on their experience, covering a victim's face after a murder may indicate a personal relationship between the murderer and the victim. Shooting someone multiple times point-blank with a shotgun could also be a crime of passion.

When officers searched Ricky's Chevy Blazer, they saw the vehicle's floorboard was soaked in blood. Using a flashlight, officers checked for weapons without disturbing any evidence. They found no firearm in the SUV and none in the house. There were no shell casings in the truck or beside the bed. Someone else had murdered the couple and partially cleaned up the crime scene.

THE INVESTIGATION BEGINS

It was a difficult day for the Brinks and for Gail's family, the Wyngardens. Police officers asked Ricky's parents about the couple's relationship and their activities over the weekend. Ricky's mother said the couple was happy, had no issues, and they had attended a wedding at a Holiday Inn on Saturday.

Detectives spoke with the neighbors on Ransom Street, and everyone agreed that the couple appeared incredibly happy and in love.

Ricky was known to be a hardworking man who spent his lunch breaks fixing things around the house. He was a valued employee of Trendway Corporation. Trendway Corporation's owners, Don and Jim Heeringa had known the Brink family for many years and said they were all "good people." Likewise, Gail's employer said she worked hard and was well-liked by her colleagues. Since neither lived a high-risk lifestyle and had a happy marriage: why would anyone want to harm them?

On Thanksgiving, Ricky and Gail Brink were laid to rest. Police officers attended the double service to look for suspicious people. They assumed whoever murdered the couple would attend their funerals as they had a feeling they were close to the couple. Following the burial, law enforcement staked out the cemetery for several days but got no new leads from visitors to the gravesite.

The Brinks were laid to rest at Lakewood Cemetery in Holland, Michigan.

LARS JOHNSTON

Detectives expanded their search for suspects among the couple's friends and coworkers. Before Gail met Ricky, she was in a relationship with a man named Lars Johnston. They dated for a while and were considered marriage, but Gail decided they weren't meant to be. There were allegations of infidelity between the couple, and they broke up. Lars didn't take the breakup well. When interviewed by police, Gail's brother, Ryan Wyngarden told detectives he saw Lars slap his sister in the face. Ryan said he helped Gail move her things out of the house that she shared with Lars the day the assault happened.

Detectives tracked down Lars and questioned him. He told them he was having dinner with friends the night of the murders and agreed to take a polygraph test. The results of the polygraph were unpublished, but his alibi was corroborated by his friends from dinner.

Ricky had an ex-girlfriend named Kathy, who he left to be with Gail. Kathy was at the wedding the couple attended at the Holiday Inn. Kathy said she was unhappy with how her relationship with Ricky ended, and she told detectives that the three of them didn't get along. Kathy's co-worker accompanied her to the wedding, and they both attended an after-party. Kathy had a solid alibi.

Two weeks after the murders, the Ottawa County Sheriff's Office received a relevant tip. Ricky and Gail lived in a house that was previously connected to a motorcycle gang. The previous owner was a member of a local charter. His name was Sid Colby, and he moved out in late 1986.

SID COLBY

Detectives interviewed Sid Colby. Throughout his interview with the police, he was very forthcoming and informed them that he had no ill will toward the couple. Colby told detectives he stopped by the house a few weeks after moving out to pick up some mail he'd left behind. The couple was pleasant and had everything ready for him when he arrived.

A detective asked Colby where he was the night of the murders. He told them he had been drinking until 11 pm at a local bar. A few hours later, he returned home to sleep. His girlfriend was with him until Sunday morning, he said.

Even though the detectives had some leads, all the suspects were cleared by alibis.

The case turned cold for thirteen years until 2000 when detectives reopened the investigation and spoke to Judy, Ricky Brink's former sister-in-law.

Judy's memory of that awful weekend in 1987 hadn't changed, but according to Judy, the Wyngarden family had some issues which she previously didn't discuss with the police.

FRICTION IN THE FAMILY

At the time of the murders, Gail's brother, Ryan Wyngarden, had been involved with drugs, and Judy heard that he owed his sister Gail money. Ryan was paying Gail for the recurring payments on the vehicle that Gail had co-signed with him. Ryan lost his job and stopped making the payments, angering Gail and Ricky. They would consistently ask Ryan for their overdue payment whenever they saw him.

There was another issue with the Wyngarden family. In 1987, Gail's parents were living in a trailer while they had their house built. Gail's parents asked Ricky and Gail if they could park their trailer in their driveway and stay with them for a few months to save money, but the couple said no. The rejection did not go over with Ryan, and he felt his sister betrayed their family.

Detectives then interviewed Gail's older sister Cheryl. Despite not living in Michigan at the time of the murders, Cheryl had a close relationship with her sister. She told police she had a conversation with her brother Ryan a few days before Gail and Ricky were murdered.

Ryan Wyngarden told his sister Cheryl that he didn't understand why Gail wouldn't help her parents when it would only be for a few months. According to Cheryl, Ryan said, "They think they're so good. They think they're better than everyone else."

After the murders, Ryan said to her, "I wonder if I could have done it?" She told detectives she found his statement horrible and bizarre. Cheryl also said Ryan had a foul temper, was a con artist, and was manipulative.

Detectives looked at Ryan Wyngarden but found no hard evidence that he committed the murders, and the case went cold again for thirteen more years.

THE BREAK

In 2013 Ryan's wife, Pam Wyngarden came forward with information that finally allowed the cops to make an arrest. Pam had a secret that she'd kept for decades. In 1987, Pam was a single mother with a young son. She was also the girlfriend of Ryan Wyngarden.

Pam told investigators that on Sunday, November 22nd, 1987, Ryan knocked on her front door, very upset. He said he'd killed his sister and her husband. She was shocked and asked Ryan to leave, but he returned later and said he had something he wanted to show her. He drove her to the

Brink's house and showed her the bullet-ridden bodies of his sister and brother-in-law. Ryan led Pam inside the house and into the bedroom. He lifted the pillow covering Gail's face and said, "If you report me to the police, this could happen to you." In 1987, under threat, Pam supplied Ryan with the alibi he needed to be ruled out as a suspect.

Pam asked Ryan why he killed his sister and her husband, and Ryan confessed to having had a sexual relationship with his sister in the past and was jealous. He also feared Gail would tell her husband.

According to Pam, on the night of the murder, Ryan drove to the Brink's home to talk to them. Ricky told Ryan to leave once the discussion turned into an argument. Ryan left but came back inside to ask for help starting his car. When Ricky went outside with him, he ordered him into his Chevy Blazer at gunpoint, and then shot him. Ryan returned to the house and shot his sister three times in the face.

Since Pam was Ryan's girlfriend, when detectives interviewed Pam in 1987, she said they were doing laundry together the night of the murders. She said she was terrified of what Ryan would do to her and her son if she told the truth. Later, Ryan and Pam married and had three children.

Ryan Wyngarden was arrested in January 2014 for the murders of Gail and Ricky Brink.

At a pre-trial hearing, an ex-girlfriend of Ryan's, Crystal

Beelen, also testified that Ryan told her about the sexual relationship he had with his sister. He did this approximately one week after the murders. According to Crystal, Ryan said that he and Gail had been in a sexual relationship as teens, and the last time they were together, he sexually assaulted her.

She also said Ryan told her he'd gone boating with the couple and Ricky noticed Ryan looking at Gail inappropriately. Ryan was afraid Ricky would confront Gail, and she would tell him the truth about her past sexual relationship with her brother.

Pam Wyngarden testified against her husband during the trial and Ryan sobbed and screamed at her from the opposite end of the courtroom. He said, "I can't believe you're saying all these lies about me. You know it's all lies."

Ryan was eventually moved into a different room to view the trial so court proceedings could continue.

During his testimony, Ryan Wyngarden affirmed his love for his sister. He maintained his innocence and rambled on for more than an hour.

The jury deliberated and returned with a guilty verdict, and 52-year-old Ryan Wyngarden was sentenced to two life sentences without the possibility of parole for the murders of Gail and Ricky Brink. He had an unsuccessful appeal attempt in 2019.

Pam Wyngarden filed for divorce shortly after the trial.

KILLER CASE FILES:
VOLUME 8

BODY IN THE MARSH

"She was a real quiet girl, not a big talker. She was real nice but she didn't come outside much. Her shades were always pulled."

MONA AUBRY, LISA'S NEIGHBOR,
GREEN BAY PRESS-GAZZETTE

AUGUST 12TH, 1986

Wayne Calewarts and Gerald Dorner were driving through the Bay Port Industrial Park in a truck that had just dumped a load of concrete. The marshland around them was still, and the only sound came from the truck's engine, chugging along the dirt road.

Gerald glanced out the window and remarked, "This is a pretty remote area. It'd be a good place to dump a body."

As they drove further down the road, Gerald suddenly hit the brakes. "Wayne, look! That's somebody's arm!

"You're nuts," said Wayne.

Gerald backed the truck up to take a closer look. And as he approached the water's edge, both men looked out the window and saw the body floating in the water.

It was a woman with long dark hair, and she was naked from the waist up. Her pink shirt floated nearby. She was facedown, and her legs were submerged in the swampy water. The arm that Gerald noticed moments earlier was twisted awkwardly behind her back.

Gerald used the two-way radio to call the company office. He told them he was near the Ken Euers Nature area off Military Avenue.

The men stayed in their truck, their eyes fixed on the life-less body floating in the water until the police arrived.

~

Lisa Ann Holstead was born in 1964, in Suffolk County, New York, to parents Frank Holstead and Judith Thompson. She grew up with three sisters and one brother and attended school in Watertown, New York. Lisa moved to California in the early 1980s and spent a few years working for an electronics firm. She moved to Green Bay, Wisconsin, to be closer to her family after giving birth to her son Jeremy in 1981.

She was known for her sweet personality but she could be shy and reserved at times. She enjoyed spending time with her son, fishing, riding horses, and playing darts in bars.

Lisa met her boyfriend, John Sot, in 1985, and the two moved in together in the Fall of the same year. However, their neighbors reported frequent arguments and shouting coming from their apartment, and the police were called to the house several times.

A FAMILY GATHERING

On August 11th, 1986, the Holstead family planned a gathering at Lisa's sister's house, which Lisa and John attended. They later moved to Dave's Bar on Main Street with some family members and friends before heading back to their apartment. However, an argument broke out between Lisa and John on the way home, and Lisa decided to get out of the car. It was 2 am, and John let her out at West Mason and Taylor Street. He saw her walking toward the highway, and it was the last time she was seen alive.

John assumed that Lisa would spend the night at her sister's house, and he wasn't overly concerned when she failed to come home the next morning. By the afternoon, he had called all her family members to see where she was. None of them had seen or heard from

Lisa, prompting Lisa's mother, Judith Thompson, to report her missing to the local police at 2 pm on August 12th.

Meanwhile, news of a body found near Green Bay was being broadcast on the radio. Reporters and police were already on the scene. Lisa's family heard the story and rushed to the Bay Port Industrial Park to see what had happened.

They arrived just in time to witness the local fire department recovering Lisa's body from the water. The family stood there trying to comfort each other while they waited. They followed the police to St. Vincent Hospital, where they were asked to formally identify Lisa's body.

THE AUTOPSY

The autopsy results revealed that Lisa had been strangled to death with her own shirt and that she'd been sexually assaulted. No other visible injuries were found on her body. Lisa had died sometime between 2:30 am and 4 am on August 12th. Fluid samples were collected from Lisa's body and stored for further analysis.

The investigators worked tirelessly to gather information about Lisa Holstead's whereabouts on the night of her disappearance. They interviewed her family and boyfriend, hoping to gain insight into her last moments.

John Sot's account of Lisa leaving his car at approximately

2 am made him the prime suspect, but investigators ultimately ruled him out due to a lack of evidence.

Lisa's mother, Judith, was distraught and wanted answers about her daughter's killer. She called the Green Bay police multiple times per day, looking for updates on the case.

Judith had recently purchased a beautiful wooden heart that she'd placed on Lisa's gravestone. It was stolen, so she spent her time making a Christmas wreath to replace it.

She told the Green Bay Press-Gazette that Lisa's son, who was now five years old, missed his mother and knew that someone "put her in the water."

Lisa's case bore similarities to Francine Stanislawski's murder, another Green Bay murder case from 1985, leading law enforcement to believe the two cases may have been connected. However, years later, it was confirmed that the murders were unrelated.

As the 1980s drew to a close, Lisa's case remained unsolved, and investigators had no new leads. The samples collected from Lisa's body remained their best hope for solving the case, but they lacked the DNA technology to identify her killer. As time went by, Lisa's murder became the oldest cold case in Green Bay.

It wasn't until 1998 that investigators were able to rule out Lisa's boyfriend as a suspect. They compared his

DNA to the foreign DNA found at the crime scene and confirmed that they didn't match. With that important piece of information, they uploaded the DNA profile to the CODIS database in hopes of one day finding a match.

In the 2010s, advances in genetic genealogy gave investigators a new tool in their search for Lisa's killer. They contacted a company that specialized in DNA testing and received information about physical traits and potential family members based on the DNA sample.

Armed with this new information, investigators contacted the numerous relatives on their list, hoping to identify the killer. Finally, they found two families in Wisconsin with a similar DNA profile to the killer. The investigators interviewed several members of these families, and Lou Archie Griffin's name was repeatedly mentioned. He had a criminal history of sexual assault and became a potential suspect.

A background check revealed that Griffin was in the area at the time of the murder and had a prior conviction for child sexual assault in 1981. He had been released on parole on May 20th, 1986, after which he moved to Green Bay. Griffin rented a house near the park where Lisa's body was found. He had since moved to Racine, Wisconsin, just south of Milwaukee.

In 2020, after several months of surveillance, investigators collected a discarded cigarette butt and beer cans from the trash can outside Griffin's home. Upon testing, the items were found to match the DNA profile recovered from the samples on Lisa's body.

Griffin was cooperative when police officers arrived at his door on October 28th, 2020, and he agreed to come to the station for questioning.

Initially, Griffin denied any knowledge of Lisa Holstead, but when presented with the DNA evidence, he admitted that he might have had a sexual encounter with her in 1986. He claimed, however, that he was under the influence of alcohol and cocaine at the time, making it difficult to recall the specifics of the encounter.

Griffin was arrested and charged with first-degree intentional homicide on October 30th, 2020. He was transported to Brown County Jail, where he remained until his trial in 2023.

Griffin's defense team planned to present an alternate suspect, accusing Lisa's boyfriend, John Sot, of the murder, but the Judge allowed the prosecution to introduce evidence from Griffin's prior conviction for sexual assault, which made the defense's case weak.

Ultimately, on January 27th, 2023, Griffin pleaded no contest to homicide by reckless conduct, and the judge found him guilty. He will be sentenced on March 27th, 2023, and faces up to 10 years in prison.

Police Chief Andrew Smith praised the officers from 1986 for preserving the DNA that eventually convicted Lisa's killer. At a press conference, he read a letter published in the paper by Lisa's mother in the days after the murder.

> "Waiting for confession. Pssst, you, talking about the horrible person that killed our loving daughter, Lisa Holstead in Green Bay on August 12th. How can you continue to live life every day knowing what you've done? Apparently, you have no conscience."

Robert Hughes, the Special Agent in Charge for FBI-Milwaukee, also spoke to the press.

> "I am really sorry that Lisa's mother isn't here to see justice served, but I'm sure she's looking down right now, and I'm sure she's appreciating what she's seeing."

Lisa's son, Jeremy, now grown, expressed relief that the case had been solved after 34 years and hoped that his family could finally find closure.

TEEN'S DARK DESCENT

> "Renette was a caring mother who did everything to help her son deal with his problems. She was a teen when she gave birth to Darrant, and she understood his behavior but wanted to keep him on the right track and disapproved of his drug use and drinking."
>
> AN UNNAMED FAMILY FRIEND

Kit Darrant was a deeply troubled 16-year-old who struggled with controlling his anger. Darrant argued daily with his mother, Renette Emile. He told his girlfriend he'd been arguing with his mother since the day he was born.

Darrant's desire to live an unrestricted life had him breaking into houses to smoke marijuana, using alcohol excessively, and even stealing his mother's car without her consent.

A family friend said Renette had considered putting Kit in a boot camp to see if it would help him. He briefly lived with his father in Naples, Florida, but when his father was deported back to Haiti, he reluctantly returned to Miami to live with his mother.

Darrant's aunt Rena recounted a harrowing incident in which the teenager, who was arguing with his mother, abruptly leapt out of Renette's vehicle and stood defiantly in the middle of a heavily trafficked road. He dared oncoming drivers to hit him. This reckless act resulted in Darrant being hospitalized in a psychiatric hospital for a week to address his aggression issues.

Rena said when Darrant was 15, he showed up on her doorstep drunk carrying several empty bottles of alcohol. She had him shower and put him to bed.

She told the Miami Herald:

> "He would tell me my sister beat on him bad. Really bad, like how they beat kids in Haiti. Like how my mom used to beat us."

According to Rena, she witnessed her sister using a belt or an extension cord to beat Darrant from the time he was a toddler.

Renette Emile was born in 1977 in Haiti. She lived in North Miami with her two sons, worked as a security guard, and attended nursing school. Her oldest son Kit was born on August 22nd, 1996, when Renette was only 19. She also had a three-year-old son she was raising along with Kit in their Miami apartment.

According to the friends of the family, Renette was a caring mother who did everything she could to help her son. Darrant hated her for not letting him do whatever he wanted.

Officers were called to the Jade Winds apartment complex several times to deal with Darrant. Once, a neighbor reported Darrant for speeding around the complex parking lot in his mother's car. He was circling the lot at top speed like it was a racetrack.

AN ACT OF VIOLENCE

On March 27th, 2012, Renette was at the apartment, waiting for Darrant to return home. It was late. He was out on a school night, and he had taken her car again without her permission.

When Darrant entered the apartment, the two argued for about 10 minutes. Darrant admitted later that during that argument, he'd decided his mother no longer needed to be in his life.

He went into his bedroom, and Renette believed that he had calmed down. However, Darrant was having suicidal thoughts. He ultimately decided he needed to kill his mother instead of himself.

Darrant waited for Renette to walk to her bedroom, and he lunged at her and put her in a chokehold. They both fell to the floor, and he held on tight until she gurgled and went limp. When he realized she was unconscious but still breathing, he ran into the kitchen, grabbed a butcher knife, and returned. He turned her over on her stomach and stabbed her more than 100 times in her torso, arms, and the back of her neck.

By the end of the attack, Darrant was covered in blood. He wiped the knife clean with his shirt and returned it to the kitchen. The bloody clothes he was wearing went into the garbage, and he took a bath. Exhausted, he went to his bedroom and quickly fell asleep.

A woman in a neighboring apartment heard two screams for help in Haitian but chose not to call the police. Darrant's three-year-old half-brother, who was in the next bedroom, slept through the murder of his mother.

The following morning, Darrant started a cleanup. He scrubbed the bedroom walls and the floor. In an attempt to hide the body, the teen covered his mother with sheets and blankets. The murder happened in her room, so he simply kept the door closed so that his little brother wouldn't see anything. Knowing that the smell might attract unwanted attention, Darrant regularly sprinkled the body with detergent powder and deodorant.

THE COVER-UP AND PARTY

Now that his mother was gone, Darrant decided to skip school, go shopping for new clothes, and drive her car whenever he wanted. He also took care of his three-year-old half-brother.

Darrant's friends recalled that he was excited to invite girls to his apartment and was in an unusually bright mood. He was planning a party for the weekend and was inviting almost everyone he knew.

Four days after the murder, he threw a party for his school friends. He opened up all of his mother's liquor bottles for the partygoers, and he seemed to have little concern that someone might find Renette's body. One of Darrant's friends even went into Renette's bedroom, where her body was still decomposing on the floor. The friend later told police he bumped into a pile of blankets but didn't realize what it was.

At one point, more than 60 students were in the fourth-floor apartment. The neighbors didn't call the police or complain about the noise, but Darrant's little brother didn't like the noise or the party and started to cry.

One of the partygoers asked about the bad smell, and

Darrant laughed and told them not to worry about it. He told them he just forgot to take out the trash.

Despite ignoring the loud high school party, the other tenants began noticing Darrant's behavior. They saw him driving his mother's car daily and sometimes late at night. He also played loud music until the early morning hours, yet no one bothered to question him about his mother's whereabouts. Darrant successfully covered up his mother's murder for eight days.

Renette's sister, Marie Altidor, was getting worried because she hadn't heard from Renette in days. She called the apartment and Darrant answered. He told his aunt that his mother couldn't come to the phone and hung up. Renette's boyfriend was also concerned that she wasn't replying to his messages and calls.

Marie Altidor went to the apartment in North Miami, and before she even knocked on the door, she could smell a foul stench. Something or someone was rotting inside the apartment. Darrant wasn't home, so she went inside. The smell was getting worse as she approached Renette's bedroom. Once inside, she could see an outline of a body covered with sheets and blankets. She knew it was her sister. She ran outside and called the police. They arrived a few minutes later and confirmed that the body was an adult female who was dead.

A TEENAGER STORY

Darrant and his younger half-brother pulled up in the Mercedes shortly after the police arrived. Darrant feigned ignorance and asked where his mother was. He then changed his story and told the police on the scene that three days ago, he had come home to find his mother on the floor bleeding. There was glass on the floor, so he wrapped his mother up in blankets and then put soap on her. Darrant claimed he had no idea who would want to hurt his mother, and he didn't want the police involved, so he didn't call anyone.

The police made the decision to take Darrant into custody for questioning. Meanwhile, Renette's other sister, Janet, was entrusted with the care of Darrant's half-brother.

At the station, Darrant realized he was caught and quickly confessed to killing his mother. He said that after the two argued on Tuesday evening, he retreated to his bedroom to think. That's when he brainstormed different methods of killing his mother and settled on strangulation. Once he'd decided that, he walked from his bedroom to hers and attacked her, strangled her, and stabbed her.

Darrant told police that he cared for his brother and ensured that they had food in the fridge. The little boy didn't suspect anything terrible had happened to his mother. He didn't ask Darrant many questions about Renette's disappearance. He likely thought his mother would be back any minute.

The autopsy confirmed Darrant's statement. Renette was savagely murdered, and there were strangulation marks on her neck. Her body showed signs of decomposition consistent with his timeline of events. Several days after the arrest, Kit Darrant was charged with first-degree murder. He faced the possibility of life in prison if found guilty. Even though he confessed and described the crime in detail, he pleaded not guilty.

Darrant was sent to jail without bail to await trial, which was scheduled for 2015. Meanwhile, Renette's sister Janet gained full custody of her three-year-old nephew, and he continued to live with her.

Kit Darrant, 19 years old at the time, appeared before a judge in August 2015. His defense lawyer, Tara Kawass, advised him to accept the plea deal offered by the prosecution, and he agreed to do so. It meant there wouldn't be a trial and that his family wouldn't have to go through another traumatic experience. If he chose a jury trial, Darrant could be sentenced to life in prison.

The prosecution had a solid case, and Darrant himself had confessed to the murder of Renette. Even if the defense tried to portray him as a mentally ill teenager, the jury might not be forgiving, considering the brutality of the crime.

Darrant took the deal and pleaded guilty to second-degree murder and was sentenced to 28 years in prison. The plea deal also included 20 years of probation after his release. Darrant's lawyer was pleased with the deal and said

Darrant regrets his actions and doesn't want to cause any more pain to his family.

Darrant himself stated that he had changed a lot in the three years after the murder and that he is a different person now than he was at the age of 16. The plea deal gave has given him hope for the future because he will still have time to rebuild his life once he completes his sentence.

Kit Darrant is currently serving time at Everglades Correctional Institution, a Level 5 security prison facility located in Miami-Dade County. This specific correctional institution focuses on rehabilitation by providing inmates with more educational programs and other activities.

Darrant's release date is set for February 20th, 2038. He will be 42 years old.

A FATHER'S BETRAYAL

> "I was evil. I exiled them, I didn't know what to do. My hands were tied. I'm not a doctor. He didn't appear at that time to be in any danger. I didn't see that he was blue."
>
> ANGELA POLLINA, STEPMOTHER OF THOMAS VALVA

There are few crimes more heart-wrenching than those that involve the death of a child. However, when such a tragedy is entirely preventable, it becomes even more devastating. This is especially true when authorities receive multiple warnings and pleas to take action but fail to do so.

THOMAS VALVA

Thomas Justin Valva was born on September 14th, 2011, to Justyna Zubko and Michael Valva. Growing up, he had two brothers, Anthony and Andrew. His father, Michael, worked as an NYPD officer, while Justyna was employed as a correctional officer.

Thomas' mother and father had high-stress jobs, and their family life was unhappy. To add to the family's struggles, both Thomas and Anthony were diagnosed with high-functioning autism, which further contributed to the dysfunction and tension in the home.

Michael and Justyna divorced in December 2015 and began a lengthy custody battle over their three boys. Justyna decided to represent herself in the court, while Michael hired lawyers. The custody hearings revealed horrible details about Justyna's life with Michael, and Justyna openly talked about the abuse she suffered during their marriage.

According to her, Michael would physically abuse her and the boys, as well as starve them. He kept the boys in the garage if they misbehaved. Michael, on the other hand, told the judge Justyna physically punished the boys and even made them sick intentionally. Valva's lawyers suggested Justyna was mentally unwell and made her sons tell lies about their father.

Justyna refused to take a psychological medical evaluation

as prescribed by the court in order to obtain custody of the children. She was willing to do the evaluation, but she asked that it be videotaped. Justyna claimed her husband's job made it impossible for her to get a fair evaluation, and a videotaped evaluation would be fair in case there was a dispute over the findings. The court refused her request, and Michael got full custody of Anthony, Thomas and Andrew in 2017.

THE BEGINNING OF THE END

The boys moved in with Michael and his new girlfriend, Angela Pollina. The family lived on Bittersweet Lane, Center Moriches, a hamlet on Long Island, New York. Angela had three children of her own, all girls, and she worked in hospital administration.

The first report of abuse to Child Protective Services (CPS) was filed in February 2018. According to the available documents, Anthony, the oldest boy, slept in the garage as a punishment for wetting the bed. His teacher and school administrator noticed that Anthony had been in dirty clothes for a week and smelled of urine. However, the most disturbing details were Anthony's hands and feet, which were red from frostbite.

The temperature in the garage was extremely low, and the boy was freezing every night. His teacher also noted that Anthony was progressively losing weight. CPS ordered Michael and Angela to attend a parenting program for one year. After completing the supervised time, the couple hired a nanny because they needed help with six children under one roof.

The nanny became a witness to harsh punishments by both Michael and Angela. The two older boys were frequent targets and often spent days in the cold garage with minimal food. Realizing how harmful these situations were for the boys, the nanny went to the police but never filed a complaint. According to her, the police officers at the station convinced her not to file the report and let CPS do their job.

The principal and teachers from East Moriches Elementary School weren't so easily persuaded. They watched the boys daily and knew something was very wrong at home. CPS received regular phone calls from them for years.

Anthony and Thomas routinely came to school in dirty clothes, and the boys were always hungry. Teachers even saw them eating from a dumpster and picking up crumbs under the school bleachers. Their special education teacher wrote a report stating the boys told her they didn't eat breakfast before school because of bad manners.

In January 2019, seven-year-old Thomas arrived at school with a black eye. His father Michael was contacted immediately, and he explained Thomas had a fight with another child at the playground. Since CPS were familiar with the Valva-Pollina family, they did a welfare check in May 2019, four months after the incident. The records show no one was at home at the time. Teachers continued to call CPS up until January 2020.

THE 911 CALL

On the morning of January 17th, 2020, the police in Suffolk County received a call from the Valva residence in Center Moriches. Below is a truncated transcript of the more than six-minute call before first responders arrived.

> Dispatch: Do you need the police?
>
> Michael Valva: I need an ambulance immediately. My son's not breathing.
>
> Dispatch: Your son who is not breathing: how old is he?
>
> Michael Valva: Eight.
>
> Dispatch: Eight?
>
> Michael Valva: Yes. He fell down. He's banged his head. He was ok. I gave him a shower to try and help him out a little bit…I'm a police officer with the city of New York. My son… I think... I don't know if he's breathing or not. I don't know if his heart stopped. He fell down on his way to the bus; he banged his head pretty good. I brought him in, and I'm doing CPR right now."

Emergency services arrived at 9:40 am and found Michael performing CPR on his son in the garage. The eight-year-old was unresponsive on the ground. Michael told them

Thomas was standing in front of the house, waiting for the school bus, when he collapsed.

Not wanting to waste time, Thomas was transported to the Long Island Community Hospital. Unfortunately, Thomas was pronounced dead soon after. Healthcare staff recorded Thomas' body temperature as 76.1 degrees, 20 degrees lower than it should have been.

After Thomas' death, Michael launched a GoFundMe page to cover funeral expenses. Family, neighbors, and friends shared the link, and the campaign was incredibly successful in a short amount of time. Michael's goal was $10,000, but he raised $14,000 in donations until the funding was revoked because he became the suspect in his son's death.

THE AUTOPSY

The autopsy revealed that Thomas went into cardiac arrest and died of hypothermia, meaning that Michael's version of the events on the 911 call was completely made-up. After examining his head injuries, the medical examiner determined that Thomas didn't fall on the driveway that morning. Instead, he had road rash on his face, suggesting he'd been dragged across the pavement.

These findings launched an investigation into the Valva family, and the police quickly discovered the accusations of child abuse that had been documented for years. Suffolk

County's CPS did very little to help the children over a two-year period.

HOUSE SURVEILLANCE CAMERAS

The investigation into Thomas' death started with reviewing the surveillance videos from inside the house. The Valva-Pollina family had covered almost all the rooms with cameras as well as the yard outside. Pollina provided the investigators with the login information during her police interview, but someone had deleted most of the video footage, before the police could access it. It was later discovered that Pollina herself deleted the footage.

However, several video clips and audio recordings were recovered from the cloud. The footage recorded two days before Thomas' death, shows Thomas on the concrete floor in the garage alongside his brother Anthony. Thomas is visibly shaking. There are no pillows or blankets in sight. It is very likely the boys were in the same position two days later when the temperatures dropped to 19 degrees Fahrenheit (-7 degrees Celsius).

On the morning of January 17th, around 8 am, Thomas defecated himself. A camera shows Valva entering the garage to scream at his son. "Little bastard sh— in his pants so much it's coming out of his pants!" He's heard telling Pollina he should make Thomas eat the feces. Valva ordered Thomas to take off all his clothes so he could clean him up. The two then walked to the backyard, and Valva doused the boy with cold water in the middle of January.

Video from the backyard camera records another child asking why Thomas can't walk. Pollina is heard replying, "Because he's hypothermic. When you're washed with cold water and it's freezing, you get hypothermia."

"You fell on concrete. Can't send you to school. You idiot!" Valva says to Thomas.

"You know why he's falling," says Pollina.

"Because he's cold," says Valva. "Boo f—ing hoo."

Pollina says, "What are you doing?"

"I'm f—ing suffocating him; that's what I'm doing," Valva responds.

"Take your hands off his mouth," Pollina says. "There are people everywhere."

Valva is heard saying to Thomas, who is on the ground, "God damn you! Get up! Get up! F—ing slob. Get up!"

He slapped the boy several times before taking him to the bathroom and running a hot bath. When that didn't revive him, Valva called emergency services.

After the police reviewed this footage, the remaining five children from the Valva-Pollina household were removed from the house. They were taken to the other parents for their safety. Even though the recordings show only Anthony and Thomas being abused, the other children might have experienced something similar and they were certainly witnesses to the abuse of the brothers.

Further review of the video and text messages between Valva and Pollina confirmed Anthony and Thomas slept in the garage for months before the younger boy died.

On January 24th, 2020, Valva and Pollina were charged with second-degree murder. Key audio and video evidence were shown at the initial hearing, as well as the prior reports of the abuse. Both Valva and Pollina pleaded not guilty.

Justyna Zubko, Thomas's mother, made a tearful statement to the media after the arrests.

> "I just kept thinking about how much abuse all my children encountered from the hands of those two abusers, Michael and Angela.
>
> For years, day after day, being deprived from food, shelter, the basics that every child should be provided with.
>
> I think about all the institutions who failed to help him completely with absolutely nothing.
>
> Now everybody's trying to do the right thing, but where were you when I begged you for help...when you could have saved my child's life?
>
> I did file a complaint with Suffolk County District Attorney's office. I did file complaints with Nassau

> County District Attorney's office, FBI, Suffolk County Police, Nassau County police, and Attorney General. Nobody helped my children."

MICHAEL VALVA'S TRIAL

Michael Valva appeared in court in September 2022. Suffolk County prosecutors had a solid case against the former NYPD officer and presented the collected evidence to the jury. The courtroom was packed with people each day of the trial. Valva's defense relied heavily on the notion that the prosecution painted the wrong picture of Valva. The defense lawyer agreed that his client was guilty. But he urged the jury to reconsider the charges.

The prosecution built its case by collecting all the evidence from the Valva-Pollina household and the prior reports of abuse. After providing the jury with the complete timeline of the events that happened on January 17th, it was clear that Valva mistreated the boys.

The trial lasted for six weeks. On November 5th, 2022, the jury deliberated for seven hours before they found Michael Valva guilty of second-degree murder and four counts of child endangerment. Valva's attorney asked for leniency for Valva's exemplary service as an NYPD officer, but the judge denied this request and instead imposed the maximum sentence. On December 8th, 2022, Valva received a sentence of 25 years to life.

Judge William Condon said in court:

> "An eight-year-old boy who right now should be getting excited for Christmas is dead. I speak for everybody out there. We can never let this happen again."

Pollina's attorney made a statement soon after Valva's trial that his client was present in the house but didn't participate in the abuse of Thomas and Anthony.

ANGELA POLLINA'S TRIAL

During Pollina's trial, a video from a garage camera was shown to the jury that captured several minutes of Thomas and his brother trying to sleep on the cold garage floor.

Pollina was watching the boys on camera and sent a text to Michael Valva that said:

> "That SOB Thomas went in the dirty laundry basket to get a dirty towel. Look how he sneaks."

After one day of deliberation, the jury found Pollina guilty of second-degree murder and four counts of endangering a child. Pollina was upset and crying as the verdict was read. She is awaiting sentencing, which will happen in April of

2023, and faces the same sentence of 25 years to life that her former partner Valva received.

Suffolk County CPS were called 17 times about the conditions the children lived in in the Valva-Pollina household.

In June 2022, the Eastern District of New York court approved Justyna Zubko's $200 million lawsuit against Suffolk County CPS for the wrongful death of Thomas Valva.

BENEATH THE SURFACE

"We do not believe it was an accident. We believe it was a murder, and we believe the evidence supports that charge."

GLEN CASH, QC DIRECTOR OF PUBLIC PROSECUTIONS FOR QUEENSLAND

In October 2003, two newlyweds traveled from Alabama to Australia. What was supposed to be a dream honeymoon soon turned into a nightmare during a dive expedition. The Watsons had been married 11 days, and only one newlywed returned home alive.

Christina Mae Watson, also known as Tina, was born on

February 13th, 1977, in West Germany. Her birth parents gave her up for adoption, and she ended up in the United States, legally adopted by Tommy and Cindy Thomas. She grew up with her younger sister in Walker County, Alabama.

Tina was diagnosed with a heart condition called paroxysmal supraventricular tachycardia or PSVT. The condition causes an abnormally fast heartbeat that could lead to fainting, dizziness, and other health problems. While Tina managed this condition with medication when she was younger, she decided to get heart surgery to help with the condition in her 20s.

TINA AND GABE

Tina enrolled at the University of Alabama and moved to Birmingham. She'd met and got engaged to a man named Scott McCulloch, but they broke off the engagement. She met Gabe Watson at a New Year's Eve party, and the two began dating in January 2001.

Tina adored Gabe even though her parents weren't fond of him. Tommy and Cindy thought that the two of them were too different to be compatible.

Despite the Thomases' concerns, the couple stayed together and graduated from college. Gabe worked for his father's company, and Tina was a manager at a clothing store. Around that time, Gabe started taking lessons to become a certified diver and he obtained his PADI certification, the first scuba certification level. Wanting to spend more time with Gabe, Tina began taking diving lessons too in January 2003. Her parents were worried because of Tina's heart condition. They talked to Gabe about it, but according to Tommy, he didn't take their concerns seriously. He told Tina's father that he did things that Tina was interested in, and she should do things that he was interested in.

THE MARRIAGE

On April 20th, 2003, Gabe prepared a surprise for Tina. Since it was Easter morning, the family gathered to participate in an egg hunt. Gabe hid an engagement ring in one of the eggs, and when Tina found it, he proposed.

The couple got married on October 11th, 2003, and two days later, they were on their way to Australia for their honeymoon. The plan was to spend two weeks in the Land Down Under, explore Sydney, and dive at some of the best diving locations in the world.

After spending a week in Sydney, Tina and Gabe traveled to Townsville in Queensland. Before their honeymoon, Gabe contacted the company overseeing diving expeditions in the area and booked a dive for both of them. Gabe wanted to dive near the wreck of the *SS Yongala,* a passenger ship that sank in 1911. It is a well-known spot for divers because the shipwreck is well-preserved.

However, this dive isn't suitable for beginners because of

the strong currents around the wreck. Even though Gabe had completed 55 dives, they were all in a lake in Oak Mountain State Park. Tina, on the other hand, had completed only five dives, and none were in open water. The couple needed to go 89 feet below the water's surface to see the wreck.

DIVE DAY

Tina and Gabe arrived in Townsville on October 21st and boarded the dive boat *Spoilsport* at 10 pm. They were accompanied by 25 other passengers and three professional divers. At 9 am the following morning, divers were instructed about the dive. The divemaster recommended using the anchor line to reach the wreck, drift over to the wreck, and grab the second line to help guide them back to the surface.

Gabe and Tina had their own equipment, so they only needed air tanks that were provided for them on the boat. Once the divers were ready, Gabe asked for an additional weight for Tina. He thought she would need it to descend. The crew then asked if they wanted to do an orientation dive first. When they refused, the couple was asked if they wanted a divemaster to accompany them, but again, they said no.

At 10:30 am, Tina and Gabe entered the water. They experienced problems right away and returned to the boat. Gabe said his dive computer was malfunctioning. He replaced the battery, and everything seemed fine. The two of them got back into the water.

Several minutes later, Gabe was back on the surface, but this time he was alone. He said Tina needed help. Upon hearing this, dive instructor Wade Singleton jumped into the water. He couldn't locate Tina at first but then saw her on the ocean floor.

Singleton pulled Tina out of the water and took her to a nearby dive boat, *Jazz II*. A doctor on board tried to resuscitate her, but she still wasn't breathing. Singleton knew that the situation was bad because Tina had spent 10 minutes in the water. The doctor attempted CPR for 40 minutes, but Tina was gone.

After Tina was pronounced dead, Gabe called his parents and was on a conference call with Tina's parents. Gabe explained that Tina was panicking, and they were on their way back up. Tina knocked off his mask and regulator, and he had to let go of her to put it back on. When he looked back at Tina, she had started to sink fast and had her arms stretched out to him. He said she blinked, so he knew she was ok, but she was sinking so quickly he thought the best thing to do was surface and get help.

On the call, Tina's mom asked Gabe if he was there with her when she died, and he said yes. He said he was there with her the whole time. This gave Tina's mother some comfort, and she consoled Gabe on the call, telling him that Tina knew he was going to get help. Gabe lied. According to witnesses, Gabe stayed on the *Spoilsport* and never requested to go over to the other boat with Tina while the doctor was trying to resuscitate her. He spent that time walking around the *Spoilsport,* asking people for hugs.

On October 23rd, 2003, a consultant forensic pathologist performed Tina's autopsy. He found evidence of an air embolism, but Tina's death had nothing to do with her heart condition. According to the pathologist, the cause of death was drowning.

Gabe spoke with the Australian authorities about what happened during the dive. According to him, the pair realized the current was too strong when they got under the surface. Tina got scared and signaled to Gabe that she wanted to go to the anchor line and return to the boat.

Gabe signaled to Tina to use her buoyancy compensator, which would get her up quicker. Tina activated the compensator, but nothing happened. Gabe approached her, but Tina was scared and knocked off his mask. While Gabe was fixing his mask, Tina started sinking. She was going down so fast that he knew he couldn't get to her, so Gabe returned to the boat and asked for help.

LEAVING AUSTRALIA

Several days later Gabe flew home along with Tina's body, and the family started the funeral preparations. The funeral director of Southern Heritage Cemetery in Pelham was told that everything on Tina would remain in the casket for the burial. However, on the day of the funeral, when the director and Gabe Watson stood by the casket, Gabe asked the director to remove Tina's diamond engagement ring and leave her wedding band on her finger.

At Tina's wake, Mrs. Watson, Tina's friend, and maid of honor at her wedding, said Gabe commented, "At least her breasts were perky" after viewing his bride in her casket. She also said at the wake, he showed pictures of his late wife, one of which was Tina standing next to a sign which read "Caution: Drowning."

SEVERAL WEEKS LATER

Several weeks after Tina's death, one of the divers, Gary Stempler, developed a film he shot underwater. He accidentally took a photo of Tina in the background of an image. She was lying on the ocean floor, face up.

While authorities were investigating the accident, crew members from the *Spoilsport,* who saw Gabe emerge from the water, told authorities he didn't seem worried about Tina and looked calm. This differed from Gabe's account and led the police to formally investigate Tina's death.

Gabe refused to go back to Australia to attend the inquiry. Despite his absence, the prosecution presented evidence that Gabe wasn't telling the truth about the diving accident.

The police tried to recreate possible scenarios that led to

Tina's death. The only one that seemed possible was that Gabe turned off Tina's regulator and waited until she lost consciousness. Then he switched on the regulator, and she sank to the bottom. Divers who were in the water with the newlyweds said they saw Gabe with his arms around Tina, and she looked like she was panicking.

After the inquiry, Gabe was officially charged with Tina's murder.

In May 2009, Gabe Watson traveled to Australia to attend his trial. The trial began on June 5th, and Gabe pleaded not guilty to murder but guilty to the charge of manslaughter. The prosecution presented the evidence in court and said that Gabe, as a diver with more experience than Tina, should've realized that the young woman was panicking. He should have removed her additional weight and inflated the buoyancy compensator.

The investigation confirmed that Tina's equipment was working and that the tank still had enough air. Furthermore, Gabe provided the investigators with 16 different versions of the event that happened in October 2003.

Gabe was found guilty of manslaughter and sentenced to four and a half years in prison. Gabe only needed to serve 12 months before being released.

After the trial, Alabama Attorney General filed an appeal to the Queensland Supreme Court. He wanted Gabe Watson's sentence to be increased. He also contacted Queensland Attorney General Cameron Dick, who said the state would file an appeal regarding Gabe Watson's sentence.

The appeal was presented to the Queensland Court of Appeals in July 2009. The attorneys asked for Gabe's sentence to be increased to two and a half years. In September 2009, Gabe's sentence was increased by six months, so he needed to spend 18 months in prison.

In May 2010, the Alabama Attorney General announced that Gabe Watson would be tried for capital murder and kidnapping because of new evidence that suggested he began planning Tina's murder in the United States. Australian authorities said they needed assurance that the prosecution wouldn't seek the death penalty. Otherwise, they would refuse to deport Gabe to his home country. The Attorney General confirmed the death penalty would be off the table.

Gabe was released from prison in Australia on November 10th, 2010. He arrived in the United States on November 25th, 2010, and was arrested. He was charged with murder and kidnapping, and his trial date was scheduled for February 13th, 2012.

While it was unclear what the new evidence was, it was believed it had something to do with statements made by Tina's father. Tommy said that Gabe had asked Tina to increase her life insurance which was approximately $200,000, to over $1 million shortly before their wedding and to also make Gabe the sole beneficiary. Tina consulted her father, and he recommended that Tina wait until she returned from her honeymoon. Tommy also said this is why Gabe removed his daughter's engagement ring from the casket. He found out that Tina hadn't increased the amount of the policy. However, Judge Tommy Nail didn't allow the testimony by Tina's father, and Gabe Watson was acquitted on February 23rd, 2012. The judge said the prosecution didn't have enough evidence to prove Gabe Watson wanted to murder his wife.

Tommy Thomas said to the media that Watson's acquittal was like losing Tina all over again.

He said:

> "I think we were all shocked by what the judge ruled. Everyone is coming up with their own reasons about why he did what he did.
>
> We expected it to go to the jury, had it gone we would have been happy. It came down to one person making a decision again. That is not what justice is about. He took a plea in Australia, and he didn't see a jury there."

After Gabe was released from custody, there was an ongoing dispute between Gabe and Tina's parents regarding her gravesite. Gabe had Tina's body exhumed and moved to a different spot. Whenever Tina's parents left flowers at her grave, they were stolen or removed. Tommy and Cindy even chained the flower arrangement down and reported the thefts to the police. Gabe was recorded by the police vandalizing the flowers and using bolt cutters to damage and remove them.

When approached by the media, Gabe provided two distinct justifications for his actions. He cited his ongoing grief for his wife's passing. And he argued that the flowers were excessive and not in line with Tina's tastes since they were plastic.

Gabe Watson said to the media:

> "When I would go out to Tina's grave I always left fresh flowers. And it struck a nerve with me that what I considered, and what I think Tina would have considered, big, gaudy, plastic arrangements that would sit out there and get faded in the sun. I don't understand what that has to do with what happened in '03. This was a year or two later. I can't grasp the relevance of that to Tina's death."

Tina's family and friends were left with many questions following her death. But as more evidence got released, diving experts started to put the puzzle pieces together. For instance, Tina and Gabe were both beginners, and neither had open water experience. Gabe wasn't a suitable dive buddy because he completed a two-day course to receive his rescue certification.

Expert divers reviewing the case say Tina should've spoken to a cardiologist and gotten approval before engaging in an activity such as diving. Neither Tina nor Gabe mentioned that she had a heart condition on their diving application.

The diving company that organized the *SS Yongala* dive was fined $10,000 because of their lack of safety standards.

BURNING SECRETS

> "Two of them are dead, and Donny's dead to me, because I do feel he is 100% responsible for this, whether he pulled it off himself or not."
>
> HANS HANSEN, FATHER OF JILLIAN AND JULIE

Two 16-year-old sisters were shot, and their house was set on fire in the quiet community of Willow Creek, California. The investigators zeroed in on a single person – their half-brother Donny. But even after his trial, the family was left with many unanswered questions. The case is considered unsolved to this day.

Jillian Lee and Julie Ann Hansen were born on December 27th, 1969, in Humboldt County, California. Their parents,

Hans and Betty Hansen, got married the same year. Betty was divorced from her first husband and had two children from that relationship, Donald and Becky. The family moved to Willow Creek, California, in 1971, and Hans opened a logging supply business.

The Hansens lived in a mobile home next to a warehouse used by Hans to run his business. Twins Jill and Julie were carefree and friendly girls loved by their classmates. They could be a bit shy sometimes but were generally outgoing and happy.

Their half-brother Donald, also known as Donny, moved out of the mobile home to Fortuna, California, after graduating from high school. While he enjoyed his independence, Donny was struggling financially. He was a short ride away from Willow Creek and visited his family often.

THE FIRE

On November 14th, 1986, Donny was in Willow Creek and staying at the mobile home. Jill and Julia went to their bedroom at around 11 pm, while their half-brother remained in the living room, where he was sleeping that night. Betty, the mother, woke up around 3 am, and she could smell that something was burning.

She woke up Hans and told him to go check it out. Once Hans exited their bedroom, he saw that the hallway was on fire. Hans found a fire extinguisher and tried putting out the flames, but it was impossible. He called out to his children and got no response. Panicked, Hans found his way to the back door and started running to the warehouse to grab more fire extinguishers.

He tripped over a gas can left on the lawn. While he didn't pay attention to that detail at the time, Hans would later confirm he knew he didn't leave the gas can there.

Meanwhile, Betty entered the living room and saw Donny standing there and yelling at someone to get out. Her son was alone, and she couldn't see anyone else. Betty also made her way to the warehouse and soon met up with Hans and Donny.

TRYING TO SAVE THE TWINS

The three returned to the mobile home, ready to put out the fire. Hans brought the ladders with him, which he used to break the window in the twins' room. He extinguished the fire inside, but the twins weren't responding to his calls. Neighbors had already called the fire department, and they were on their way.

A neighbor saw a figure in the field by the mobile home. As they made their approach, they realized it was Julie. She had a large wound in her stomach and was bleeding heavily, but she was still alive. Once Donny saw his sister, he immediately told his parents that he had pulled her out of the burning home.

Julie was taken to the hospital, and a close examination

revealed that she was shot with a 12-gauge shotgun. Jill was found in her bedroom the morning after the fire. Her body was badly burned, but it was clear she had a wound in her abdomen similar to Julie's.

The charred remains of the mobile home provided investigators with more evidence about what happened the previous night. They found three shotgun shells and two gas tanks. One was inside the mobile home, and the other was on the lawn. The investigators searched the nearby warehouse and discovered the potential murder weapon – a 12-gauge shotgun tucked away behind crates. They didn't tell the family they had found the gun.

One day later, the police were guarding the warehouse when Donny sneaked in. The officers stopped him, and he said he was there to feed the family dog, even though Donny knew the dog was with their neighbors. Since the investigators didn't tell anyone about the shotgun, they assumed Donny wanted to get the murder weapon out of the warehouse.

The ballistics confirmed that the shotgun was used to kill Jill and wound Julie. The weapon wasn't registered to Donny, so they questioned his friend, who was the owner. They said Donny borrowed the gun on November 12th but didn't say why he needed it.

The police dug deeper into the purchases made by Donny in the days before the fire and found out he had bought five gallons of gas. The investigators found receipts that confirm this. Furthermore, he was seen by eyewitnesses at the gas station.

Three shotgun shells were found in his car, and they matched the ones recovered from the mobile home. All the physical evidence pointed in Donny's direction.

Two weeks after the fire, Julie was strong enough to communicate with the investigators. She first told her doctor that she remembered smelling smoke and opening the door to her room. Julie then heard a shot and felt pain in her abdomen. Initially, that was everything she could recall. Julie didn't even remember how she crawled out of the burning home but was positive Donny didn't get her to safety.

When she spoke to the detectives working on the case, Julie said she did remember seeing Donny's face right before she was shot.

Shockingly, Donny appeared in the courthouse on December 2nd, wanting to be interviewed by investigators. His story was full of contradictions, so he requested a polygraph test. Donny failed twice. He was arrested and charged with murder and arson.

Even though Julie was slowly recovering in the hospital, she suddenly passed away on December 19th, 1986. It was revealed that an air bubble formed in her intravenous feeding tube and entered her bloodstream, which resulted in her death.

Without Julie as their star witness, the prosecution had a difficult task ahead of them. They knew her changing story might be too much for the jury to convict Donny.

Donny Hansen's trial began in April 1987, and the prosecution was asking for the death penalty for the murder of his twin sisters. They had the evidence on their side: Donny was seen purchasing gasoline at the gas station. He borrowed the shotgun, which was the murder weapon, and also bought shotgun shells. But the defense surprised everyone with their alternative theory.

They called two neighbors who remembered the night of the fire. According to them, they saw two unknown men near the Hansen residence. They left in their vehicle after the shots were fired and returned to the scene as the mobile home was burning.

The defense then suggested these two men were responsible for the arson and murders. According to Donny's lawyer, the unidentified men broke into Donny's car and took the shotgun and gasoline cans. They gained access to the mobile home and poured gasoline all over the living room as Donny slept on the couch.

One of the men entered the twins' bedroom and shot Julie first and then Jill while the family was waking up. The shooter exited the mobile home, returned the weapon to Donny's car, and drove off with his accomplice. Donny explained he hid the shotgun in the warehouse because he feared someone might steal it. He allegedly didn't know it was used in the murders.

The jury believed the story presented by the defense and Donny Hansen was found not guilty. Soon after, Donny moved from Humboldt County and changed his name. It is rumored he now lives in Happy Camp, California, and has three children of his own.

Hans and Betty Hansen believe that Donny is guilty of murder and arson. They suspect he planned to kill the whole family and collect the life insurance money. Even though the case is marked as unsolved, it is unofficially closed because law enforcement believes they caught the right person. However, Donny can't be accused of this crime again because of double jeopardy.

The police also think that Donny might have had help. The neighbors who said they saw two unknown men near the Hansen residence weren't lying. The two were later identified and taken to the station to be questioned. While investigators believe they didn't tell the truth about their whereabouts on the night of the fire, they couldn't prove the men were involved.

Betty herself saw Donny shouting at someone when she entered the living room, so he perhaps didn't act alone. Soon after the tragedy, Hans and Betty stopped talking to Donny. They moved to Eagle Point, Oregon.

DEADLY BELIEFS

"The Scientology community was not happy with the story, which raised the possibility that Elli Perkins might not have been murdered had her son been given psychiatric treatment."

CBS BROADCASTING

The Church of Scientology has been curating its public image for decades now. But in 2003, a gruesome murder shocked the citizens of Buffalo, New York, and made the public more aware of Scientology's aversion toward modern medicine.

Elli Perkins was born in 1949 in Rochester, New York. She grew up in a Jewish family and was very popular in school. Elli was artistic, fun, and creative. Art was her first love, but she also enjoyed reading. During her time at the Rochester Institute of Technology, Elli felt uninspired and had a hard time focusing on her work. She struggled a lot before discovering one of L. Ron Hubbard's books about Scientology.

The teachings of this new religion resonated with her, and Elli felt like her creativity was coming back. Wanting to be even more involved in Scientology, she started attending Scientology classes. There she met her future husband, Dan Perkins, a fellow Scientologist who worked as a carpenter and ran his own small business.

The two got married and had two children together – a boy named Jeremy in 1975, and Danielle, a girl born in 1976. Determined to make money as an artist, Elli continued painting, but there wasn't a lot of interest in her work. Around this time, she discovered glass painting and saw it as a challenge. Elli would create hundreds of tiny glass objects and then travel upstate to sell them at the Sterling Renaissance Festival.

CLEAR

In 1979, Elli and Dan reached *Clear* status in Scientology, which meant they got rid of all their past trauma. The family moved to California at the start of the 1980s, and Elli found work at the Scientology Celebrity Center in Los Angeles. By the end of the decade, the Perkins family returned to Buffalo, New York.

Jeremy was still a young boy when his family relocated to California. He had an artistic streak, just like his mother, but he didn't do well in school because of learning problems. Jeremy dropped out of high school before graduation and focused on playing drums in his rock band. During his teens, Elli and Don suspected Jeremy had mental health issues but decided to ignore the signs because of the beliefs of the Church of Scientology.

When Jeremy was 24 years old, his condition worsened seemingly overnight. He told his dad he heard voices in his head and was sent to join Scientology's Sea Org in California instead of going to therapy. Elli and Dan hoped Scientology would help Jeremy overcome his mental health issues. So he signed the Sea Org contract in the spring of 2001 and flew out to Los Angeles.

Jeremy didn't get along with fellow Sea Org members and even filed a report on his partner, who didn't attend mandatory Scientology classes. In the end, Sea Org didn't do anything to help Jeremy with his problems, so he was sent back to Buffalo after three months. He returned to work for his father as a carpenter.

On August 14th, 2001, Jeremy was arrested for trespassing outside the University of Buffalo. A court-ordered psychological exam confirmed he suffered from schizophrenia. Elli then convinced the judge to release Jeremy into her custody, promising she would provide all the help he needed. In reality, Elli did this to prevent Jeremy from taking any medication. And so Jeremy's mental illness went untreated for months.

At the beginning of 2002, Jeremy suffered a head injury at work, which worsened his symptoms. In the summer, Dan fired Jeremy because his condition was getting out of hand. At that time, the family talked to Dr. Conrad Maulfair, a fellow Scientologist and an osteopathic physician, who suggested that Jeremy should take vitamin therapy because of the built-up toxins in his body.

The Church of Scientology was keeping a close eye on Jeremy and concluded the members should distance themselves from the young man. He was classified as level III or *Potential Trouble Source,* and the other members were advised not to have contact with Jeremy.

Elli focused on the recommended vitamin therapy and gave Jeremy his daily dose of pills. But he became suspicious of her quickly. Jeremy's hate towards his mother grew because he believed she was poisoning him. In February 2003, Elli found yet another alternative form of treatment. This time she consulted with Albert Brown, a so-called natural healer. Brown wasn't a Scientologist, but the Church approved of his practice.

Brown had a farm in Springville, New York, just south of Buffalo. His patients stayed there, and Elli wanted Jeremy to spend a few days at the facility. The young man met with Brown before the treatment and agreed that the natural healer might help him. He seemed hopeful at that time, but things quickly went bad.

Jeremy was scheduled to arrive at Brown's farm on the

evening of March 13th, 2003. That morning, Elli and her son got into an argument. Elli had to call Dan to come home from work and calm Jeremy down. Once the situation cooled off, Dan returned to work, and Elli told Jeremy to take a shower.

THE MURDER

Elli was talking on the phone with her best friend around 10 am when Jeremy got out of the shower. He stood by the door and watched his mother before walking into the kitchen and grabbing a 12-inch steak knife. Jeremy flew into a rage and attacked his mother, stabbing her until she was motionless on the bedroom floor. Jeremy kept stabbing her, even though it was evident she was dead.

Elli's friend and neighbor came over and knew something was wrong. She immediately called the Buffalo Police Department and then the local Scientology Organization. Jeremy was taken into custody at 10:30 am. He gave a full confession to the police and told them exactly how he killed his mother.

This is a partial excerpt of his confession:

> "...I then went downstairs to watch a little TV when my mom asks me to take my vitamins. I take a handful every day, maybe 10-15. I don't like to take these because I always feel better if I don't. I told her I didn't want to today, and I ended up taking them and flushing them down the toilet without my mom

> knowing. She then told me to take a shower. I don't like it when she tells me to take a shower. I know when to take my own shower. I got mad, but I went upstairs to get my clothes. I went back downstairs to use the shower. My mom was in the kitchen painting. She paints on glass as a hobby.
>
> When I got out of the shower, I saw my mom was on the phone in the kitchen. I went into the kitchen and took a pointed knife about 12 inches long with a brown handle. I got this from the drawer to the left of the sink. We have about 10 of these knives. They may be steak knives. I held the knife in my right hand behind my back, and she hung up the phone. I tried to slit my wrists after the shower with a utility knife, but I wouldn't die, so I decided to do my mom instead.
>
> I pushed her into her bedroom downstairs and stabbed her in her chest and arms. She was screaming, "No don't, Jeremy, no don't." I stabbed her about 4-5 times before she fell down. I was using a cross-stabbing motion when she was standing. I then stabbed her about 10 more times in the stomach after she fell to the ground. I knew she was a goner. I then tried to cut out her right eyeball, but it would not come out. I believed her eyes were evil."

The Church contacted Elli's friend, telling her not to speak with the media about the attack but that she should cooperate with the investigators.

At 1:30 pm, Jeremy gave a written statement describing the attack in detail. According to the young man, he wanted to slit his wrists when he got out of the shower but then changed his mind and attacked his mother instead. He admitted attempting to gouge his mother's right eye out because he thought it was evil.

Jeremy didn't remember how many times he stabbed Elli, but the autopsy confirmed she had 77 wounds on her body. When asked about the motive, Jeremy said his mother was strict and didn't allow him to play drums in his room. He couldn't stand taking orders from her anymore. Jeremy was ordered to attend another psychiatric evaluation.

Jeremy's previous diagnosis was confirmed again. On July 28th, 2003, he was found not responsible by reason of mental disease or defect and was placed on probation. On January 24th, 2004, it was determined that Jeremy was severely mentally ill and should be committed to a secure facility.

As soon as they learned about the case, the church leaders started distancing themselves from the Perkins family. Members who knew them were forbidden from commenting on the murder. The Church of Scientology was worried that their stance on psychology would end up on the front pages of magazines, which would be bad publicity.

Additionally, Elli had obtained high *Operating Thetan* levels. According to the teachings of Scientology, she was supposed to have special powers and be able to cheat death.

The murder was a blow to the church members because it was clear that high *Operating Thetan* levels couldn't save themselves from an attack.

Of course, the details of the murder soon leaked out, and the public learned about the advice given to Elli Perkins by Dr. Conrad Maulfair, one of the high-ranking members of Scientology, who suggested that she give Jeremy vitamins to detox his body instead of seeking professional help. Dr. Maulfair appeared in Jeremy's court hearing and confirmed he was contacted by the Perkins family regarding their son. However, he never met the young man himself, and Jeremy wasn't his patient.

Meanwhile, Jeremy was in a secure mental health facility, where he was monitored around the clock. His psychiatrist finally found the right pharmacotherapy, and the young man was doing better. He even admitted that he wouldn't have hurt his mother if he had been on meds from the start.

The murder of Elli Perkins would pop up in the media years after the crime itself. In 2006, LA Weekly published an advertisement that blamed actor Tom Cruise for Elli's death. Cruise was the face of Scientology at that time and is the most well-known member of the church to this day. The ad reminded the readers that Jeremy was given vitamins instead of antipsychotic medication.

In October 2006, the famous true-crime show, *48 Hours* covered the case and received backlash from the Church of Scientology. They tried to change the content of the episode and even blamed CBS for being biased because they advertised various medications on their channel.

Two years after the death of Elli Perkins, the Church of Scientology used a video clip of her daughter Danielle in a DVD. In the clip, Danielle says,

> "Any PC who sits down in front of me, I know I can do something to help that person. I know that I can take that person's aberrations and use standard tech, apply it to that person. And, I can make that person saner."

THE LAST BREATH

"This case is so huge, so overwhelming, it's like nothing we've ever had before."

GLENDALE POLICE SGT. RICK YOUNG, *LOS ANGELES TIMES*, APRIL 29TH, 1998

When most of us think of the most prolific serial killers, we think of hardened lifetime criminals who thrive in the shadows. But perhaps there is a name you've never heard before, and perhaps he killed over 200 people while being well-paid and wearing a clean, crisp medical uniform.

EARLY LIFE AND ENTRY INTO THE MEDICAL FIELD

Working in the medical field comes with a lot of responsibilities. Medical professionals are supposed to help their patients, but some do the opposite. Efren Saldivar, a respiratory therapist, decided to take fate into his own hands.

Efren Saldivar was born on September 30th, 1969, in Brownsville, Texas. His parents, Alfredo and Isaura, soon relocated the family to Los Angeles in hopes of finding better job opportunities. Saldivar had good grades in school and was a friendly and talkative teen. But he felt like an outcast in high school because of his weight.

STRUGGLING WITH DEPRESSION

His grades started to drop, and he wasn't allowed to graduate because he failed English. In 1989, Saldivar worked at a supermarket and occasionally shoplifted small items from the store. But running into a friend who attended the College of Medical and Dental Careers changed Saldivar's life forever.

Saldivar liked his friend's uniform, and from that moment on, he was determined to find a job in the medical field. He began studying like never before and passed a high school equivalency test. In 1988, Saldivar became a student at the College of Medical and Dental Careers. He lived with his parents and brother during that time, and his family supported his goal. In February 1989, Saldivar received a certificate after completing his training.

When he was 19, Saldivar began working at the Glendale Adventist Medical Center as a respiratory therapist. Despite his age, he was punctual, reliable, and kind to patients. His colleagues loved working with him too. Saldivar struggled with depression during this time. According to some sources, he attended therapy. But Saldivar quickly gave up and stopped taking the prescribed antidepressant too.

One evening while flicking through channels, Saldivar saw a news report about a doctor in Chicago who was killing his patients. It gave him an idea as he realized he could do the same because he was alone during night shifts and without supervision. Also, most of his patients were close to death. Saldivar believed he would have more free time and fewer responsibilities by killing them.

THE DISCOVERY OF SALDIVAR'S CRIMES

On December 30th, 1996, Saldivar used Pavulon on an elderly woman named Salbi Asatryan. He entered her room at 4 am when there weren't many people around and used Pavulon again. More and more of his patients would simply die, but no one thought it was strange because all of them were sick and suffering from respiratory problems.

In February 1997, Jean Coyle, a regular patient of the Glendale Adventist Medical Center, arrived at the hospital. She knew the entire staff and felt right at home there. Coyle didn't hesitate to press the call button frequently, which enraged Saldivar, who was working the night shift.

Saldivar entered Coyle's room while she was sleeping and gave her a small dose of succinylcholine chloride. Instead of going into cardiac and respiratory arrest, Coyle started suffocating and making loud noises. That attracted the attention of other nurses working the night shift, and they managed to stabilize her condition. One of the people there was Ursula Anderson, Saldivar's co-worker. The two were in a secret relationship. Since Coyle was there because of respiratory problems, nobody investigated the incident.

INVESTIGATION AND DISCOVERY OF SALDIVAR'S SECRET

By April 1997, the hospital staff was talking and gossiping about Saldivar. Some of them noticed that the patients who were in his care died more frequently. The co-workers were talking about Saldivar's magic syringe. Bob Baker, another colleague, took these rumors seriously. He reported Saldivar to a supervisor who examined his work history and found nothing suspicious. Several weeks later, Baker and a co-worker opened Saldivar's locker as a prank and found morphine, suxamethonium chloride, and syringes inside. Saldivar wasn't supposed to have them, but Baker couldn't report him again because he did open the locker himself and could get into trouble.

Meanwhile, Saldivar was focused on his affair with Anderson, and the two spent a lot of time together during night shifts. Anderson believed that Saldivar had something to do with some of the deaths in the hospital and confided in one of her friends. She didn't say much, but it was enough to raise the alarm. In February 1998, Anderson's friend contacted the hospital administration anonymously and suggested they should look into Saldivar.

POLICE INVOLVEMENT AND SALDIVAR'S ARREST

The local police were contacted by the supervisors from the Glendale Adventist Medical Center, who informed them about Saldivar and the accusations. The hospital gave him a week off and urged the police to interview him. Saldivar was contacted by law enforcement on March 11th, 1998, and he arrived at the station the same day.

After talking to police officers for several hours, Saldivar admitted he had killed many patients. According to him, those were mercy killings because the patients were in pain, and he couldn't watch them suffer anymore. He carefully selected his victims and killed those who were close to dying. The police arrested him that night, but since Saldivar didn't provide any names and there was no physical evidence, the investigators had no idea how to proceed. They released Saldivar from custody two days later and started working on finding the proof he was responsible for the murders.

Below is a short transcript of the initial polygraph test Saldivar agreed to take for the police.

> Examiner: Efren, do you understand why you're here today?

Saldivar: To clear me up.

Examiner: To clear you up about what?

Saldivar: What he told me is that an anonymous call came in saying that I'm walking around injecting people for the purpose of killing them. Like an Angel of Death kind of thing.

Examiner: Are you an Angel of Death, Efren?

Saldivar: No.

Examiner: Have you done anything like that?

Saldivar: This is my reservation — there's been a lot of times where I've not actually done it, but kind of assisted it either directly or indirectly. That's why I know it's gonna say, yeah, that I'm lying.

Examiner: The only way you would fail my test tonight is if you deliberately lie. Why don't you tell me about the times that you help-assisted?

Saldivar: Oh, God. All right. I'll start with the very first time. I was 19 years old — fresh out of school. At about 11 o'clock, one of the ICU nurses tells me that there's a patient on life support that was assigned to me.

The patient had cancer — spread out to the whole body. The family was saying their goodbyes, and the doctors were planning to turn off the breathing machine. But when he peeked through the curtains, it was still on. I see the patient doing, like, you know, mild breathing motions and I told the nurse. She goes, 'Oh, we can't have that.' She says, 'The patient's going to die.' I go in there. I get both tubes, and I connect them.

Examiner: What did that do?

Saldivar: The patient basically suffocated.

Examiner: When was the second time?

Saldivar: Ok. Now, the other times...

Examiner: About how many occasions can you recall where you just didn't do anything?"

Saldivar: Oh, geez, in the nine years — and it's not just me, the nurses do it too.

Examiner: Um-hum.

Saldivar: I'd have to say at least 100.

Examiner: OK. When is the last time?

Saldivar: Last week.

CONFESSION, TRIAL, AND SENTENCING

Shockingly, Saldivar appeared on TV several weeks later and retracted his confession. He allegedly confessed because he was depressed and wanted to die, so he made the whole thing up. But the investigators weren't convinced.

Saldivar was fired from the Glendale Adventist Medical

Center, and his license was suspended. He wasn't able to work as a respiratory therapist anymore. Meanwhile, law enforcement was determined to find proof that Saldivar had murdered his patients. They combed through his records and focused on the last two years at the hospital.

The investigators exhumed 20 potential victims of Saldivar and sent their liver tissue for testing. A medical examiner found large doses of Pavulon in six of them. Efren Saldivar was arrested on January 8th, 2001, while on his way to work. He was employed as an electrician. During the second interview, he again confessed to the murders but offered a new explanation.

NEW EXPLANATION AND CHARGES

Saldivar claimed he was under a lot of stress because he was working around the clock. His schedule was hectic, and he wanted to have more time to rest.

> "We had too much work," Saldivar told police. "When I was only at my wits' end on the staffing, I'd look at the patient board. Who do we gotta get rid of? OK, who's in bad shape here?"
>
> EFREN SALDIVAR

On January 10th, 2001, Saldivar was charged with six counts of murder and one attempted murder. His victims were Eleanora Schlegel, Jose Alfaro, Salbi Asatryan, Balbino Castro, Luina Schidlowski, and Myrtle Brower. Jean Coyle was the only one who survived the poisoning.

Saldivar was facing the death penalty, so he agreed to a plea deal in March 2002. He pleaded guilty to six counts of murder and one attempted murder. On April 17, 2002, Efren Saldivar was sentenced to seven life sentences without the possibility of parole. He's now been in prison for 21 years and is 53 years old.

UNREQUITED LOVE

> "I'm not a good person. It is not your fault. Something in me just doesn't work. I've always had terrible thoughts. I've always had these feelings. I just kind of felt off. I think this is the end for me. I'm either going to prison or going to die. I know I'm going to get caught."
>
> BRANDON THEESFELD'S NOTE TO HIS PARENTS

It's always a heartbreaking situation when a person loves someone who doesn't love them back. But few could have guessed how far one young man would go to avoid commitment.

In the summer of 2019, Ally Kostial was a junior, attending

lectures at Ole Miss and teaching fitness classes on campus. She had no idea that her on-and-off boyfriend was planning her murder.

Alexandria Madison Kostial, also known as Ally, was born on September 11th, 1997, in St. Louis, Missouri. She attended Lindbergh High School and dreamed of going to the University of Mississippi or Ole Miss. During high school, Ally participated in cheerleading, track and field, and was a member of the golf team. She volunteered as an English teacher in South America and Africa.

After graduating from high school, she got accepted to her dream college and was excited to move to Oxford, Mississippi, in the fall of 2016. Ally was very friendly, and she quickly made a lot of friends. She majored in business marketing and loved taking part in various school activities.

Ally was the president of the Ole Miss Golf Club and a member of the Alpha Phi sorority. She enjoyed yoga and pilates, so she taught fitness classes on campus. In her spare time, Ally liked to take photos of beautiful sunsets. She posted them on Instagram regularly.

Ally met Brandon Theesfeld in the fall of 2016, soon after the start of her freshman year. He was born on April 5th, 1997, in Fort Worth, Texas. His father was a doctor, and Brandon enjoyed soccer and hunting. He also majored in business. The two began dating casually, but Ally hoped they would soon be in a real relationship. However, that didn't happen. Her friends noticed that the two never went on dates and hung out only when Brandon called Ally.

The two had a falling out during their sophomore year and didn't speak for a long time. According to Ally's friends, Brandon blocked her phone number and was unreachable. They started talking again during junior year, but things stayed the same. Ally was in love with Brandon, but he clearly didn't feel the same.

In the summer of 2019, Ally stayed on campus to take classes. Her parents visited her at the beginning of July and spent a couple of days with her daughter. Ally's mother, Cindy, helped her pick out new decor because Ally enjoyed rearranging her furniture and changing the look of her room. Two weeks later, the Kostial family received a call from the police.

DISCOVERY OF A BODY

On the morning of July 20th, 2019, a police officer patrolling the area around Sardis Lake discovered a female body at an abandoned fishing camp. This part of the lake is popular among college students who come here on weekends to ride ATVs when the water is low. However, the water was high on July 20th, and there weren't many people at the lake.

The female victim was shot nine times, and there were 11 shell casings on the scene. An ambulance driver saw a purse in a ditch and informed the officers. The police quickly learned that the victim's name was Alexandria Kostial, a student at the University of Mississippi.

The investigators informed the Kostial family and then drove to the campus, which was 45 minutes away from the crime scene. They talked to Ally's friends, hoping they might know who was with her last night. Ally's friends mentioned a young man named Brandon, who was Ally's on-and-off boyfriend.

The police reached Brandon on Sunday, July 21st, and asked him to come to the station for an interview. He said he would be there at 8:30 am on Monday. However, Brandon didn't show up, and the investigators started tracking him. They discovered he was on the move, traveling to Memphis on Interstate 55. Brandon was running away to Texas. He was seen at a gas station in South Memphis and quickly taken into custody by Lafayette County deputies. The officers searched his vehicle and found a .40 caliber gun. Brandon also had traces of blood on him.

He remained calm during the arrest and asked for a lawyer right away. His father, Daniel Theesfeld, spoke to the media afterward and said that his son is innocent until proven otherwise.

The police tried to find Ally's phone, hoping it would tell them more about the events that led to her murder. Its last location was in Oxford, and that was everything they knew. But a search of Ally's room uncovered another piece of evidence — her Apple Watch. Even though the investigators didn't have her phone, they could read her text messages because the two devices were connected.

Brandon's room was searched too, and the police found a goodbye letter written on July 20th and addressed to his parents. It suggested Brandon was planning suicide. His computer and phone were analyzed, and the investigators finally had all the clues they needed to assemble the whole story.

THE UNRAVELING RELATIONSHIP

In April 2019, both of them were busy studying for exams. On April 14th, Ally sent Brandon a photo of an inconclusive pregnancy test.
Brandon texted her twice.

> It's so early you just take a pill not keeping it at all I do not want a kid at all

> I am serious no kid at all it will ruin my life I will not help at all. Not to be mean but this is how I feel and I'm not changing my mind.

Ally said he couldn't tell her what to do. Brandon replied she should get an abortion.

He began ignoring Ally's texts, and she did everything to grab his attention. Ally sent him long texts saying she was drinking a lot of alcohol, hoping Brandon would be sympathetic toward her. He read her messages but didn't reply. Ally informed him that she experienced light bleeding at the beginning of July and might have lost the baby. Again, she didn't hear back from Brandon.

On July 12th, Brandon was on his way to Fort Worth when Ally sent him a photo of two inconclusive pregnancy tests. It likely upset Brandon, who posted a Snapchat of his gun two days later. The caption said: "Finally taking my baby back to Oxford."

The following week, Brandon was back on campus. He was searching the internet for advice on concealing a crime and getting away with murder. Ted Bundy was also in his search history. On July 18th, Ally sent Brandon a photo of her belly.

On July 19th, Brandon messaged Ally asking if he could drop by her room so they could talk. He also wanted to know where her roommates were. Ally spoke with her mom later in the evening and told her she was going out with her friends to a bar.

At 11:52 pm, she was seen on a surveillance camera at Oxford Square leaving one of the bars in that area. Ally called an Uber, and she returned home alone. The investigators discovered that Brandon picked up Ally at 1:28 am on July 20th. The pair drove to the abandoned fishing camp near Sardis Lake. Brandon was familiar with the area because he spent some time there with his friends during freshman year.

The two stopped at Lakeside Market in Como, close to the lake. Once they arrived at the fishing camp, Ally and Brandon sat on a picnic table and drank White Claw Hard Seltzer. In his testimony, Brandon said he was drinking the whole day and even did cocaine at the fishing camp. He took the gun out of his car and fired one shot toward the lake. Brandon then proceeded to shoot Ally. The police received a call from a local walking their dog and learned they heard shots between 2:15 am and 2:30 am.

Brandon drove back to campus, returned to his room, and wrote the goodbye letter. Realizing he couldn't kill himself, Brandon spent the evening with his friends, and they went bowling. On Sunday, Brandon dropped by another friend's place with his gun and a pack of beers. He slept there that night and decided to go to Texas on Monday morning.

TRIAL AND SENTENCING

On August 30th, 2019, Brandon Theesfeld was indicted on a capital murder charge. He pleaded not guilty. The prosecution had a solid case against him since it was confirmed Brandon had planned the murder for several weeks. His internet searches confirm that he wanted to eliminate Ally because he saw her as a problem. Furthermore, he searched for a remote spot where they could be alone.

Ally trusted him and didn't hesitate to go with Brandon to Sardis Lake. The autopsy confirmed Ally wasn't pregnant at the time of her death. There is a possibility she had a miscarriage at the beginning of July. Ally's parents didn't know what she was going through even though they talked often. They had never met Brandon but had heard Ally talk about him.

Brandon Theesfeld's trial was delayed because of the pandemic. He appeared in front of a judge on August 27th, 2021, and pleaded guilty to first-degree murder as a part of a plea deal. He was sentenced to life in prison without the possibility of parole.

Ally's mother, Cindy, made a statement in court.

> "I wish I could have kept her away from this evil, callous, scheming, ungrateful, sinister and violent and corrupt monster. He had every opportunity to do good in the world, but he chose to do evil. Brandon, you belong in jail each day for the rest of your life for the heinous act you committed to such a sweet soul in Ally."

SEX AND MURDER

"I have been telling the truth from the beginning, Bob has used me and threatened me. He told me he had friends in the mafia and would have me killed. I went to the police, no one believed me."

JOE GENTZ, HANDYMAN AND MURDERER

A secret sex life, a fed up wife, and reliance on untrustworthy friends led a conniving husband right into the prison cell where he belonged.

The Bashara family lived a good life. They were well-known residents of Grosse Pointe, an affluent suburb of Detroit. However, Robert Bashara led a secret life that few knew about.

THE INDEPENDENT AND FOCUSED WIFE

Jane Engelbrecht Bashara was born on June 22nd, 1955, in Mount Clemens, Michigan. She was the oldest of four children. Jane enjoyed school from a young age and attended Mount Clemens High School. She enrolled in Central Michigan University after graduation. In 1977, she earned a BA in Business Administration. Jane quickly found a job, bought her first house, and started studying for her Master's Degree at the University of Detroit.

Attending classes at the university was complicated because Jane had a full-time job, but six years later, she had her MA in Business Administration. Fiercely independent and reliable, Jane was focused on her career. But in 1983, she met a man named Robert Bashara.

Jane and Bob Bashara got married on April 25th, 1985. Both were doing great at that time as Bob got into the real estate business, and Jane received a huge promotion at work. The happy couple had a baby boy named Robert Junior in 1988. In 1989, the family moved into a large house at 522 Middlesex Road. Their second child, Jessica, was born in 1992.

Bob was involved in the community and was the president of the Grosse Pointe Rotary Club. Jane was the president of the Grosse Pointe South High School Mothers' Club and raised money for scholarships. She enjoyed volunteering and inspired those around her to do the same. After some time, it was clear that Jane was a responsible parent who was making money for the family. Bob, on the other hand, was the opposite.

THE UNRAVELING: BOB'S MISTRESS AND JANE'S DIVORCE REQUEST

In the 2000s, Bob managed an apartment building in Grosse Pointe and often hung out at the Hard Luck Café. The Internet allowed him to explore BDSM and find partners online. It's possible that Jane didn't know about this side of her husband at all. Bob's online name was Master Bob, and he started chatting with Rachel Gillett, who became his mistress.

The two met in the basement of Bob's apartment building, where he made a small dungeon with hooks on walls and swords as decorations. According to Rachel, Bob told her he was married to his wife Jane, but the two were in the process of getting a divorce. She soon learned that Jane and Bob weren't getting separated and broke things off with Bob.

That didn't last long because the two couldn't stay away from each other. Bob asked Rachel to move into one of the apartments above the BDSM dungeon, and she agreed. This time he claimed that he had an open marriage. His mistress didn't know that Bob was spending a lot of money and also didn't pay his taxes. Jane was furious at him because he relied on his mother for financial help and took the family money to support his lifestyle. Realizing that Bob didn't want to change, Jane asked for a divorce.

THE UNLIKELY DUO: BOB AND JOE GENTZ

Steve Thibodaux, a used-furniture salesman, introduced Bob to Joe Gentz. Steve thought Bob could find Joe work because he was a good handyman. In exchange, the man could live at one of Bob's apartments.

Joe grew up in a poor family in Warren, Michigan, and attended a residential school for developmentally disabled children. After graduation, he got addicted to drugs and alcohol. Joe got sober in 1990 and met his wife in 2000. The two lived in Washington D.C., and had a daughter soon after the wedding. The couple divorced in 2003, and the girl stayed with Joe.
She was soon taken away from him because Joe was an unfit parent. Even though he tried his best, he couldn't take care of the household and the little girl. Joe relapsed and started drinking again. Wanting to be closer to his family, he returned to Michigan. That's how Joe ended up living in one of Bob's units and working as his handyman.

Jane was pressing Bob for a divorce, but he knew he didn't have the money to go through it. He started talking to Joe about murdering Jane. Bob thought Joe should do it. Joe kept refusing, but Bob was persistent. One evening, Bob called Joe and asked him to come to his house and help him move some boxes out of the garage.

On January 24th, Joe Gentz arrived at the Bashara residence on Middlesex Road. He entered the garage with Bob, and Jane joined them. When she entered the room, Bob pulled out the gun and pointed it at Joe. He ordered the handyman to kill his wife or Bob would shoot him. Jane and Joe stared at Bob, terrified.

Believing that his threat was real, Joe hit Jane, and the woman fell to the ground. He then placed his heavy work boot on her neck and pressed as hard as he could. Jane suffocated soon after. They placed Jane in her car, and Joe drove toward northeast Detroit. Bob followed closely behind in his vehicle.

They left Jane's car in an alley, and Bob left Joe to find a way home. Bob drove straight to the Hard Luck Café to create an alibi. Other customers noticed Bob and remembered the man was walking in and out of the café that evening. He was also sweeping around the building, which was something he had never done before. At around 11 pm, Bob returned home and called the police to report his wife missing.

The call was made at 11:30 pm, and Bob stated that he'd last heard from Jane at 5 pm when she called to tell him she was going home from work. According to him, he arrived at the house at 8 pm and expected to see Jane because the TV and the lights were on. He went to the café, expecting she would be back soon.

THE DISCOVERY OF JANE'S BODY

In the early hours of January 25th, 2012, Frank Leone, a tow truck driver, was in east Detroit. He spotted a black

Mercedes SUV and thought it was stolen. The tow truck driver contacted the police and told them the license number. Soon after, a police officer checked the car and saw a female body in the back seat. They believed she overdosed because of pills that were scattered around the vehicle. Her purse was next to her body, and the officer soon learned her identity – Jane Bashara.

The police knew that her husband Bob reported Jane missing last night. The medical examiner ruled that Jane died of strangulation. A couple of her fingernails were broken, suggesting she fought her assailant. The pills were hormone drugs.

Since the Bashara family lived in Grosse Pointe, the media picked up the case quickly. The community was in shock, and a candlelight vigil was organized at Grosse Pointe South High School on January 25th.

THE INVESTIGATION

On January 27th, the police called Bob Bashara in for an interview. He provided them with the entire timeline of his movements on the evening of January 24th, which was immediately strange to the investigators. The police knew Jane wasn't killed in her SUV, so they were trying to find the crime scene.

After searching the Bashara residence, the investigators determined that Jane was killed in the garage. They found tiny blood stains on the ground and sent them for DNA testing. Joe was questioned on February 1st, 2012, and soon confessed to helping Bob remove Jane's body from the garage. He also said he was offered $2,000 and a Cadillac to murder Jane. However, the investigators didn't take him seriously because of his low IQ.

The media dug deeper into Bob's life, and soon the entire city of Detroit knew about his fascination with BDSM, the mistress, and the sex dungeon. The home of Rachel Gillett was searched by the police in March 2012, but they didn't find any proof she was involved in Jane's murder.

On March 3rd, 2012, Joe Gentz was arrested in Mount Clemens. The investigators received the DNA results earlier that week and confirmed that the blood found on the garage floor at the Bashara residence belonged to Jane and Joe. He was charged with first-degree murder.

Scared that Joe would start talking about the murder, Bob went to his friend Steve Thibodaux and asked him to find someone to shut Joe up. He offered $2,000 for the hit. Steve agreed, took Bob's money, and went to the police station to turn him in. Bob Bashara was arrested and charged with first-degree murder.

THE TRIAL AND SENTENCING

Joe Gentz was offered a plea deal by the prosecution and agreed to spend 17 to 25 years in prison in exchange for testimony against Bob Bashara. The trial began in October

2014, and numerous witnesses, including Rachel Gillett and Frank Leone, appeared on the stand.

Bob's statement at the trial:

> "I know I absolutely did wrong, what I did was inexcusable, and I have no one to blame but myself. I understand that I must pay before what I've done. I absolutely stand before you and my family and the world to take responsibility for my actions."

Even though Bob apologized for the crime, the jury couldn't be swayed. On December 18, 2014, he was found guilty of the murder of his wife, Jane Bashara. One month later, Bob was sentenced to life in prison without the possibility of parole.

Bob Bashara died in prison on October 15th, 2020 at the age of 62. He died of natural causes.

THE WEALTH AND THE TRAGEDY

> "I would gladly have given every cent I have in the world and everything I could borrow to save my boy, but it was not to be."
>
> ROBERT GREENLEASE SR.

In September 1953, two decades after the famous Lindbergh kidnapping, the public was shocked to learn that a six-year-old boy from Kansas City was abducted from school. His family didn't hesitate to pay the ransom, hoping to see their boy alive again. Unfortunately, that never happened.

A SELF-MADE MAN

Robert Greenlease Sr. was born on August 25th, 1882, in Saline County, Missouri. He grew up in an underprivileged family and dropped out of school in the sixth grade. He found a job and helped his family out financially.

Robert's parents moved the family to Kansas City when he was in his teens, and there, he saw cars for the first time. Mesmerized by automobiles, Robert spent all his time studying how they worked and eventually opened an auto repair shop.

When he was 21 years old, he constructed his first car, the Kansas City Hummer, but it wasn't successful. However, Robert was interested in the new mass-produced vehicle called the Cadillac and signed up to be their representative in the Midwest. He opened a dealership in Kansas City, and soon enough, Robert was making a lot of money.

He partnered with other dealerships in the area and even bought stock in General Motors. Soon, Robert became a multimillionaire and was one of the wealthiest people in Kansas City.

A SECOND FAMILY

He was married to Betty Rush until 1939. They had one son, Paul, who attended Kemper Military School in Boonville, Missouri. There, Paul Greenlease befriended another young man named Carl Hall.

After his divorce from Betty, Robert met a woman named Virginia Pollock, who worked as a nurse. Despite a significant age difference, the two fell in love and married soon after. The family moved to Mission Hills, an affluent neighborhood on the outskirts of Kansas City. The couple had two children – Virginia Sue, born on December 22nd, 1941, and Bobby Junior, born on February 3rd, 1947.

The Greenlease children attended the French Institute of Notre Dame De Sion, a private Catholic school, but Virginia Sue transferred to a nearby Sunset Hill Girls' School as she got older. Robert Sr. would drive little Bobby to school every morning, and his mother, Virginia, would pick him up in the afternoon. The family followed the same routine every day.

On September 28th, 1953, at around 10:55 am, a woman who introduced herself as Bobby Greenlease's aunt spoke to Sister Morand at the school entrance and said that Bobby's mother had a heart attack and was at St. Mary's Hospital. Sister Morand pulled Bobby from class while the unknown woman waited in the chapel.

According to Sister Morand, Bobby walked towards the woman and didn't look confused or scared. Bobby and the woman walked out of the school and entered a taxi. Half an hour later, Sister Marthanna contacted the Greenlease residence to ask about Virginia. Virginia herself picked up the phone, and after the initial shock, Sister Marthanna told her that Bobby was picked up from school by an aunt. Panicked, Virginia called her husband Robert, who was at work. He rushed home and alerted the chief of police.

Knowing they had a kidnapping on their hands and that Bobby might already be out of state, the chief contacted the FBI.

Sister Morand mentioned that the unknown woman entered a taxi, so the police quickly identified the driver. Willard Creech confirmed he gave a ride to a woman fitting the description provided by the school. She entered the taxi with a little boy and wanted to go to Katz Drug Store on Main Street.

CARL HALL AND BONNIE HEADY

The kidnappers who took Bobby out of school were Carl Austin Hall and his girlfriend, Bonnie Heady. Hall was born on July 1st, 1919, and grew up in a wealthy family. His father was a famous lawyer, and his mother had a large inheritance. Hall's parents indulged Hall when he was young, probably because they lost one child due to a birth injury.

Hall's father passed away unexpectedly when he was only 13 years old. His mother didn't want to take care of him anymore, so Hall was sent to live on a farm. He then went to Kemper Military School, where he had classes with Paul Greenlease. Hall later said Greenlease was a celebrity at the military school, and everyone knew his father was a multi-millionaire.

Hall enrolled in William Jewell College in Liberty, Missouri, but dropped out after the first semester. Feeling lost and unable to repair the relationship with his mother, Hall enlisted in the Marines and was shipped to Asia to fight in World War II. He started drinking heavily and was discharged.

His mother and grandmother died soon after, and Hall inherited the family money. By then, he was an alcoholic who sometimes used drugs, such as amphetamines and morphine. Hall attempted to invest the money in several businesses, but they all failed. He started gambling and, after several years, lost the entire inheritance. Broke and desperate, Hall robbed several taxi drivers and was arrested. As a result, he was sent to Missouri State Penitentiary in Jefferson City.

During his time in prison, Hall began planning a kidnapping that would make him rich again. He remembered Paul Greenlease and his father. Paul had a much younger half-sister and half-brother who would be easy to snatch. After serving only one year, Hall was released, and he moved to St. Joseph, just a short drive away from Kansas City.

While sitting in a bar, he met a woman named Bonnie Heady. She was born on July 15th, 1912, and was a bit older than Hall. Heady had a similar background. She grew up in a well-to-do family and married a successful farmer. However, her husband cheated on her, and Heady filed for divorce. She received a house and a large amount of money in the settlement. When her father passed away, she inherited his farm.

But Heady wasn't good with money and quickly spent

everything she had. Renting out her father's farm was her only source of income before deciding to go into sex work. Two days after meeting Hall, she allowed him to move into her house. The pair drank all the time, and Hall soon shared his kidnapping plan with her. Even though Heady was hesitant, Hall promised he would do everything to protect her in case they got caught.

Once Heady was on board, she called the Greenlease residence while the family was on holiday and told the maid she was doing a survey about schoolchildren in Kansas City. The unsuspecting maid answered the questions. The kidnappers knew where the children went to school, so they began trailing the family in a rented vehicle.

While their primary target was Virginia Sue, Hall decided they would take Bobby because he was younger. He wasn't sure if Heady could do her part because she was an alcoholic.

Knowing that children are difficult to deal with, Hall planned to kill Bobby from the beginning. Once Heady brought the boy to the parking lot in front of Katz Drug Store, all three drove across the nearby border to Kansas. Meanwhile, Heady was talking to little Bobby and got some personal information from the boy. She knew the names of his pets, which they could use to prove they had Bobby.

Bobby seemed content but was asking questions about where they were going, so the pair told him they would get ice cream and then see his father. Instead, they drove back to Missouri to a secluded area near Heady's house.

Once there, Hall got out of the car and got in the back with six-year-old Bobby. He first tried to strangle the child with a piece of rope. The rope was too short for Hall to grip it properly, and Bobby was now kicking and screaming, so Hall took out his .38 revolver and fired two shots at close range at the child's head. The first shot missed, but the second shot killed Bobby. He took Bobby's body out of the car and laid it on a tarp, and then buried his body in a shallow grave.

After the murder, Hall and Heady returned to Kansas City, where they started making ransom demands. They demanded $600,000 from the Greenlease family, which was a staggering amount of money at the time. The Greenleases were desperate to get their son back and agreed to pay the ransom.

Hall and Heady gave the Greenleases specific instructions on delivering the money. They told them to place the cash in a bag and leave it in the trunk of a car parked at the park entrance. Hall's plan was to pick up the ransom and then send Heady to St. Louis, where she would mail a letter revealing Bobby's whereabouts.

However, things did not go according to plan. After Hall picked up the money, he noticed that he was being followed by a police officer. Panicking, Hall sped away, ultimately losing the officer. He then met up with Heady, and the two fled to St. Louis.

In St. Louis, they rented an apartment under fake names and continued their drinking and drug use. They didn't know what to do with the ransom money and eventually decided to split it between themselves. Hall took his share and left Heady, planning to go to Mexico.

However, they were tracked down by the FBI, who had received a tip from the landlady of the apartment building they were staying in. The landlady recognized them from the news and contacted the authorities. The FBI arrested Heady first and then caught Hall before he could leave for Mexico.

Both Hall and Heady were charged with the kidnapping and murder of Bobby Greenlease.

Carl Hall and Bonnie Heady were arrested, they both confessed to their involvement in the kidnapping and murder of Bobby Greenlease.

Hall provided the information about the location of Bobby's body, which led the FBI to Heady's backyard at 1201 South 38th Street. The FBI found Bobby's body buried in a shallow grave, wrapped in a plastic bag and covered with a thick layer of lime.

THE TRIAL

U.S. Attorney Edward L. Scheufler represented the federal government in the case, as the crime involved crossing state lines, making it a federal offense under the Federal

Kidnapping Act, also known as the Lindbergh Law. During the trial, the prosecution laid out a detailed and chilling account of the events that had led to Bobby's death.

Scheufler made his case and showed how Carl Hall, a career criminal, had meticulously planned the kidnapping and murder of Bobby with the help of Heady.

They were both found guilty and sentenced to death.

In the days leading up to their deaths, Hall and Heady were held in separate cells at the Missouri State Penitentiary. Prison officials reported that neither showed any signs of fear or regret. On December 18th, 1953, the two were led into the gas chamber and executed.

The Greenlease family, forever changed by the loss of their young son, eventually established a foundation in Bobby's name to aid children in need.

TALL CORNFIELDS

"I do hope, one day, (your daughter) Paulina has an opportunity to become a mother. But how will she ever explain to her children who their grandfather is?

This is the legacy you left behind for your only child, Mr. Rivera."

LAURA CALDERWOOD, MOTHER OF MOLLIE TIBBITS

A young woman from a small town in Iowa went running on a typical summer day in 2018 and her lifeless body was found one month later. This is what happened to Mollie Tibbets.

Mollie Cecilia Tibbets was born on May 8th, 1998, in San Francisco, California. She lived in the Bay Area with her parents, Rob and Laura, and two brothers, Jake and Scott. Her parents divorced in 2007, and Laura decided to move to Brooklyn, Iowa, to have a fresh start. The children were thrilled with this change of scenery and loved living in a small community.

Even though they were in Iowa, Rob Tibbetts stayed close to his children and regularly saw them. Mollie signed up for a cross-country team because she enjoyed running. She wasn't the fastest runner out there, but Mollie had fun training with her friends.

In high school, she met her boyfriend, Dalton Jack, a football player. The two started dating in 2015. After graduation, Mollie got accepted at the University of Iowa, and was a psychology major. In the summer of 2018, she was home in Brooklyn and working at a children's day camp at Grinnell Regional Medical Center. Mollie used the sunny weather to run almost daily and was looking forward to starting her sophomore year in the Fall.

On July 18th, 2018, Mollie was housesitting for her boyfriend, Dalton. He was a construction worker and was in Dubuque, Iowa, which is around 130 miles away from Brooklyn. Mollie looked after his dogs since one of them had epilepsy. The weather outside was quite warm, and she was waiting for 7 pm to go on a run.

Dalton's house was in west Brooklyn, and Mollie had her shoes laced up and was ready to start her run at 7:30 pm.

She planned to go on her usual route towards east Brooklyn and cover six miles. Mollie wore her typical running gear and had her phone and a Fitbit watch.

A black Chevrolet Malibu passed her shortly after the start of her run. Mollie's hairdresser saw her from her car at approximately 8 pm, and they waved at each other. Then the Chevrolet Malibu returned. The driver stopped the vehicle and started running alongside Mollie. She tried to keep it cool initially, but the man's presence bothered her. The girl stopped and asked him to leave her alone. When he refused, she said she would call the police. Then he grabbed Mollie and dragged her into his vehicle.

Mollie was scheduled to work on July 19th, and her co-worker got worried when she didn't show up in the morning. Since she didn't call in sick, the co-worker called Dalton, who was her friend. He said he hadn't heard from Mollie since yesterday and had no idea where she was. Dalton called Mollie's family and then returned to Brooklyn with his brother to see what was happening.

Meanwhile, Mollie's family called her friends. After failing to locate their daughter, they filed a missing persons report.

Dalton and his brother spent the day driving around Brooklyn and the surrounding area searching for Mollie. They thought something had happened to her on the run, and she might be hurt.

The local law enforcement contacted the Iowa Division of

Criminal Investigation, and their agents arrived in Brooklyn to help look for the missing young woman. They coordinated searches of the area, but there were still no clues that could lead to Mollie's whereabouts.

Thousands of tips came in, and the investigators checked every single one. But they still couldn't find Mollie. A reward was offered, and it reached $366,000 through donations that were coming in from all over the United States.

Dalton Jack was questioned by the police, which was a standard part of the investigation, and was ruled out as a suspect right away. However, the public believed he was somehow involved, resulting in harassment and online bullying. On July 25th, the police made a statement that Mollie's boyfriend wasn't a suspect.

The police didn't have the information recorded by Mollie's Fitbit that could provide them with her exact running route on July 18th. But they had the old data, which helped them create a map of Mollie's favorite routes. The officers started searching along the roads for surveillance cameras, hoping some of them recorded Mollie at the time of her disappearance.

They spotted her in the footage, which gave the police hope they could find more clues. The investigators went through the available videos and wrote down every vehicle and person in the area before and after Mollie passed by. The black Chevrolet Malibu was spotted immediately, and law enforcement believed the driver could know more about what happened to Mollie on July 18th.

The police were searching Brooklyn for the Chevrolet Malibu and spotted the vehicle from the surveillance footage. After checking the license plate number, they discovered the car was registered to a woman from a neighboring town; however, the driver was a man. The officers approached him, and he said he didn't speak English. Luckily, a bystander was fluent in Spanish and helped the officers communicate with the driver.

He said his name was Cristhian Bahena Rivera and that he was familiar with Mollie's disappearance. However, he claimed he had nothing to do with it. The police later learned he grew up in a poverty-stricken family in El Guayabillo, Mexico. Rivera illegally entered the United States in 2011 on an inflatable raft.

He had relatives in Iowa, so he joined them and started working on the farms around Brooklyn. Rivera was an undocumented worker who avoided the authorities for seven years. His daughter was born in 2015, and Rivera shared custody of her with his ex-girlfriend.

Rivera was called in for questioning on August 20th. Detectives suspected he knew more about Mollie's disappearance and was ready for a lengthy interview. Rivera was shown the surveillance footage showing him driving the Malibu and changed his story. He now told the investigators he did see Mollie on July 18th because he was delivering a vacuum cleaner to his uncle, who lived in the east part of Brooklyn.

Afterward, Rivera shared more details about his encounter with Mollie, admitting he noticed how attractive she was. He then said he stopped his car at one point and ran beside her. This revelation led to him saying Mollie threatened to call the police and that they argued by the road. According to Rivera, Mollie screamed and tried to slap him. Then he blacked out.

The next thing he could remember was that he was driving his car with Mollie's earbuds in his lap. He then remembered Mollie was in his trunk. After 11 hours of interrogation, Rivera agreed to take the investigators to Mollie's body.

On August 21st, 2018, Rivera and the investigators left the police station at 4:30 am. He told them to drive southeast, 15 miles out of town. They stopped near some cornfields, and Rivera said they would find Mollie's body there. The officers discovered her body lying on the ground with her clothes neatly folded beside her.

Mollie's autopsy revealed she was stabbed nine times, and these injuries killed her. The removal of her clothes suggested she was sexually assaulted. On August 22nd, Cristhian Bahena Rivera was charged with first-degree murder. His bail was $5 million because he was a flight risk. On September 19th, he pleaded not guilty.

The disappearance of Mollie Tibbetts was heavily covered

by the media at the time. When the public learned her killer's identity, the murder quickly became politicized. He was an undocumented worker employed by Yarrabee Farms. The owner, a prominent Iowa Republican, Craig Lang, said they used the federal E-Verify program to confirm his immigration status. It was later discovered that Yarrabee Farms wasn't a part of the E-Verify program, so Lang accused Rivera of providing them with false information.

Rivera's trial began on May 17th, 2021, in Davenport, Iowa. The prosecution had a solid case against him because of all the physical evidence collected from Rivera's car. However, Rivera's defense tried introducing an alternative suspect, Dalton Jack, Mollie's boyfriend. They learned the couple had problems one month before the murder as Mollie found out he was cheating on her. No physical evidence supported these claims, and Dalton Jack had a good alibi.

The courtroom was stunned when Rivera introduced a second version of the events that led to Mollie's murder. According to him, two unknown men appeared in his living room on July 18th, 2018, held him at gunpoint, and forced Rivera to drive around Brooklyn. When the men saw Mollie, they hopped out of the car and chased her down the road with a knife. They placed her in the trunk and asked Rivera to take them to a remote location. He drove to the cornfield where she was later found.

After killing Mollie, the men threatened Rivera by saying they would hurt his little girl if he went to the police. The two walked away, leaving him next to the cornfield. Since he was an undocumented worker and was afraid for his daughter's safety, Rivera didn't tell anyone what happened. Rivera's defense lawyers said the forensics discovered two unknown DNA profiles in the trunk and claimed the evidence supported Rivera's claims.

The jury began deliberating on May 28th, 2021, and it took them eight hours to reach the verdict. Cristhian Bahena Rivera was found guilty of first-degree murder and was sentenced to life in prison on August 21st, 2021. He is currently at the Iowa State Penitentiary in Fort Madison, Iowa.

THE LAMBETH POISONER

"He [Dr. Cream] is a monstrous product of the nineteenth century; a man absolutely without mercy and with an insatiable lust for killing."

SIR ARTHUR CONAN DOYLE

While Jack the Ripper is the most famous serial killer of the Victorian Era, London was terrorized by another criminal several years later. The newspapers called him *The Lambeth Poisoner,* but his real name was Thomas Neill Cream, a physician and surgeon from Canada.

Thomas Neill Cream was born in Glasgow, Scotland, on May 27th, 1850, to Mary and William Cream. He was the oldest of eight children and William's favorite. The family moved to Canada in 1854 and resided near Quebec City.

William was a well-known shipbuilder, and the Cream family was quite wealthy. Thomas Cream was exceptionally intelligent and loved spending time with his father, who showered him with expensive clothes and gifts.

Even though he did well at school, Cream was known as a troublemaker. No matter what he did, his father, William, never punished him. So when Cream announced he wanted to study medicine, William was there to support him financially. Cream's siblings worked at the shipyard and helped their father.

In September 1872, Cream arrived at McGill University in Montreal. He was hard to miss because of the fancy clothes and jewelry. Cream was always in the company of women, and he attended many parties. Somehow his grades remained high, and he graduated on March 31st, 1876. During his time at McGill University, Cream showed interest in chloroform and covered the subject in his senior thesis.

RELATIONSHIP WITH FLORA BANKS

After graduation, Cream lived in Waterloo, Quebec, where he met Flora Banks. Her father was a hotel owner, and the Banks family was known in the area. The young woman fell madly in love with Cream, and she was sure he loved her back because he promised to marry her. What Flora didn't know was that most everything Cream said was a lie. Cream was leaving and was already planning to travel to London, England, for his post-graduate studies.

One evening, Flora informed Cream that she was pregnant. Cream refused to marry her and insisted that she abort the child. When she refused, he blackmailed her by saying he would tell everyone she got pregnant out of wedlock.

Since that would be a huge scandal, Flora agreed to an abortion. But there was yet another obstacle – abortion was illegal in Canada. Not wanting to go to another doctor, Cream decided to perform the abortion himself. After all, he was now a doctor.

Everything seemed fine until several days after the procedure. Flora had a high fever, and her family doctor discovered the young woman had an abortion. Flora's father was furious. On September 11th, 1876, he dragged Cream back to his house and forced them to marry. But Cream made other plans, and on the morning after the wedding, he was sailing to London to attend St. Thomas's Hospital Medical School.

He stayed in touch with Flora while overseas. The young woman's condition was getting worse, and she was now suffering from bronchitis. Cream sent her a letter and included small white pills to help her with the pain. Flora took them but felt sick and told her family doctor that her husband had sent the medication from England. Tragically, Flora passed away in August 1877. The official cause of death was bronchitis, but Flora's family believed Cream had something to do with it because of the pills.

During his time at St. Thomas's Hospital Medical School,

Cream became even more interested in chemistry, especially after learning that one of his professors was an expert witness in a strychnine poisoning murder case.

Cream completed his post-graduate studies and returned to Canada. He opened a medical practice in London, Ontario.

Cream was charming and friendly to his patients, so they continued coming to his practice even after it was discovered that he was operating without a license. Well aware that performing illegal abortions pays a lot, he did them after hours.

In the summer of 1879, Cream began an affair with Catharine Hutchinson Gardner. She got pregnant, and Cream asked her to have an abortion. Catharine refused, and then she disappeared. The woman was discovered several days later in a small shed behind Cream's practice on 204 Dundas Street. The police talked to the doctor, and he denied having a relationship with her.

However, Cream confirmed Catharine was his patient and that she came to the office asking for an abortion. When he refused, the young woman said she would poison herself. The autopsy said she was killed by a handkerchief soaked in chloroform. Cream gave the investigators a letter allegedly written by Catharine in which she named a businessman who lived at her hotel as the baby's father. However, Catharine's friends and family said someone forged her signature.

The police ended their investigation, and the murder of Catharine Gardner was never solved. Cream wasn't arrested for this crime. Now specializing in abortions, Cream moved to Chicago, where he set up his practice near the red-light district.

While in Chicago, Cream performed illegal abortions on sex workers. One of his alleged patients, Mary Anne Faulkner, passed away in August 1880, and Cream was investigated by the police. However, the investigators couldn't prove that Cream had harmed the woman. In December of the same year, Miss Stack, Cream's patient, mysteriously died, but he wasn't investigated.

Yet another unsolved death related to Cream happened in April 1881. Alice Montgomery was discovered dead in her boarding house, and the police learned she recently had an abortion. The cause of death was strychnine poisoning. The police couldn't find any evidence that connected Cream to the death of Alice Montgomery.

In the summer of 1881, Cream began an affair with Julia Stott, the wife of Daniel Stott. Daniel had epilepsy, and Cream and his mistress allegedly planned his murder together. Julia gave him medicine that was supposed to help with his condition. Unfortunately, Daniel Stott died on July 14th, 1881. Even though the coroner ruled his death a natural cause, the investigators soon got interested in Julia and her lover.

As soon as the duo was arrested, Julia turned on Cream and testified that he was the only person behind the murder of Daniel Stott, who died of strychnine poisoning. Cream was sentenced to life in prison but was released in July 1891 after serving 10 years. It is suspected that Cream's brother bribed the Governor.

William Cream passed away in 1887 and left quite a lot of money for his eldest son. Thomas Cream purchased a ticket to England and arrived in Liverpool on October 1st, 1891. Since he was familiar with London, Cream relocated to the city and rented a place at 103 Lambeth Palace Road. This part of London was known for high crime rates and sex work.

MURDERS IN LONDON

By this point, Cream hated women and wanted to inflict pain. On October 13th, 1891, he was in contact with Ellen Donworth, also known as Nellie. Nellie was a 19-year-old sex worker. She had heard about the new doctor who moved to Lambeth, accepted his invitation, and the two went for a drink. Soon after, Nellie felt sick and passed away the same night.

The coroner concluded that Nellie died of strychnine poisoning. The police received a letter from someone named A. O'Brien, who said he would reveal the name of the killer for £300,000. Additionally, Cream anonymously blackmailed W.F.D. Smith, who ran bookstalls all over London, and said he would turn Smith in for the murder because he could prove he did it.

On October 20th, Matilda Clover, a 27-year-old sex worker, spent an evening with Cream. The doctor gave her some pills and told her to take four before bed. Matilda passed away during the night after experiencing painful spasms. The coroner ruled she died of heart failure. Cream then anonymously blackmailed Dr. William Broadbent, a physician.

According to Dr. Broadbent, the blackmailer claimed to have physical evidence that he was involved in the murder and asked for £25,000. The doctor contacted Scotland Yard, and the investigators suggested they try to catch the blackmailer together. But the plan didn't work, and Cream wasn't caught.

In March 1892, Cream briefly returned to Canada but was back in London, England, by April 2nd. He met with Louise Harvey, a sex worker, and gave her two pills. The doctor was pushing her to take the medication in front of him, and she became suspicious. The woman put the pills in her mouth but didn't swallow them. Instead, she tossed them in the river while Cream wasn't looking.

On April 11th, 1892, Cream was with Alice Marsh and Emma Shrivell in their rented apartment. As he was getting ready to return to his place, he offered them a can of salmon and pills. Marsh and Shrivell knew that Cream was a doctor, so they thought it would be okay to take the medication. But both of them felt sick as soon as they swallowed the pills. The coroner first believed that the women ate bad tuna, but he soon discovered they were poisoned with strychnine.

The newspapers in London were covering the case of the Lambeth Poisoner, and the murders were soon the talk of the town. The police cleared the people who were blackmailed by the anonymous person, but they still had no idea who sent the letters. However, the blackmailer wrote about Matilda Clover's death, the sex worker who died of heart failure.

Around the same time, Cream met a New York City policeman who was in London for a vacation. The two talked about the murders, and Cream offered to give him a tour of Lambeth. He took the policeman to the homes of the murdered sex workers, which immediately made him suspicious. The policeman mentioned Cream's name to a British policeman, and he was soon placed under surveillance.

ARREST AND TRIAL

Scotland Yard learned that Cream lived in Lambeth and frequently visited sex workers. The investigators contacted the police in the United States and Canada and discovered that Cream served time for poisoning.

Meanwhile, Matilda Clover's death was reinvestigated, and it was determined she died of strychnine poisoning. Cream was arrested on June 3rd, 1892, and was charged with four counts of murder 10 days later, as well as one attempted murder and blackmail.

Thomas Neill Cream's trial began on October 17th, 1892,

and lasted four days. He was found guilty and sentenced to death. On November 15th, 1892, Cream was hanged at Newgate Prison. The man who executed Cream claimed that he admitted to being Jack the Ripper seconds before his death. But no one else heard this statement.

Even though it is a compelling theory, Thomas Neill Cream was in Joliet Prison in 1888 and wasn't responsible for Jack the Ripper's murders.

THE EMPTY BED

> "I'd like to talk to Jackie now. If I did, I'd ask her if she killed Nima. I'd hope she would tell me the truth."
>
> GEORGE CARTER, NIMA'S FATHER

Two eerily similar crimes happened in Lawton, Oklahoma, in the mid-1970s. A survivor and an eyewitness claimed that a babysitter was behind one of the murders. The police didn't have any physical evidence to connect her with the second murder, but they believed the teen was guilty because of how similar the crimes were.

Nima Louise Carter was born on March 23rd, 1976, to parents George and Rose Carter. The family lived in

Lawton, Oklahoma, 87 miles southwest of Oklahoma City. The Carters liked to go out and have fun now and then. So they hired a teen named Jaqueline Roubideaux, who was a neighbor, to babysit their little girl when they wanted to socialize with their friends.

HALLOWEEN NIGHT

On October 31st, 1977, George and Rose decided to stay in. The couple was getting ready to go to bed, and they placed little 19-month-old Nima in her crib. Nima started crying as soon as they closed the door. Rose and George decided to let her cry herself to sleep because they were trying to teach her to stop crying without their help, which she did a few minutes after they put her to bed.

Rose and George didn't hear her cry again throughout the night. The next morning, Rose entered Nima's room and found the crib empty. Thinking she was with George, she entered the bathroom where he was shaving. However, Nima wasn't there with him.

Nima didn't have a habit of climbing out of the crib, but they still searched the entire house, hoping to find her hiding in a closet or cabinet. But there was no sign of her. The Carters quickly realized their daughter had been taken sometime during the night. They contacted law enforcement and reported Nima missing.

The officers who arrived at the scene noted there were no

signs of forced entry. The Carters confirmed that all doors and windows were locked before they went to sleep. They told the police that the family dog had been poisoned one month prior to Nima's abduction, and recently, graffiti had been sprayed on their house.

The police couldn't find any evidence that someone else was in the house, so they zeroed in on the parents, believing they had something to do with Nima's disappearance. Rose and George were questioned by the investigators several times, and they both agreed to take a polygraph. The Carters passed and were removed from the suspect list.

CHILLING CONNECTION TO ANOTHER KIDNAPPING

The investigators were still without a solid lead, so they started questioning those closest to the Carters. One of them was Nima's babysitter, Jaqueline Roubideaux, also known as Jackie. The police were familiar with her because she was potentially involved in the kidnapping and murder of a girl she babysat in 1976. However, that case wasn't covered by the local media, and it's unclear why the police didn't charge her back then. It's possible the Carters didn't know about Jackie's possible involvement in the death of another child she babysat. They likely thought she was just a regular teenage girl from the neighborhood.

THE PREVIOUS MURDER

More than one year before Nima's disappearance, the city of Lawton experienced another shocking crime. On April 8th, 1976, twin girls, Mary Elizabeth and Augustine Lena Carpitcher, were at home watching TV. They were almost three years old and living with their grandmother and aunt. Jackie Roubideaux looked after them often, so the girls weren't surprised when she appeared at the front door. Jackie invited the twins out, and they said yes.

According to reports, the babysitter supposedly took the two girls to an abandoned house and left them inside an old-fashioned refrigerator with external locks or latches. Prior to locking the fridge, Jackie allegedly lied to the girls by saying that their aunt would be coming soon to take them to an ice cream parlor.

The family reported the girls missing the same evening, and the police began searching for them. On April 10th, kids were playing in the same empty house when they heard a voice from the fridge. One of them was brave enough to open the latch. Augustine leaped out, scared and gasping for breath. The kids could see another girl inside, but she wasn't moving.

Law enforcement confirmed that Mary Elizabeth Carpitcher suffocated in the locked fridge. Her twin sister survived by breathing in the air coming from a tiny hole near the door hinges. They had been locked inside the fridge for two days.

Police asked Augustine if she could tell them more about the person who locked them inside the fridge, and she said it was their babysitter, Jackie.

Thelma McCaig, a neighbor, confirmed she saw Jackie with the twins on the day of the disappearance but didn't think twice about it because she was often at the Carpitcher house. She confirmed they were going in the direction of the abandoned house where the twins were found.

The investigators talked to Jackie, who was still a minor at the time of the crime, but the teen wasn't very talkative. The police didn't have physical evidence that Jackie locked the girls inside the fridge and couldn't charge her with Mary's murder, so she continued working as a babysitter.

When the police learned that Jackie was Nima's babysitter, they wondered if she might have something to do with her disappearance as well. It was now the end of November, and they hadn't found Nima.

DISCOVERY OF THE BODY

Almost four weeks after Halloween, two boys were playing in an abandoned house four blocks away from the Carter's house. One of them opened the refrigerator, and the body of a small girl fell out. The boys were terrified and ran out of the house without telling anyone what they saw. A few days later, a man went into the abandoned house and found the body on the ground. He contacted the police right away.

Even though the body was heavily decomposed, Rose and George recognized Nima. The striking parallels between the murders of Mary Carpitcher and Nima Louise Carter led investigators to focus their efforts on Jackie Roubideaux.

The teenager was familiar with the floor plans of both victims' homes. In each case, the bodies were discovered in deserted properties and locked inside antiquated refrigerators.

The investigators interviewed Jackie again, and the teen remained emotionless. She said she was playing bingo on Halloween night. While this wasn't the strongest alibi, they didn't feel they had enough to make a murder charge stick. The only evidence police had was eyewitness testimony for Mary's murder. No one saw Jackie near the Carter residence on the night Nima disappeared. Law enforcement couldn't explain how she took Nima from a locked house. They believed she snuck into the girl's bedroom during the day and waited for the parents to go to sleep to kidnap the little girl.

George Carter thought the murder was committed by someone close to the family. An unknown person poisoned their dog first to have easier access to the house and took Nima from her crib without anyone noticing.

THE CONTROVERSIAL TRIAL AND CONVICTION OF JACKIE ROUBIDEAUX

Even though Jackie Roubideaux wasn't charged with murder in 1977, the police finally arrested her in 1982 at the age of 22. They decided the testimony given by Thelma McCaig was credible and would stand up in court. Thelma's husband, who was a retired fire chief, supported his wife and believed she saw Jackie take the twins on the day of their kidnapping.

The prosecution could only charge Jackie with the murder of Mary Carpitcher, but the judge allowed the district attorney to talk about Nima's case because of the similarities. The trial began in the spring of 1982, and 69 witnesses appeared on the stand, including the surviving Carpitcher twin who was now nine years old. Augustine repeated the story she told to the police in 1976, and she was still sure the person who kidnapped them from the house was Jackie.

When Augustine was rescued, she had what appeared to be human bite marks on her arm. Police took photographs of the bite marks in 1976. The prosecution claimed the bite marks matched the dental impressions taken of Jackie's mouth.

The defense said the bite marks could have come from Augustine's twin Mary. To counter this, Mary's body was exhumed, and impressions were made from the child's mouth, which clearly showed the bite marks on Mary's arm did not come from her sister.

The prosecution's expert dental witness could only say that the bite marks in the photos were consistent with Jackie Robideaux's mouth.

Jackie kept quiet during the testimonies and didn't speak with anyone, including her lawyers. The jury began their deliberation on May 20th, 1983. It took them six and a half hours to find Jackie Roubideaux guilty of first-degree murder. She was sentenced to life in prison.

Jackie Roubideaux died in prison on August 26th, 2005, from liver cirrhosis. She filed appeals several times, asking for a shorter sentence, but was denied. The murder of Nima Louise Carter is still officially unsolved, even though authorities believe that Jackie was responsible for this crime.

Nima's grandmother, Audrey Carter, had a completely different opinion. When talking to the media, Audrey said Jackie was weird and could be a killer.

Nima's mother, Rose Carter, passed away in 2000.

Nima's father, George, thinks Jackie didn't kidnap and kill his little girl. He said that the teenager he knew wasn't capable of murder. George, now a minister, told the media he had forgiven the person who killed Nima but could never forgive the act itself.

"My wife and I lived for years with the what-ifs. Nima cried that night when we put her down to sleep. We never got up to check on her. We figured we didn't want to spoil her; that she would eventually go to sleep. I now believe that person was already in her room, probably hiding in the closet. What if we had opened the closet? What if we had gotten up to check on her that night? What if we had brought her in to sleep with us?

"What if? What if?"

LOCKED UP AND TORTURED

"Never in Hong Kong in recent years has a court heard of such cruelty, depravity, callousness, brutality, violence and viciousness."

PETER NGUYEN, CROWN PROSECUTOR OF HONG KONG

Hong Kong faced considerable challenges with organized crime in the 1990s. In March 1999, a gruesome murder was discovered after a teenager informed the police she was haunted by a ghost.

This chilling case involves the tragic life of Fan Man-yee, who was born in 1975 and abandoned by her parents. She grew up in an orphanage, and after leaving the institution, she had to navigate homelessness, sex work, and drug addiction.

Fan eventually found employment at the Empress Karaoke Nightclub, where she worked as a dancer. It was here that she met her future husband, with whom she shared an interest in drugs. They married in 1996 and had a son in 1998, but their marriage was tumultuous, with neighbors frequently hearing arguments and screaming throughout the night.

Seeking to turn her life around, Fan found work as a hostess at the Romance Villa in Kowloon. Her new job did not involve sex work, but the income was insufficient to support her family. Fan stopped using drugs during her pregnancy but started spending more time with one of her regular customers, Chan Man-lok, a 34-year-old drug dealer and Triad gang member. He frequently invited Fan to join him in using drugs, particularly crystal meth, and she found it difficult to resist. Fan began hanging out with Chan after work and soon met individuals from his inner circle.

One fateful evening, Fan made the terrible decision to steal Chan's wallet, which contained around $400. When Chan discovered the theft, he was enraged. Although Fan promised to repay him and did so, Chan demanded more money and added a fee. As the fee continued to increase, Fan struggled to make enough money in time.

In March 1999, Chan instructed two of his associates, Leung Wai-lun and Leung Shing-cho, to kidnap Fan Man-yee. They took her from her apartment to 31 Granville Road in Tsim Sha Tsui, where they were joined by 14-year-old Ah Fong, one of Chan's girlfriends. The apartment was spacious and decorated with Hello Kitty items, including plushies, figurines, and bedding.

Chan and his associates planned to keep Fan captive in the apartment, force her to work around the clock as a sex worker, and use her earnings to pay off Chan's ever-increasing fee. However, as the days passed, Chan became increasingly angry with Fan and incited the group to physically assault her.

Fan suffered extensive bruising and injuries, and she was in constant pain. Despite her condition, the group continued to bring clients to the apartment. Ah Fong, the teenager staying in the apartment, took pleasure in torturing Fan, participating in the abuse and laughing throughout the ordeal.

The torture inflicted upon Fan grew more severe over time. She faced daily attacks, including being tied up and used as a punching bag, sexually assaulted, and struck with metal bars. They burned her feet with candle wax and rubbed spices, dirt, and salt into her wounds to intensify the pain. If she pleaded for them to stop, her tormentors would punish her more severely.

As Fan's condition worsened, the group withheld food, leaving her weak and immobile from the combination of her injuries and malnourishment. Clients stopped coming to the apartment due to Fan's deteriorating state, but none of them reported anything to the police. They likely feared the consequences of reporting a Triad member.

While Fan languished in pain on the apartment floor, the group continued to take drugs, play video games, and watch TV, seemingly indifferent to her suffering.

One night, the group went out clubbing and left Fan tied up and mostly unconscious in the bathroom. It is unclear exactly when she died, but it is believed to have occurred around April 15th, 1999, after almost a month of torture.

The group returned to the apartment three days later and found Fan dead in the bathroom. They assumed she had overdosed on drugs, unable to comprehend that their torture and starvation could have killed her. They then began discussing how to dispose of Fan's body.

DISMEMBERMENT

The three men placed Fan in a bathtub and used a saw to dismember her. Meanwhile, Ah Fong prepared pots of boiling water in the kitchen. They decided to cook individual parts of Fan's body on the stove and dispose of the bones as garbage. They fed Fan's remains to stray dogs.

Disturbingly, they prepared their dinner while boiling Fan's head and used the same utensils. Unsure of what to do with the skull, the group sewed it inside a Hello Kitty mermaid plush toy. They disposed of most of the evidence but kept one tooth and a few internal organs, possibly as souvenirs.

THE CONFESSION

One month later, Ah Fong walked into a Hong Kong police station. She appeared distraught and frightened. The teen began describing a female ghost that visited her at night, seeking revenge. Initially, the officers thought it was a joke, but when Ah Fong claimed to know the ghost, they pressed her for more details.

Ah Fong eventually divulged the horrific events that transpired at 31 Granville Road. Police asked her to lead them to the crime scene, which she did willingly. Upon arrival, the apartment's odor was overwhelming due to piles of garbage in the kitchen. Despite the mess, they soon discovered a human tooth and internal organs hidden in the refrigerator. Ah Fong pointed to the Hello Kitty plush toy and revealed that Fan's skull was inside.

When they dismantled the toy, the police confirmed Ah Fong's account. Neighbors identified the victim as 23-year-old Fan Man-yee. Due to the absence of her entire body, it was impossible to determine the exact cause of death. Fan's husband, who believed she was on a drug binge and avoiding their son, had not reported her disappearance to the police.

Ah Fong agreed to testify against the three men involved in Fan Man-yee's torture and death. In return, she received immunity, and her identity was protected due to her status as a minor. Ah Fong is not her real name. Chan Man-lok, Leung Shing-cho, and Leung Wai-lun were arrested and taken into custody.

Their trial began in October 2000 and lasted six weeks. Each man claimed innocence, blaming the others for the crimes. The lack of physical evidence posed a challenge for the prosecution, who could not conclusively prove that the men had murdered Fan. On December 6th, 2000, all three were found guilty of manslaughter, false imprisonment, and preventing the lawful burial of a body. They were sentenced to life in prison with the possibility of parole after 20 years.

Leung Shing-cho filed an appeal and was granted a retrial. This time, he pleaded guilty and was sentenced to 18 years in prison. Leung was released in 2011 but was arrested again in August 2022. He was accused of inappropriate contact with a 10-year-old girl, the daughter of Leung's friend. Leung massaged and touched the girl. He was sentenced to 12 months behind bars. Chan Man-lo and Leung Wai-lun are still in prison.

The so-called Hello Kitty Murder inspired two movies, *Human Pork Chop* and *There is a Secret in my Soup,* both released in 2001.

Even though these claims can't be confirmed, the residents of the building on 31 Granville Road did experience strange things in their apartments and could hear a woman crying in the middle of the night. But some of them knew a gruesome murder happened in the building.

As for Ah Fong, the teenager who reported the crime to the police, she was placed into protective custody, and her identity remains a secret. It is unknown if she has managed to rebuild her life.

The apartment at 31 Granville Road was demolished, and a hotel now stands on the site.

THE HUSTLER

"I never wanted this to be my life. You don't wake up one day and decide to become a serial killer."

GARY RAY BOWLES, SERIAL KILLER

Gary Ray Bowles was born on January 25th, 1962, in Clifton Forge, Virginia. He was the youngest of four children and grew up in a dysfunctional household. Bowles' father was physically abusive, and his mother struggled with mental health issues. Bowles' parents divorced when he was young, and he was raised primarily by his grandparents.

As a child, Bowles was known to be manipulative and would often lie to get what he wanted. He had a history of stealing and was expelled from school in the seventh grade for stealing money from a teacher's purse. Bowles ran away from home when he was a teenager and began traveling around the country, taking odd jobs and living on the streets.

Bowles' criminal history began in his early twenties when he was arrested for the first time for stealing a car. Over the next several years, he was arrested multiple times for crimes such as assault, theft, and drug possession. He was in and out of jail for much of his adult life, serving time in Virginia, Georgia, and Florida.

In 1982, Bowles was arrested for the beating and sexual assault of his girlfriend. He received a six-year sentence in prison. Eventually, in 1991, he was released and quickly resumed his life of crime. He robbed an elderly woman and was sentenced to four more years in prison but was released after two.

Bowles' criminal behavior was often linked to his struggles with his sexuality. He was attracted to men but struggled with his identity, particularly in the conservative communities where he grew up.

YEARS IN FLORIDA

Bowles moved to Daytona Beach, Florida, where he worked as a male prostitute. He became involved in a long-term relationship with a wealthy older man named John Hardy Roberts, a 59-year-old insurance salesman. He provided Bowles with financial support, and Bowles provided sex and eventually moved in with Roberts.

Bowles had a girlfriend at the time who was pregnant with his child, and he still wanted to see her. The older man gave him an ultimatum, and the relationship ended badly. Bowles chose his girlfriend and lost his source of income.

Bowles ended the relationship by murdering his benefactor. He smashed his head in with a lamp and rolled up a hand towel and shoved it down Roberts' throat.

Bowles left something very important at the crime scene — his probation paperwork. During the murder, the paperwork had found its way underneath Robert's body. The police had a suspect but he was long gone with Roberts' credit cards and car. The police tracked Bowles to Nashville through credit card use but lost him after that.

Shortly after that, his girlfriend found out about his prostitution although she didn't know about the murder. She got an abortion without Bowles' knowledge. When he found out, he was livid and it was around this time that Bowles started his killing spree.

He later claimed that he hated gay men because they kept him from having a good life. However, it is clear that his actions were also influenced by his long history of violence and criminal behavior, as well as his struggles with his sexuality and identity.

David Jarman was a 39-year-old loan officer in Washington, DC. Bowles met Jarman at a gay bar and went back to his house. Just like the murder of Roberts, Bowles beat Jarman severely before strangling him and stuffing a rag down his throat. Jarman didn't report for work, and a maintenance man discovered his body. Again, Bowles had stolen Jarman's credit cards and car.

Milton Bradley was a 72-year-old man from Savannah, Georgia who had served in the US Army during the Korean War. Bradley was slightly affected by a shrapnel head wound he received in the war. Bowles volunteered to drive Bradley home after they'd met in a pool bar. Instead of taking him home Bowles took him to a golf-course and behind a shed he beat Bradley with an old toilet. He then stuffed his mouth with leaves he found on the ground.

Alverson Carter Jr. was a 47-year-old man from Montgomery, Alabama, living in Atlanta. Bowles met Carter at a gay bar and lured him to a remote area, where he stabbed him to death and stole his car.

Albert Morris, a 47-year-old man from Jacksonville, Florida was the next victim. Bowles met Morris at a bar one night, where the two men bonded over drinks and shared stories. Morris invited Bowles to live with him in his trailer in Hillard, Florida, not realizing the danger that lurked behind Bowles' friendly facade.

At that time, Bowles was going by the alias "Joey Pearson" because he knew the FBI was after him. In that two-week period before Morris was murdered, he asked his friend Jackie Strickland to give "Joey Pearson" a ride somewhere.

During the ride, Strickland made small talk with Pearson, who was looking at the landscape as they drove. He said, "You're going to stay with Al and do work around there?"

Pearson answered, "Well, I'm gonna do a little bit of construction, and then I think I'll move on.

Pearson yelled at Strickland to stop the car and pull over. Strickland watched as he jumped out of the car and ran towards the woods, pointing like he'd seen something.

Pearson turned around and tried to get Strickland out of the vehicle by telling him he should come and look at what he found.

Strickland didn't trust Pearson and stayed in his car. Eventually, Pearson came back to the car, got in, and said he'd seen a tent that he wanted to show Strickland.

Strickland claimed to the media after Bowles was arrested that he was close to becoming one of Bowles' victims.

> "This guy was looking to probably kill me and run off with my car and the money that I had."

Less than two weeks later, Bowles had murdered Strickland's friend Albert Morris. Morris was shot, beaten, and strangled by Bowles. Again, Bowles placed something in his victim's mouth. This time it was a sex toy.

Walter Hinton, a florist, was the final victim of Bowles' killing spree. His brother-in-law found him in his bathroom covered in blankets several days after losing contact with him. He'd had a concrete stepping stone dropped on his face, which had caused multiple jaw fractures and had left Hinton almost unrecognizable. But that's not what killed him. After the facial injury, Hinton had been strangled, and a roll of toilet paper had been wedged partway down his throat.

When police started the investigation, friends said Hinton had recently had a house guest named *Timothy Whitfield.*

On November 22nd, 1994, in Jacksonville, Florida, they finally apprehended *Whitfield* as he hid in a makeshift campsite under a bridge. They brought him in for questioning as a suspect in the murder of his roommate Walter Hinton.

Not realizing who he really was, Bowles told the police he was tired and wanted to move the process along. He told them his real name and, after a cigarette, confessed to the murders of six men.

The police were stunned. The FBI and various local police had been chasing Bowles up and down the I-95 corridor for eight months, and once they had him, they didn't even realize who he was.

Bowles said, "It's time. I want the killing to stop. I'm either getting six life sentences or the electric chair."

He was charged with the murder of Walter Hinton and found guilty of Hinton's murder in 1996. He was sentenced to death.

Despite his brutal crimes and confession, Bowles tried to appeal his conviction. He argued that he had a traumatic childhood and that his crimes were the result of his troubled upbringing. However, his appeals were unsuccessful, and he was executed by lethal injection on August 22nd, 2019, at the Florida State Prison.

On the day of his execution, he was brought into the death chamber, where he lay on a gurney with IVs inserted into his arms to deliver the lethal cocktail of drugs. His last words were an apology to the family of Walter Hinton, expressing remorse for the pain he had caused.

A VAMPIRE CLAN

"I've never seen anything worse. It was a very gruesome situation. That was probably the worst case I've had."

AL GUSSLER, LAKE COUNTY SHERIFF'S OFFICE

Listening to alternative music and pretending to be a vampire doesn't make you a criminal. However, a small town in Kentucky was shocked to learn that four local Kentucky teens who called themselves the Vampire Clan committed a gruesome double murder in Florida.

Roderick Justin Ferrell, also known as Rod, was born on March 28th, 1980, in Murray, Kentucky. His parents, Sondra and Rick Ferrell, were teens when Rod was born.

The couple got married when Sondra learned she was pregnant, but the marriage didn't last long. Rick left, and Sondra moved back in with her parents, who helped her with the baby.

Rod would later say he learned about the occult at a very young age, thanks to his grandfather, who was in a cult. He allegedly witnessed human sacrifices at the age of five and was sexually assaulted by the cult members.

As a boy, Rod loved playing Dungeons and Dragons. Role-playing games were his favorite. Then his mother introduced him to Vampire: The Masquerade. Rod created a character named Vesago with an entire backstory. He was a 500-year-old vampire who could see into the future. He soon started to believe that he was, in fact, Vesago.

In 1995, Rod met a teen named Jaden Stephen Murphy. Both attended Calloway County High School and dressed similarly. Jaden hung out with his group of friends, but they quickly accepted Rod as one of them. The teens were obsessed with vampires, industrial music, and gothic fashion. Rod finally felt like he belonged somewhere.

Jaden organized a crossing-over ceremony for Rod that officially made him a part of the group. The two teens drank each other's blood. As Jaden spent more time with Rod, he became concerned about his friend. He noticed that Rod was cruel to animals. Jaden witnessed Rod kill a kitten by throwing it against a tree because it scratched him.

MEETING HEATHER WENDORF

Rod's mother, Sondra, met a man who lived in Eustis, Florida and moved there for a couple of months. While there, Rod attended Eustis High School and met a girl named Heather Wendorf. She lived with her parents, Richard and Naomi, and an older sister, Jennifer. Richard worked as a warehouse manager, and Naomi was a stay-at-home mom.

Heather was a moody, withdrawn teenager. She would fight with her parents regularly. She didn't want to spend time with her friends and was considered a loner. But when she met Rod, the two started hanging out. They became friends and then dated briefly, but Rod moved back to Murray, Kentucky.

Heather and Rod continued to talk over the phone. The families noticed large phone bills, so the pair started communicating via letters. Rod found out that Heather didn't like her parents because, according to her, they were abusive.

Heather told Rod her father was sexually abusing her, and her mother knew about it and did nothing. Rod became fixated on driving to Eustis and rescuing Heather.

Meanwhile, Jaden and Rod weren't on good terms. Their friendship ended after someone broke into an animal shelter in October 1996 and mutilated all the puppies. Rod was questioned by police about the incident but not charged. Rod was exiled from the group and started to look for new friends to make his own vampire clan.

Sixteen-year-old Scott Anderson was another outcast who wanted to feel he belonged somewhere. His family lived in a small house, and he worked at McDonald's. He enjoyed hanging out with Dana Cooper, Rod Ferrell, and his girlfriend, Charity Keesee.

In November 1996, the group started planning their road trip to New Orleans, the vampire capital of the world, according to Rod. They would stop by Eustis, Florida, and pick up Heather. Heather's best friend, Jeanine LeClaire, was familiar with the plan.

The group left Kentucky on November 22nd, 1996, in Scott Anderson's Buick. They had car problems along the way but managed to reach Eustis on November 25th. They contacted Heather earlier that day from a payphone, and she gave them her address. They picked her up in front of her house and went to a graveyard.

According to Rod, they spent several hours there, and Heather took a blood oath. Heather later said this was the first time she learned about Rod's intentions to kill her parents. She allegedly told him not to harm Richard and Naomi. She said they should steal her family's Ford Explorer and take it to New Orleans. The keys were in the bedroom, and Rod and Scott intended to break into the house and steal them.

When the group arrived back at Heather's house, they

agreed that the three girls would stay in the car. Rod and Scott entered Heather's house through the garage and looked for weapons. The two teens had agreed that Rod would go after Heather's father, Richard while Scott would kill Naomi. Rod picked out a crowbar he found in the corner
of the garage.

When they entered the house, Richard was watching TV in the living room. The volume was up, and he didn't hear the teens come in. Rod hid behind the couch and then began hitting Richard in the head. Once the man was unconscious, Rod stabbed him in the ribs. Scott watched everything unfold from the corridor. He was shocked and knew he couldn't do the same to Naomi.

Naomi had just gotten out of the shower and was making coffee in the kitchen. Rod startled her, and she poured hot coffee on him. The two started fighting, and Naomi scratched Rod's face. They wrestled on the floor as Rod hit Naomi with the crowbar. He bashed her head in as she lay motionless on the kitchen tiles. Scott and Rod found the car keys in the bedroom and searched the house for any valuables they could find. They grabbed a necklace, a hunting knife, and Richard's credit card. Rod's clothes were covered in blood, and when the girls saw him, they realized something awful had happened. Even though Dana and Charity knew about his intentions, they just thought he was role-playing.

The group took both the Buick and Ford Explorer but

stopped and switched the license plates after several miles, dumping the old car.

Jennifer Wendorf arrived home at 10 pm and saw her father in front of the TV. She thought he was sleeping. Jennifer then went to the kitchen and discovered her mother lying in a pool of blood. When she ran to get her father, Jennifer realized he was dead too.

The police arrived at the Wendorf house soon after and spoke to Jennifer, who told the officers her younger sister Heather wasn't home and the family car was missing. Jennifer believed that Heather and her friends had something to do with the murders.

The officers soon located Heather's best friend, Jeanine LeClaire, who told them about a boy from Kentucky named Rod Ferrell. An abandoned Buick with Richard's license plates was found close to the house, and the VIN revealed it was registered to Scott Anderson from Murray, Kentucky.

Richard's autopsy revealed he had 22 wounds on his body and a fractured skull. He had the letter V carved into his chest. Naomi had 23 wounds, most of them on her head. The forensic team found skin cells under her nails and it was later confirmed that the DNA belonged to Rod Ferrell.

The group of teens was on the road at that time, traveling to New Orleans, Louisiana. Rod then decided they should head to Baton Rouge first. They were broke and didn't know what to do. Charity said she would contact her grandmother, who lived in South Dakota, and ask her for money. The grandmother agreed to meet them at Howard Johnson's hotel.

Charity had no idea her grandmother had contacted law enforcement and told them about the meetup. The police set a trap for the teens, who arrived at the hotel's parking lot. They were taken into custody right away and taken to Baton Rouge jail. The group was extradited to Florida and questioned at the Lake County Jail.

During the questioning, Rod confessed to the murders. It seemed like he was proud of what he'd done and showed no remorse. He told police, "I went to her dad and smacked the f— out of him until he finally quit breathing, so, yes, I'm admitting to murder. Actually, it took him about 20 f—ing minutes to stop. I swear, I thought he was immortal or something."

He did say that his friends had nothing to do with the murders, hoping they would be released. Dana and Charity confessed they knew about the plan but thought Rod wouldn't go through with it.

Scott told them the plan was for him to murder Naomi, but he couldn't do it after witnessing Rod's attack on Richard. He also said that he believed Heather was the one who orchestrated the murder of her parents. Heather claimed she had nothing to do with the crime and was surprised to see Rod covered in blood as he exited her family home.

Rod was charged with two counts of first-degree murder,

armed robbery, and burglary. On February 12th, 1998, he pleaded guilty to all charges, hoping he would avoid the death penalty. His defense claimed Rod suffered from a schizotypal personality disorder and Asperger syndrome. Regardless, the judge sentenced him to death.

Scott Anderson was charged with two counts of first-degree murder, armed robbery, and burglary. He also pleaded guilty but managed to avoid the death penalty because he was presented as Rod's accomplice. He was sentenced to life in prison.

Charity Keesee was charged with two counts of third-degree murder, robbery, and burglary. She was sentenced to 10 and a half years in state prison.

Dana Cooper faced identical charges and was sentenced to seven and a half years behind bars.

A grand jury cleared Heather Wendorf of any charges related to the death of her parents. They ended their statement with this paragraph:

> While she certainly acted inappropriately in planning to leave home and arguably so in remaining with the others after learning what had been done, we acknowledge that these acts are not crimes. We also wish to unequivocally state that these actions were wrong. Heather Wendorf, her sister, and the families of both Richard Wendorf and Naomi Ruth Queen will live the rest of their lives with the conse-

> quences of Heather's choices of associates and activities. Nothing that anyone can say or do will change the loss they have suffered. We wish them God's mercy and grace in the recovery that must follow.

Rod Ferrell was the youngest inmate on death row for two years. In November 2000, his sentence was reduced to life in prison by Florida's Supreme Court because he committed the crimes as a minor.

On December 3rd, 2018, Scott Anderson attended a hearing and was resentenced to 40 years in prison. He will be released in 2030.

DON'T DO DRUGS

"He wanted to feel some sort of power. There's some messed up part of his head that said if I can kill these people and get away with it, it must be right. But really he was just a skinny, frail boy who lived out East of St. John's, Arizona."

NICK FLORES, RICKY'S BROTHER

In the late 2000s, Apache County was a quiet and remote region in Arizona, with a population of just over 71,000 people. But the peace of this tight-knit community was shattered when three gruesome murders occurred.

The murders seemed to be connected, but the police had no leads and the cases remained unsolved for months.

Then, on a hot August afternoon, a young man walked into the police station in Springerville and confessed to the murders. It was a shocking revelation — the killer was just 21 years old and had become the youngest serial killer in the state of Arizona.

The young man was William Inmon, known to his friends as Willy. Born in Phoenix in 1988, Inmon's family had moved to Springerville when he was still a child. Growing up, he had a tough life — his parents were drug addicts who were frequently absent, leaving him to fend for himself. Inmon had always been fascinated by guns and the military, often talking about them to anyone who would listen.

Inmon's solitary existence meant he had few friends, but he loved spending time with his dog and walking the surrounding countryside. In order to make ends meet, Inmon worked in a local general store and took on odd jobs throughout Apache County. It was during one of these jobs that he met his first victim.

WILLIAM MCCARRAGHER

William "Stoney" McCarragher was a man with a dark past. Born in 1935 in Waterbury, Connecticut, he had been a member of the Boy Scouts of America under multiple names and moved up and down the East Coast. However, McCarragher's involvement with the Boy Scouts was not without controversy. He had been accused of illegal conduct involving young boys several times and was found

to be in possession of obscene photographs at the time of his arrest.
Despite serving time in prison and being released on parole, McCarragher remained fixated on the Boy Scouts. He continued to be active in the organization under an alias, showing a persistent and disturbing pattern of behavior. In the 1960s, he arrived in Litchfield, Connecticut, where he met Mary Laurancy Wray and the two got married. However, McCarragher's problems persisted, and he was ordered by the court to attend therapy.

Eventually, McCarragher decided to leave his past behind and move to the arid landscape of Arizona. He purchased a large plot of land in St. John's, a small town just north of Springerville. Living alone, McCarragher would frequently hire young men to help around the ranch, including William Inmon.

In April of 2007, Inmon was working at the ranch when McCarragher made his move and began inappropriately touching the teen. Inmon felt violated and discussed the incident with another young man who worked on the ranch, who confirmed that he had experienced the same thing.
Inmon was angered even more by this revelation and decided to take matters into his own hands.

That same night, he returned to McCarragher's ranch, where the man was already asleep in his bed. Inmon cut several holes in the window screens and fired his rifle 12 times. McCarragher was hit seven times and died.

After committing the murder, Inmon entered the house and threw things around to make it look like a robbery. McCarragher was known to have a lot of cash in his home, and Inmon hoped investigators would think that was the motive.

Investigators talked to all the men who had worked at the ranch at that time, including Inmon. He was even taken to the station for an interview, where he denied shooting McCarragher. Investigators couldn't find a solid lead, and the case went cold.

THE SECOND MURDER

Daniel Achten was a 60-year-old Vietnam war veteran who lived close to Inmon. In the months leading up to Achten's murder, the tension between Inmon and Achten was high. The two often argued about Inmon's dog and the trash on the young man's property. After Inmon's dog went missing in March 2009, Inmon accused Achten of killing it. Inmon had even gone so far as to file a report with the local authorities regarding the missing dog. Achten denied having anything to do with the dog's disappearance, which enraged Inmon.

The loss of his pet had fueled Inmon's resentment towards Achten, and Inmon knew he couldn't let Achten go unpunished. Inmon, armed himself and went to speak with Achten. The two engaged in a heated argument, and Inmon lost control and pulled the trigger. The loud crack of the gunshot stopped the argument. Achten fell to the ground, dead.

Realizing the gravity of his actions, Inmon knew he had to act fast to avoid being caught by police. Inmon, with the help of his friend Joseph Douglas Roberts started a bonfire, dragged Achten's body over to it and set it ablaze. They stood and watched as the flames consumed most of the flesh and bones. Once the fire had burned out, Inmon and Roberts gathered the remaining ashes and bones, and buried them in a shallow grave near Achten's home.

Achten was reported as missing by a relative, but police found no clues that could lead them to Achten or a suspect. It seemed as though Achten had simply vanished into thin air.

THE MURDER OF RICKY FLORES

Ricky Flores was a 16-year-old who lived with his family in St. John's. Flores and Inmon knew each other and often hung out. The teen was a high school dropout who planned to get a job and provide for his newborn child. Unfortunately, Flores was also a drug user. On August 13th, 2009, Inmon picked up Flores in front of his house, and the two went for a drive.

Flores didn't know that Inmon was in contact with Jeffrey Johnson, the 43-year-old father of Flores' girlfriend. The two knew each other from Jeffrey Johnson's tire shop. The Johnson family didn't approve of Flores, especially after their teenage daughter, Jessica, gave birth to the couple's child in 2008. The father wanted Flores dead and was willing to pay Inmon to murder him.

Once the young men were in the car, Inmon told Ricky he was there to talk about his drug use. Inmon told Ricky he had to stop using drugs.

Meanwhile, he was driving towards a rural part of St. John's. Inmon let Ricky get out of the vehicle but then shot him once with a shotgun. Flores' body was taken to Jeffrey Johnson's house as proof he was dead. Inmon then burned Flores and buried his remains in a shallow grave in a forest in Greenlee County.

Ricky Flores' mother contacted the police on August 14th, 2009, and told them her son was missing. He left all his things at home, including the phone charger, so she believed something had happened to him. She said that Flores sent her a message saying he was with Inmon. That was the last time she heard from him.

THE CONFESSION AND TRIAL

On August 29th, 2009, William Inmon sprinted into Springerville Police Station, demanding to speak with Chief Steve West. He said the police from St. John's were at the house he shared with his 44-year-old girlfriend, Storm Williams. They had a search warrant and were going through his things. Inmon asked Chief West to stop the search because those police officers weren't from

Springerville.

Despite Chief West's inability to halt the search, he was intrigued by Inmon's demeanor and asked him to sit down for a conversation. Over the next several hours, Inmon opened up about his difficult upbringing and revealed that the police were searching his home in connection with the disappearance of Ricky Flores.

Investigator Brian Hounshell joined Chief West and Inmon in the interrogation room. After some initial hesitation, Inmon ultimately confessed to the murder of Ricky Flores, retracting his previous story about dropping Flores off in St. John's. Inmon then claimed that he was hired by Jeffrey and Melissa Johnson to commit the murder.

Inmon's confession led to the arrests of Jeffrey and Melissa Johnson, along with Inmon's girlfriend, Storm Williams. Inmon, facing the possibility of a death sentence, made a deal with the prosecution to confess to two more murders in addition to the murder of Ricky Flores. His revelations finally gave the police closure on the mysterious disappearances of William "Stoney" McCarragher and Daniel Achten. Inmon claimed to have shot Achten, citing him as a drug dealer and a horrible person.

Despite being charged with first-degree murder, Storm Williams was deemed incompetent to stand trial, and her case was dismissed.

The police focused their attention on Jeffrey Johnson, who was charged with soliciting the murder of Ricky Flores, while his wife Melissa was charged with not reporting the murder to the authorities.

The Johnsons accepted plea deals, with Jeffrey Johnson receiving a sentence of seven years, five years probation, and a $150,000 fine. Meanwhile, Jessica Johnson, and her newborn daughter, moved in with Flores' mother.

During his confession, Inmon implicated his friend Joseph Douglas Roberts in the murder of Daniel Achten because Robert helped him conceal the body. Roberts was arrested and charged with first-degree murder and concealment of the body.

Inmon's initial plea deal would have landed him behind bars for 25 years, but he agreed to testify against Roberts, which resulted in the prosecution lowering his sentence to 24 years. However, to the surprise of many, all charges against Inmon's friend were ultimately dropped by an Apache County judge.

The investigators discovered that Inmon saw himself as a vigilante killer, targeting drug users and people he thought were unimportant or should be murdered. It appeared that his hatred toward an addict like Ricky Flores could have been rooted in his own troubled upbringing and how his parents treated him as a child.

During his confession, Inmon expressed pride in killing William "Stoney" McCarragher, but he expressed regret over the murder of Ricky Flores. The investigators also uncovered that Inmon had planned to kill two more people in 2009, but their identities were never revealed.

William Inmon is now serving his 24-year sentence at the Arizona State Prison Complex Safford and is scheduled for release in 2030.

GREYHOUND HORROR

"I got sick after I saw the head thing. Some people were puking, some people were crying, some people were shocked. He just looked at us and dropped the head on the ground, totally calm."

GARNET CANON, PASSENGER ON THE GREYHOUND BUS

On that summer afternoon in July 2008, the passengers of Greyhound bus 1170 had no idea that their uneventful journey would soon turn into a horrific nightmare.

Timothy Richard McLean Jr., or Tim as he was known to his friends, was one of the passengers. Tim was a young man with a bright future ahead of him. Born on October 3rd, 1985, in Winnipeg, Manitoba, he grew up in a small town called Elie, surrounded by the beauty of the wilderness. Tim was loved by everyone who knew him, and his friendly, outgoing nature made him a popular figure in his community.

As a child, Tim developed a deep love for the outdoors, and he spent much of his time exploring the natural wonders around him. He was active and enjoyed playing sports, particularly soccer. Tim was also an avid motorcyclist, and he loved nothing more than hitting the open road on his bike.

In the summer of 2008, Tim took a job working at a carnival. One of his friends, who worked at the Red River Exhibition in Winnipeg, had asked him to join her. Tim was always up for an adventure, and the chance to see new places was too good to pass up. The carnival traveled along the west coast, and Tim had a chance to visit British Columbia. He fell in love with the province and decided he would move there one day.

Working at a carnival was a unique experience for Tim, and he quickly made friends with his co-workers. By the summer of 2008, he was preparing to move to British Columbia. But first, he needed to stop by his home in Winnipeg to pack his things and spend time with his family. Tim's girlfriend was also pregnant with their child, so he wanted to see her before he left.

In July 2008, Tim was in Edmonton, Alberta, with the carnival. His friends wanted to buy him a plane ticket to Winnipeg, but Tim declined. He was used to traveling long distances by bus and planned to listen to music and nap until he reached his destination.

THE BUS RIDE

Tim boarded Greyhound bus 1170, taking his seat at the rear of the vehicle with his headphones in. The journey was uneventful at first, with the bus making several stops along the Yellowhead Highway to pick up more passengers.

In the small town of Erickson, Manitoba, a man by the name of Vincent Weiguang Li boarded a Greyhound bus at 6:55 pm. He was an imposing figure, tall with a shaven head and dark sunglasses. Vince didn't talk to anyone, which was not uncommon when traveling by bus. However, what the passengers didn't know was that Vince was struggling with a severe mental illness – schizophrenia.

Vince was born on April 30th, 1968, in Dandong, China. He graduated from the Wuhan Institute of Technology with a BA in computer science in 1992. He met his future wife, Anna, and began working as a software engineer in Beijing. However, the couple wanted to move to North America, and they settled in Winnipeg in 2001. Vince had difficulty finding work in his field due to the language barrier and ended up working menial jobs.

In 2004, Vince began experiencing hallucinations and delusions, believing that he was Jesus and that the voices he heard were coming from the sun. These symptoms led to a diagnosis of schizophrenia, but Vince refused to take medication and acknowledge his illness.

His wife filed for divorce, and Vince moved to Edmonton in 2006, where he found work at Walmart and attended church regularly.

In 2008, Vince heard voices again, and he was fired from his job at Walmart. One month later, the voice told him to leave Edmonton, and he boarded a Greyhound bus to Winnipeg.

On July 29th, 2008, he got off the bus in Erickson, Manitoba, and spent the day walking around town. That evening, he boarded bus 1170 with 35 other passengers.

Vince concealed a hunting knife under his jacket and initially sat close to the driver. He later moved to a seat next to a passenger named Tim and dozed off with his headphones on. At around 8:30 pm, the other passengers were awakened by a scream, and they turned to see Vince stabbing Tim in the neck with the knife. The passengers watched in horror as Vince attacked Tim, who fell to the floor.

The bus driver stopped the bus on the side of the Trans-Canada Highway, and the passengers fled the bus. Vince continued his attack, decapitating Tim and mutilating his body. The driver used the emergency immobilizer system to prevent Vince from leaving the bus, and he was later arrested by the police.

The Royal Canadian Mounted Police arrived at the scene after 8:45 pm as the bus driver, several passengers, and a truck driver tried to contain Vince, who was in the midst of a terrifying psychotic episode. Despite their best efforts, law enforcement decided not to enter the bus, resulting in a standoff with Vince, who was incoherent, talking to himself and unable to communicate.

The officers watched in horror as Vince consumed parts of Tim's body and roamed the bus, proclaiming that he had to stay inside forever. The tense situation continued until 1:30 am the following day when Vince attempted to escape by breaking a window. At this point, the officers were forced to use a taser twice to subdue him and take him into custody.

During the search, police officers discovered Tim's tongue, nose, and ear in Vince's pockets. Shockingly, Tim's eyes and several parts of his heart were missing, and it was suspected that Vince had consumed them while locked in the bus.
The other passengers were eventually taken to the police station to provide statements. Greyhound employees arranged for new clothes to replace the ones left on the bus, and they arrived in Winnipeg at 3:30 pm, still shaken from the traumatic events they had witnessed.

When police interrogated Vince, he denied cannibalizing Tim, but the evidence against him was overwhelming. He was charged with second-degree murder and appeared in court on August 5th, 2008. The judge ordered a psychiatric evaluation, and the trial began on March 3rd, 2009.

Vince pleaded not guilty due to a mental disorder, and the psychiatrist who evaluated him testified in court that he murdered Tim because he believed God was speaking to him. According to Vince, God had ordered him to kill Tim, whom he believed to be a demon. Vince also claimed that he needed to mutilate Tim's body to prevent him from being resurrected.

Despite pleading not guilty, the judge accepted the psychiatric evaluation, and Vince was sent to the Selkirk Mental Health Centre. The McLean family was outraged by this decision since Vince had admitted his guilt. Nevertheless, Vince's mental health began to improve during his time at the facility, and he was eventually granted more freedoms.

In February 2016, Vince changed his name to Will Lee Baker and was granted permission to live alone. The Manitoba Criminal Code Review Board discharged him on February 10th, 2017, and decided to keep all of his health documents private.

The tragedy continued to take its toll on those involved, with Corporal Ken Barker, one of the first officers at the scene, taking his life in July 2014 after suffering from post-traumatic stress disorder for years.

Tim's friend Jossie Kehler said in an email to CBC News: "He has a lot of friends, and they all are very upset he's gone, and they would like to say they miss him and he will always be in their hearts. People say no one's perfect, but Tim, he was. He did nothing bad to anyone."

THE LAST THANKSGIVING

"Flush chunks down toilet, not garbage disposal … don't have to get rid of body if no forensic evidence…Remove her clothes and take them with me for disposal."

MURDER PLANNING NOTES
WRITTEN BY JOEL GUY JR.

Thanksgiving, a time for family gatherings and heartfelt celebrations, was forever marred for the Guy family in 2016. On the last Thursday of November that year, they gathered in their family home for one final Thanksgiving feast, blissfully unaware that their youngest son had already planned a chilling double murder.

Joel Michael Guy Sr., born on February 10th, 1955, and his

wife, Lisa Guy, born on August 8th, 1961, were a loving couple who had been married since 1985. Three years into their marriage, they had a baby boy, Joel Michael Junior. Joel Sr. had three daughters, Tina, Angela, and Michelle, from a previous marriage. The girls adored Lisa and eagerly embraced their new little brother.

FAMILY LIFE

The family made their home in the picturesque Hardin Valley, Tennessee, west of Knoxville, in a spacious two-story house on Goldenview Lane. Lisa, wanting to devote her time to raising her son, became a stay-at-home mom, while Joel Sr. worked as a pipeline engineering designer. Determined to provide the best possible education for Joel Jr., they sent him to Hahnville High School and later to the Louisiana School for Math, Science, and the Arts, where he graduated in 2006.

Joel Jr. initially enrolled at George Washington University in Washington D.C., but his academic journey soon took a detour. After just one semester, he dropped out and transferred to Louisiana State University, where he pursued his dream of becoming a plastic surgeon. Living alone in Baton Rouge, Joel Jr. relied on his parents to pay for tuition and rent, which allowed him to focus solely on his studies.

Once Joel Jr. was settled in college, Lisa returned to the workforce, taking a job at Jacobs Engineering in Oak Ridge. As the years passed, Joel Sr. and Lisa began to look forward to retirement, making plans for a simpler, nature-filled life in a smaller home. While the decision to leave their beloved family home in Hardin Valley was difficult, they eventually found a charming property in Surgoinsville, Hawkins County. Their three daughters were thrilled for the couple, but Joel Sr. and Lisa had yet to break the news to their son, Joel Jr., who was deeply attached to the family home.

A CHANGE IN LIFESTYLE

As part of their retirement plan, Joel Sr. and Lisa decided to stop financially supporting their son, who was 28 in 2016. Believing that it was time for him to take on more responsibility, they planned to inform him of the upcoming changes during their final Thanksgiving celebration in the old house, with the whole family in attendance.

On November 23rd, 2016, Joel Jr. arrived in Hardin Valley. His half-sisters Tina and Angela were unable to attend, but Michelle was there with her boyfriend and their three children. Michelle later noted that Joel Jr. seemed unusually cheerful, a stark contrast to his typically grumpy demeanor. Instead of retreating to his childhood bedroom, as he usually did during family gatherings, he spent his time playing with Michelle's children.

After the long drive from Baton Rouge, Joel Jr. decided to extend his stay with his parents for the weekend. On November 25th, the three of them visited the new house in

Hawkins County, and Joel Jr. appeared genuinely happy for his parents' upcoming retirement.

On November 26th, Lisa's absence from work raised concern among her colleagues. Known for her reliability, Lisa would have called in sick if she was unwell. As the day passed, Lisa's supervisor grew increasingly worried and contacted the police to request a welfare check.

A HORRIFYING FIND

When officers arrived at the Guy residence, they found both family cars parked in the driveway, suggesting that the family was home. Yet no one answered the door. Inside, they could hear the family dog barking, but there was no other sign of life. Peering through a window next to the front door, they saw groceries scattered on the floor, prompting their suspicion that something was amiss.

Fearing that Lisa or Joel Sr. might be in danger, the officers entered the house. They were immediately met with sweltering heat and a nauseating stench. The thermostat had been cranked up to 90 degrees, and there were blood stains and cleaning supplies in nearly every room.

As they ventured upstairs, the officers found the dog locked in a bedroom. Just around the corner, they made a grisly discovery: a pair of severed arms meticulously arranged on the floor of the exercise room. In an adjacent room, two large plastic bins filled with acid contained two human torsos. The horror continued in the kitchen, where

Lisa's severed head was found inside a large pot on the stove.

The search of the home turned up a backpack containing a notebook with a detailed to-do list for the murders, as well as a list of each victim's assets and the life insurance payout for Lisa. This evidence led the police to suspect that the killer was none other than Joel Michael Jr.

Investigators quickly discovered that Joel Jr. lived in Baton Rouge and contacted the local police to check his apartment. As they arrived, they found Joel Jr. entering his car, a meat grinder stowed in the trunk. It seemed he was returning to the family home to finish his grisly task.

The medical examiner assigned to the case faced a daunting challenge due to the state of the dismembered bodies. Joel Sr.'s arms and legs had been removed from his torso, and his head had been reduced to a skeleton. The examiner noted a possible blunt-force trauma to his forehead. The torso was not as decomposed as the rest of the body, revealing 34 stab wounds in Joel Sr.'s back.

Lisa's body had also been dismembered, her arms and legs severed at the joints. Examination of her skin and muscle tissue showed 25 stab wounds on her back, and her internal organs, including her heart, had been damaged during the attack.

Joel Michael Jr. was charged with the first-degree murder of his parents, Joel Sr. and Lisa Guy. Initially, the prosecution believed they had a strong case, but their confidence was shaken when Joel Jr. filed a motion to dismiss the evidence found in the family home, citing the lack of a search warrant. The motion was granted.

Despite the setback, the trial commenced on September 28th, 2020. Over the four years he spent in prison awaiting trial, Joel Jr. attempted to claim the $500,000 life insurance policy on his mother. He also clashed with fellow inmates and requested a private cell.

The prosecution opened the trial by introducing the jury to the chilling case, arguing that Joel Jr. had planned the murders weeks before Thanksgiving, anticipating that his parents would cut him off financially. According to his notebook, Joel Jr. intended to frame his father for the murders.

The prosecution pieced together a harrowing narrative of the attack, suggesting that Joel Jr. had ambushed his father in the exercise room upstairs and stabbed him repeatedly with a kitchen knife. He then began dismembering the body, starting with Joel Sr.'s hands. Based on the scattered groceries found at the scene, investigators believed that Joel Jr. had attacked his mother as soon as she entered the house.

Joel Jr.'s plan to dissolve the bodies in acid and flush the remains down the drain would have obscured the timeline of the murders, giving him ample time to cover his tracks. Although they couldn't use all the physical evidence found in the Guy residence, the prosecution presented receipts from a local Walmart that showed Joel Jr. had purchased large quantities of chemicals, as well as a first aid kit shortly after the murders, suggesting he had been injured during the attacks on his parents.

Michelle, Lisa's daughter from her first marriage, took the stand and testified about her half-brother's unusually friendly demeanor during Thanksgiving. Normally avoiding family events, Joel Jr. was actively engaging with everyone and having fun. The defense used this testimony to argue that Joel Jr. was happy despite learning he would be cut off financially and therefore had no motive to kill his parents.

However, the prosecution countered by asserting that money was the sole motive for the murders. They argued that Joel Jr., with no intention of completing his college degree, wanted to live off his mother's life insurance payout, which he had documented in his notebook.

On October 2nd, 2020, Joel Michael Guy Jr. was found guilty of two counts of first-degree murder and three counts of abuse of a corpse. He received two life sentences plus four years. In November 2022, Joel Michael Jr.'s attorney filed an appeal for a new trial on behalf of his client, but the appeal was denied.

Joel Michael Jr. is currently serving his sentence at the Northwest Correctional Complex in Tiptonville, Tennessee, where he will likely spend the rest of his life behind bars for his crimes. His release date is 2135.

CONFESSIONS FREELY GIVEN

> "God damn, will you find me? I just stabbed somebody with an ice pick. I can't stop myself. I keep killing somebody."
>
> PAUL MICHAEL STEPHANI

In the 1980s, Minnesota police were dealing with a mysterious killer who targeted young women wearing red clothes. He called 911 after every murder and confessed over the phone. His high-pitched tearful voice earned him a nickname — The Weepy Voiced Killer.

Paul Michael Stephani was born in Austin, Minnesota, on September 8th, 1944. He was one of 10 children who grew up in a very religious family. The family lived on a farm outside the city limits, and the family went to church every weekend. Stephani's parents divorced, and his mother remarried when Stephani was only three years old.

His stepdad was also a devout catholic and got along with Stephani's mother just fine. However, he was very abusive towards the children. He would often hit them and even throw them down the stairs. Unable to cope with such an environment, Stephani moved out after graduating high school in the early 1960s.

He rented an apartment in Saint Paul, the state capital, and worked various jobs before landing a position at the Malmberg Manufacturing Company. Around the same time, he met his future wife Beverly, and the two got married. Soon after, they had a daughter. Unfortunately for Stephani, his marriage didn't work out. Beverly asked for a divorce, and Stephani didn't see his daughter after that.

In 1977, Stephani was fired from the Malmberg Manufacturing Company, and that triggered his underlying mental illness. Stephani kept his aggression in check for years, but the divorce and firing were a huge shock for him. He was arrested for an assault soon after losing his job.

Determined to get back on track, Stephani began a new relationship and found employment. His new girlfriend was from Syria, and it turned out her parents had arranged a marriage in her home country. When Stephani's girlfriend left the United States, he felt broken and betrayed.

THE MURDERS BEGIN

On December 31st, 1980, Stephani was driving through downtown Saint Paul. At around 1 am, he saw a young woman walking alone on the street. She was wearing a red dress and no coat, even though it was freezing cold outside. Her name was Karen Potack, and she was a 20-year-old student who came to Saint Paul to celebrate the New Year.

Karen had a disagreement with her sisters and left the club without her coat. Stephani assumed she was cold, so he used that to get Karen inside his car. He pulled up next to her and offered the young woman a ride. She agreed, and the two started driving around.

Stephani drove towards the Malmberg machine shop where he used to work. He knew the place would be deserted at this time of night. After parking in a secluded place, he exited the vehicle and went to grab a tire iron from his trunk. Stephani then ordered Karen to step out, but she refused. He started hitting her with a tire iron.

Karen was lying unconscious on the ground while Stephani continued to hit her. He abruptly stopped and drove away, leaving the injured girl in the dark. Suddenly, Stephani had a change of heart and stopped to find a phone booth. He called 911 and told them Karen's location, stating she was injured.

Police officers found Karen Potack, and she was rushed to the hospital. They were puzzled by the attack because she wasn't robbed or sexually assaulted. When she recovered, Karen couldn't remember anything about the man who attacked her due to the head injury. Stephani got away this time.

On June 3rd, 1981, Stephani was at a diner when he saw 18-year-old Kimberly Compton. The teen was a student from Pepin, Wisconsin, who had graduated from high school a few weeks prior. The two began talking, and Stephani learned that Kimberly had moved to Saint Paul that day. He used this information to offer Kimberly a tour of the city.

Stephani suggested they go to the river and enjoy the views. Kimberly accepted, and the two drove away in Stephani's car. When they arrived at the riverbank, Stephani took an ice pick from his trunk and attacked the girl while she was sitting on the ground. He stabbed her 61 times and then strangled her with a shoelace. Stephani tried to hide Kimberly's body by placing her in tall grass.

Three boys, who were playing near the river, discovered Kimberly and called the police. Meanwhile, Stephani felt guilty and contacted law enforcement. He almost sounded like he was crying while saying he was sorry for killing the young woman. The police believed it was a prank call, but they remembered the caller said he murdered her with an ice pick.

The medical examiner confirmed an ice pick was the murder weapon, and the investigators believed the killer himself called them. Since they didn't discover any physical

evidence at the scene, the police focused on the phone call. They released the audio recordings to the public, hoping someone might recognize his voice.
911 call from Stephani:

> *"Don't talk; just listen. I'm sorry for what I did to Compton. I couldn't help it. I don't know why I had to stab her. I am so upset about it. I keep getting drunk every day, but I can't believe I did it; it's like a big dream....I can't think of being locked up, if I get locked up I'll kill myself, I'd rather kill myself than get locked up. I'll try not to kill anyone else."*

Two days later, he called 911 and apologized for the murder. On June 6th, he contacted law enforcement again to tell them the newspapers got the details of the crime wrong. On June 11th, he said he was sorry for what he had done to Kimberly.

A second call to 911 from Stephani about Compton:

> *"Please don't talk; just listen. I'm sorry I killed that girl. I stabbed her 40 times. Kimberly Compton was the first one over in St. Paul. I don't know what's the matter with me. I'm sick. I'm going to kill myself, I think. I'm just going to... If somebody dies with a red shirt on, it's me. I've killed more people... I'll never make it to heaven!"*

The police anticipated the call on June 11th and traced it to a bus station. When the patrol car arrived there, they didn't find the caller. Investigators believed this wasn't his first murder, so they combed through the calls from the past year. They stumbled upon the call that was received after the attack on Karen Potack and realized the voice was identical.

The investigators did everything to identify Kimberly's killer, but there weren't any new calls. Stephani laid low for more than a year. Then on July 21st, 1982, he was driving through Roseville, located just outside Saint Paul, when he saw 33-year-old Kathleen Greening. Stephani parked his vehicle and watched the woman as she carried her suitcases.

She was going in and out of her house. Stephani noticed she went inside and didn't come out for several minutes. He approached her front door and entered the house since it was unlocked. Kathleen was getting ready for a bath when Stephani entered her bathroom, grabbed her, and shoved her head underwater.

After a couple of minutes, Kathleen stopped moving, and Stephani knew she was dead. For some reason, he didn't call the police this time. Instead, he went to his local church and spent hours crying. Kathleen was discovered dead in her home, but the police had no reason to connect the so-called Weepy-Voiced Killer to this murder.

Two weeks later, on August 5th, 1982, Stephani was in the Hexagon Bar when he noticed Barbara Simons, a 40-year-old nurse from Minneapolis. He asked the woman for a cigarette, and the two began chatting. They talked for hours, and Barbara really liked Stephani. He offered her a ride home, and before the two left, Barbara told the waitress that she was about to leave with Stephani.

But instead of dropping her home, Stephani drove Barbara to the banks of the Mississippi river and stabbed her more than 100 times with an ice pick. He threw the murder weapon into the water. The following morning, Barbara's body was discovered by a paperboy.

As expected, Stephani called the police two days after the murder. He was weeping and said he was scared to go to prison. But again, the investigators had no idea who the killer was. Barbara's family told the police she was at the Hexagon Bar on the night of the murder.

The waitress remembered the man who chatted with Barbara and provided the police with a detailed description. The investigators searched their records and presented the waitress with photos of local criminals that fit the description. Since Stephani was arrested for assault in the 1970s, his image was included. The waitress picked him out of the photo lineup.

But again, the police didn't have any physical proof he was the killer. So they decided to follow Stephani. A patrol car was in charge of surveilling his apartment. Police followed their suspect after he entered his vehicle on August 21st, but they lost him.

On August 21st, 1982, Stephani was on his way to east Minneapolis. There he came across 19-year-old Denise Williams, a sex worker. She agreed to go to Stephani's apartment. Afterward, he offered to drive her home. While everything seemed fine initially, Denise noticed Stephani wasn't going toward Minneapolis.

He suddenly stopped at a dark parking lot and demanded she pay him for the ride. Denise refused and started to exit the car. Before she could do that, Stephani opened the glove compartment, grabbed a screwdriver from it, and stabbed Denise in her stomach. Knowing she had to defend herself, Denise found an old glass bottle on the floor and hit Stephani with it.

Denise used the broken bottle to slice Stephani's hand and face. He opened the passenger door, and the two fell out of the vehicle. Denise's screams were heard by a man who lived in a nearby house. He ran to the parking lot to help Denise, but Stephani attacked him with a screwdriver. The man returned to his house and called the police.

Stephani got into his car, leaving Denise behind, and drove straight home. He couldn't stop the bleeding but knew that hospital wasn't an option. Instead, Stephani called 911, claiming he was beaten up on the street. He provided his address, and the dispatcher informed the police about the call because they were informed Stephani was under surveillance.

Meanwhile, Denise spoke to the investigators and identified Stephani as the man who attacked her. After being treated for his wounds, Stephani was taken to the police station to talk to the officers about his alleged attack. He claimed he was robbed, but they knew he was lying.

Detectives working on the case of the Weepy-Voiced Killer showed Stephani photos of his victims, and he immediately jumped from his seat and started talking in a high-pitched voice. It was the voice of the person who called 911 and confessed to the murders.

Paul Michael Stephani was charged with the murder of Barbara Simons and the assault of Denise Williams. He pleaded not guilty. As the investigators dug deeper into his background, they discovered he worked at the Malmberg Manufacturing Company, where Karen Potack was attacked.

Detectives also discovered that the murders began after his girlfriend moved to Syria and assumed this event triggered Stephani to start killing. Both his ex-wife and sister appeared in the courtroom during the trial and confirmed that the Weepy-Voiced Killer sounded like Stephani. He was found guilty on both counts and sentenced to 18 years in prison.

In 1997, Stephani was diagnosed with skin cancer and was told he was going to die within a year. Knowing he had nothing else to lose, Stephani contacted the police and offered to tell them about all of his crimes. He asked for a photo of his mother's headstone in return.

Stephani was a suspect in the attack on Karen Potack and

the murder of Kimberly Compton, and he confessed he was responsible for those crimes. However, he also mentioned that he drowned a woman in a bathtub but couldn't provide her name.
The police identified her as Kathleen Greening.

When asked about the motivations behind his killings, Stephani just said there was a voice in his head telling him to kill. He died on June 12th, 1998, in the Oak Park Heights maximum security prison.

KILLER CASE FILES: VOLUME 9

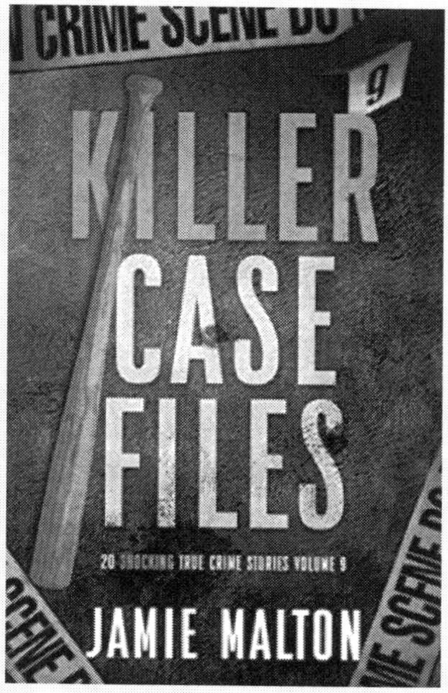

SCUTTLE THE SHIP

"Picked up blonde girl, brown eyes, from small white raft, suffering exposure and shock. Name Terry Jo Duperrault. Was on *Bluebelle*."

TELEGRAPH FROM THE GREEK FREIGHTER, *CAPTAIN THEO,* TO THE US COAST GUARD IN MIAMI

What started as a family cruise on a sailboat called Bluebelle ended in tragedy. One survivor was located a day after the accident. Miraculously, a second survivor was found three days later, and the investigators finally learned what really happened to the passengers of the Bluebelle.

The Duperrault family consisted of the father, Arthur, who was 40 years old, his wife, Jean, who was 38, and their three children, Brian, 14, Terry Jo, 11, and René, who was only seven years old. The family lived in Green Bay, Wisconsin.

During World War II, Arthur had enlisted in the Navy and worked as a medic. Around that time, he met his future wife, Jean, and the two got married in 1944. After the war, Arthur graduated from college and started his career as an optometrist.

Jean was into gardening, interior design, and playing musical instruments. When Arthur was in his mid-thirties, he expressed a desire to take his whole family to sail around Florida and the Bahamas. He visited this part of the world with the Navy and wished to experience it again. Jean supported this idea, and the family started saving money for the trip.

In the summer of 1961, Arthur and Jean began planning their seven-day cruise. They wanted to spend a week on a sailboat and enjoy the warm weather. The Duperrault family arrived in Fort Lauderdale, Florida, in November 1961 and rented a sailboat named Bluebelle from the owner Howard Pegg for $515. It was large enough for six people and the crew. Arthur hired 44-year-old Julian Harvey as the skipper and paid him $100 daily.

Harvey invited his 34-year-old wife, Mary Dene Harvey, to work as a cook on the Bluebelle. She was Harvey's sixth wife, and the two were married just two months before the voyage. The Duperraults left the Bahia Mar Marina on November 8th, 1961.

The Bluebelle sailed around the Bahamas for four days and made stops at Bimini and Sandy Point. The Duperrault family was determined to have fun on their vacation and went swimming and snorkeling. They purchased souvenirs and collected seashells on the beaches. On the evening of November 12th, Arthur was so thrilled with the overall experience that he said the family would return to the Bahamas for Christmas.

Since it was their final night before sailing back to Florida, the Duperraults had dinner with the Harveys on the deck. Terry Jo decided to go to bed early, so she went below the deck to her cabin. Her brother and sister stayed on deck with their parents.

On November 13th, 1961, around noon, the crew of a tanker called *Gulf Lion* spotted a dinghy in the water. Inside was a man who was waving and shouting. Once they helped him get on board, they saw he had a small girl with him. She was wearing a life jacket, but it was clear the child was dead.

The man said his name was Julian Harvey, a skipper of a sailboat called Bluebelle. According to him, at 8:30 pm on November 12th, Bluebelle was somewhere between Great Stirrup Cay and Abaco Islands when it was hit by strong winds. The mast snapped in half and made a hole in the hull. Two passengers were injured, and he couldn't reach them because of the broken mast. While Harvey was looking for tools to help him clear his way to the passengers, the sailboat caught on fire.

Knowing he couldn't do anything, Harvey boarded a nearby dinghy and watched the sailboat sink. He saw the body of young René Duperrault float by, and hoping she was still alive, Harvey pulled her out and tried to revive the little girl. Unfortunately, she was already gone.

Harvey was left in Nassau, the capital of the Bahamas, where he talked about the accident to the authorities. He seemed willing to help and shared many details about the night of the accident. However, those who spoke to him noticed his stutter. But it was somewhat understandable because he just went through a traumatic experience.

There was one detail that was suspicious – the dinghy Harvey was rescued from was equipped with supplies. Since there were no witnesses, authorities had to believe Harvey, at least for now. He returned to Miami on November 15th and was scheduled for an interview with the U.S. Coast Guard the following day.

On November 16th, a Greek freighter, *Captain Theo,* was on their usual route in the Northwest Providence Channel. The second officer noticed something resembling a fishing boat floating more than a mile away from the ship. Knowing that such a vessel couldn't survive the high waves, the second officer was curious about the small boat. Then he spotted a person inside the boat.

He called the captain, and the two realized they were looking at a small dinghy with a girl inside. She had blonde hair and was trying to wave to them. She was badly sunburned and wearing a white shirt and pink cropped pants. The raft was small and her legs dangled over the side. The freighter stopped, and a make-shift raft made of oil drums was lowered into the water. The crew saw sharks circling the dinghy, so they asked the child to wait for the crew member to come and pick her up. While the girl floated on the raft waiting to be rescued, one of the sailors took a photo of her. It was later seen and printed in newspapers around the globe with the title, "sea waif."

The child was heavily dehydrated and sunburned, but she was still able to speak. She said her name was Terry Jo Duperrault. She was out in the sea for several days after her sailboat Bluebelle sank. Soon after, she couldn't talk anymore but continued communicating with gestures. She was asked if she had any family, and the girl, visibly upset, gave the "thumb down" sign and shook her head no. The Greek sailors nursed the girl giving her sips of water and juice to drink.

Meanwhile, the freighter contacted the U.S. Coast Guard, who sent a helicopter to pick up the survivor and bring her to the hospital. Despite being in a bad state, the girl started recovering quickly. But she still couldn't talk.

Harvey was interviewed on November 16th by the U.S. Coast Guard, and this time he told them that the broken mast ruptured the sailboat's gas tank, which resulted in a sudden fire. The flames separated him from the rest of the passengers and his wife.

Harvey's story changed, but the investigators were still willing to give him the benefit of the doubt because the man did survive a shipwreck. Since he was an experienced skipper, the investigators wanted to know why he didn't use flares to alert the nearby ships. Harvey said he panicked and forgot to look for them, which was odd.

On November 17th, Harvey had been giving his statement about the accident when he was informed that Terry Jo Duperrault was alive. Harvey was visibly shocked and said, "Oh my God!" Realizing how it sounded, Harvey quickly added, "Isn't that wonderful?" The U.S. Coast Guard now had a second witness, and Harvey knew they would soon learn the real story.

Several minutes later, Harvey asked the investigators if he could rest because he was tired and wanted to speak with his wife's family. He drove to the Sandman Motel on Biscayne Boulevard, where he checked in under a fake name, John Monroe. Later in the afternoon, a maid entered Harvey's room and discovered his lifeless body in the bath.

Harvey committed suicide in an unusual way. He slashed his ankles, wrists, and jugular vein with a razor blade. Harvey wrote a suicide letter but didn't provide details of the accident or the events that happened on Bluebelle. Instead, the letter simply suggested he was nervous and potentially depressed. Harvey left a tip for the maid alongside the letter.

WHAT REALLY HAPPENED ON THE BLUEBELLE

On November 20th, Terry Jo was ready to speak with the

investigators. Her condition had improved significantly since her arrival at the hospital. The girl recalled going to her cabin on the evening of November 12th. She was scared by shouting and screaming and heard her older brother calling for their father. Terry Jo snuck out of her cabin and saw her brother and mother dead near the galley. They were lying in pools of blood.

She saw Harvey with a bucket, and at first, he didn't even notice her. When he did, Harvey pushed the girl below the deck. Not sure what was happening, Terry Jo returned to her cabin. She saw oil and water coming in from under the door soon after. At one point, Harvey came to her cabin. He was carrying a rifle but didn't shoot her. He assumed she would go down with the sailboat.

Her cabin was filling up with water, so Terry Jo returned to the upper deck. Harvey had lowered a dinghy and was loading it with items. The girl approached him and asked if the boat was sinking. He calmly said yes. The dinghy floated away, and Harvey jumped into the ocean. Terry Jo was left alone on a sinking sailboat. There was no fire.

She remembered a small life raft tied to the deck and went towards it as the sailboat sank. Terry Jo reached it just in time. She floated for three and a half days in the open water. The raft was tiny, even for a child, and Terry Jo had to sit upright. Her survival was a miracle since she didn't have food or water and couldn't protect herself from the sun. After the rescue, Terry Jo's raft was lifted from the water and began falling apart.

According to Terry Jo, the sea was calm on the night of the accident, and there weren't any winds. When she climbed to the deck, the mast wasn't broken, which meant Harvey's version of the events was fabricated.

WHO WAS JULIAN HARVEY?

The investigators wanted to learn as much as possible about Julian Harvey and his background, hoping it would provide them with the motive. They quickly discovered Harvey had financial problems and found it impossible to keep a job.

Harvey married his 6th wife, Mary Dene, in July 1961 and had a double indemnity life insurance policy on her in September of the same year. After the incident on the sail-boat, the investigators were approached by Mary Dene's brother, who told them all about Harvey's financial strug-gles. Before the wedding to Mary Dene, Harvey pretended to be wealthy, but his wife soon found out he was broke.

At the beginning of October, Harvey was hired as a skipper by Harold Pegg, the owner of Bluebelle. The Duperrault family were his first clients. Their family cruise created the opportunity for Harvey to stage an accident and try to collect the insurance money for his wife, who came along as a crew member. Perhaps Harvey didn't intend to murder the Duperrault family, but maybe Arthur saw him kill Mary Dene or dispose of her body.

Additionally, Harvey had received three prior insurance

settlements. Most notably, he survived a car crash that killed his second wife and mother-in-law in 1949.

TERRY JO

Once she recovered, Terry Jo returned to Green Bay and moved in with her aunt, grandmother, and three cousins. The family resided in De Pere. In 1962, she changed her name to Tere Jo. She studied X-ray technology in college but decided to switch to cultural geography because the field of medicine proved to be too stressful for her.

Tere Jo earned a bachelor's degree from the University of Wisconsin in Green Bay. She was employed by the Wisconsin Department of Natural Resources. Tere Jo moved with her husband, Ron Fassbender, and their three children to Kewaunee, Wisconsin.

She didn't talk about the trauma she went through until the 1980s. In 2010, Tere Jo released a memoir called *Alone: Orphaned on the Ocean*. She stated that she didn't want to be seen as a victim but as someone who lived a happy life despite what happened to her.

SERIAL POLICEMAN

"Schaefer is the most sexually deviant person I had ever seen. He made Ted Bundy look like a Boy Scout."

PROSECUTOR ROBERT STONE

Nestled within the Sunshine State, Martin County, Florida, is known for its awe-inspiring landscapes, sandy beaches, and its year-round temperate weather. In the 1970s, droves of young people from across the United States were attracted to this idyllic corner of the state, nicknamed the Treasure Coast. Little did they know a serial killer wearing a cop's uniform lurked among them.

A KILLER IS BORN

Gerard John Schaefer Jr. was born on March 26th, 1946, in the quaint town of Neenah, Wisconsin. He was the first-born and had two younger sisters. His father, Gerard Sr., made a living as a traveling salesman, while his mother, Doris Marie, spent her time caring for the children at home. The family frequently relocated before ultimately settling down in Fort Lauderdale, Florida, in 1960.

The Schaefer family had money and frequented the local yachting and country clubs. They kept up appearances, but the family was dysfunctional. Schaefer's father was an alcoholic who routinely subjected Doris Marie and the children to verbal abuse. Despite his frequent absences, he showed little affection for his son, instead favoring his daughters, which fueled Schaefer's jealousy. Schaefer remained deeply attached to his mother as a child, but he eventually felt like neither of his parents cared for him.

DARK DESIRES

While at St. Thomas Aquinas High School, Schaefer was somewhat of a loner, keeping to himself and having few friends. He was fond of solitary activities such as hunting, fishing, and immersing himself in the natural world. On these outings, he would tie himself to trees and fantasize about dying because it sexually excited him. While in high school, he had a girlfriend, Cindy, who participated in his "rape fantasies." She broke up with him after three years.

Schaefer continued to pursue his fantasies that revolved around bondage and sadomasochism. He was frequently seen peering through windows in his neighborhood and even broke into some homes to steal women's underwear. He began cross-dressing while still in high school, although he later said this was to avoid being drafted into the Vietnam War.

After graduating in June 1964, he enrolled at Broward Community College in the Fall, where he pursued a teaching degree. In 1968, Schaefer received a scholarship to attend Florida Atlantic University in Boca Raton.

A SERIES OF FAILURES

In December 1968, Schaefer married Martha Louise Fogg, a woman two years his junior. Their marriage didn't last long and ended on May 2nd, 1970. Fogg cited Schaefer's excessive demands for sex and extreme cruelty as reasons for the divorce.

Schaefer started teaching in March 1969, but he was dismissed from two schools within two years due to unprofessional behavior and insufficient knowledge of his subjects. Schaefer took some time off after his dismissal and traveled through Europe and North Africa before returning to Florida.

He applied to become a police officer at the Wilton Manors Police Department. Even though Schaefer failed the psychological part of his police exam, he was officially appointed a patrolman for Broward County in September 1971. That same month, Schaefer married his second wife, Teresa Dean.

Schaefer's tenure at the Broward County Police Department lasted six months. He was fired when it was discovered that he regularly stopped female drivers, recorded their license plates, and contacted them to arrange sexual encounters.

Remarkably, his career in law enforcement continued. Schaefer became a deputy at the Martin County Sheriff's Department. He provided a counterfeit letter of recommendation, and since his record showed no previous convictions, he was hired by Martin County in June 1972.

THE ABDUCTION OF NANCY AND PAULA

On July 21st, 1972, Gerard Schaefer, while on duty, encountered two hitchhiking teenage girls, Nancy Trotter, and Paula Wells. He escorted them back to their lodging in Stuart, where he lectured them on the perils of hitchhiking, even falsely claiming hitchhiking was illegal in Martin County. When the girls discussed their plans to visit the beach the following day, Schaefer offered to drive them there.

The next day, Nancy and Paula met Schaefer on East Ocean Boulevard around 9 am. Rather than driving the girls to the beach as promised, Schaefer took them to Hutchinson Island, all the while continuing to lecture them about the dangers of hitchhiking. He stopped the vehicle and threatened the girls with his gun. Schaefer led them into a thickly wooded area after handcuffing them. He separated them, tying each girl to a different tree, and he placed nooses he'd made around their necks. They stood precariously on exposed tree roots, and any wrong step or attempt to escape would result in their deaths.

Unexpectedly, Schaefer received a radio dispatch summoning him to the police station. He told the girls that he would return shortly and warned them not to try and escape. Ignoring his threats, both Nancy and Paula desperately worked to free themselves. It was dark, and they couldn't see each other in the dense forest. They went their separate ways upon escaping. Paula managed to reach the highway, where a truck driver stopped to assist her. He brought her to a nearby police station — the very one where Schaefer worked. Nancy was soon found near a creek with her hands still bound behind her back. Upon learning that Paula was safe, she was overcome with relief.

Schaefer returned to the forest two hours later only to find the girls had escaped. Panicked, he contacted his boss, Sheriff Robert Crowder, and confessed to tying up the girls in the woods to teach them a lesson about hitchhiking.

At the station, Nancy and Paula recounted their harrowing ordeal, describing their abductor and detailing their escape. They identified Gerard Schaefer as the man who had tied them to a tree in the forest and threatened to sexually assault and murder them.

Despite Schaefer's insistence on trying to scare the girls, his boss wasn't convinced. He was immediately fired, arrested, and charged with false imprisonment and aggravated assault. Schaefer spent two weeks in jail before posting bail. He found work at a Kwik Chek minute mart and awaited his trial, scheduled for November 1972.

In September 1972, Schaefer enrolled in classes at an adult education center in Fort Lauderdale under the alias Jerry Shepherd. There, he befriended 17-year-old Susan Place and 16-year-old Georgia Jessup. The teenagers were captivated by their new acquaintance, who claimed to have traveled extensively and harbored an interest in the supernatural. On September 27th, 1972, Susan's mother, Lucille, discovered her daughter hurriedly packing her belongings. Susan explained that she intended to accompany Georgia on a road trip with their friend Jerry.

Lucille briefly spoke with Jerry outside her home and also noted the license plate number of Jerry's 1969 Datsun. She bid her daughter farewell, and Susan assured her mother that they would stay in touch. After four days without contact from Susan, she and Georgia's mother reported the teenagers missing to the Oakland Park police. Although Lucille provided the license plate number, the investigation stalled due to incorrect jurisdiction.

THE FIRST TRIAL

In November 1972, Gerard Schaefer accepted a plea deal that reduced his sentence. Pleading guilty to aggravated assault, he was given a one-year sentence in county jail, with eligibility for parole after six months. Schaefer requested that the judge postpone his sentencing for a few weeks so he could help his wife, Teresa, relocate to Fort Lauderdale. Teresa wished to live closer to Schaefer's mother while he was in jail. The judge granted the request, given Schaefer's status as a police officer with no prior convictions. Schaefer remained free until January 15th, 1973, when he began serving his sentence in Martin County jail.

CONNECTING THE DOTS

In March 1973, Lucille Place, Susan's mother, discovered a letter sent by Jerry Shepherd (Schaefer's alias) in Susan's bedroom. Hoping to find her daughter, whom she still believed had run away, Lucille and her husband, Ira, drove to the address in Stuart, Florida. There, they learned that Jerry Shepherd was an alias used by Gerard Schaefer, who had been in jail since January for abducting two teenage girls. Realizing the connection between Schaefer and the disappearance of Susan and Georgia, Lucille contacted the police.

DISCOVERY OF THE BODIES

On April 1st, 1973, two men stumbled upon human remains in a shallow grave in Oak Hammock Park in Port Saint Lucie. The police were contacted, and the bodies were identified as Susan Place and Georgia Jessup. Both girls had been decapitated, and their bodies had been mutilated. They were found only six miles from where Schaefer had abducted Nancy Trotter and Paula Wells in July 1972. Given the similarities between the cases, investigators obtained search warrants for Schaefer's residence and his mother's house.

The search uncovered various weapons, Schaefer's "fictional" stories detailing kidnappings, sexual assaults, and hangings, over 30 Polaroid photos of mutilated women, and a box of items or trophies he'd taken from his victims. Most of the items were jewelry and teeth. This evidence linked Schaefer to several disappearances and murders. On May 18th, 1973, Schaefer was charged with the first-degree murder of Susan Place and Georgia Jessup and was sent for a psychiatric examination.

THE SECOND TRIAL

In September 1973, Schaefer's second trial began in St. Lucie County. Teresa Dean, Schaefer's wife, was initially unaware of her husband's crimes, but she became suspicious when he was fired from the police force. She testified against him at his trial. Her testimony focused on a photo album containing pictures of women in bondage and torture poses in their home.

The prosecution presented evidence of the gruesome double murder, while the defense attempted to prove that Susan Place's parents had identified the wrong person. After five hours of deliberation, the jury found Schaefer guilty of two counts of first-degree murder, and the judge sentenced him to two terms of life in prison.

Teresa Dean divorced her husband after the trial and refused to speak about their relationship.

HOW MANY WOMEN DID HE KILL?

The exact number of Schaefer's victims remains unknown, but the police compiled a list of potential victims after searching his homes. It is also unclear when Schaefer began killing women.

The first murder that can be connected to Schaefer was Leigh Farrell Hainline Bonadies, who disappeared on September 8th, 1969. Other potential victims include Carmen Marie Hallock, Bonnie Taylor, Mary Alice Briscolina, and Elsie Lina Fermer.

Four years after the trial for the double murder, a set of bones and teeth belonging to Barbara Ann Wilcox and Colette Goodenough were found. The two teenagers from Iowa had been missing since 1973.

The bodies were found by a hog hunter near the C-24 Canal located in western Port St. Lucie. The girls had last been seen in Mississippi, hitchhiking to the east coast of Florida. The remains of the girls were discovered scattered around a large tree, and investigators' reports indicate that the tree showed signs of being used to hang one or both of the girls. According to the reports, an orange crate was found nearby, as if it had been used as a seat for a spectator. Although Schaefer was considered a likely suspect, the case remains unresolved.

SUZANNE GALE POOLE

The remains of a young female, later identified as Suzanne Gale Poole, who was also referred to as "Singer Island Jane Doe," were found by the Palm Beach County Sheriff's Office in a swampy area on Singer Island in June 1974. Suzanne had been tied to mangrove trees with wire. Despite numerous attempts to identify her over the years, including the development of a DNA profile for CODIS in 2015 and facial reconstruction in 2019, prior attempts had been unsuccessful.

In December 2021, the Sheriff's Office sent the remains to Othram Labs for genetic genealogy analysis for new leads. In March 2022, the in-house genealogy team at Othram found potential family members. The breakthrough came on June 2nd, 2022, when the young girl was identified as 15-year-old Suzanne "Susan" Gale Poole, who had been reported missing in 1972, just before Christmas.

Authorities believe that Poole was a victim of Gerald John Schaefer, and they are conducting further investigations to hopefully provide closure for Poole's family.

PRISON LIFE

While in prison, Schaefer relied heavily on mail to communicate with the outside world, and he wrote stories that often included murders. Schaefer was an avid writer, both before and after his arrest. His writings included graphic accounts of his crimes, as well as numerous fictional stories that contained similarly disturbing content. He also wrote letters to various individuals while in prison, including other known serial killers and true crime authors. He also helped the police break a child pornography ring from inside the prison in 1983.

Schaefer was mistrusted by fellow prisoners, who suspected he was an informant for the police. On December 3rd, 1995, Gerard Schaefer was stabbed to death in his cell by fellow inmate Vincent Faustino Rivera. Rivera stabbed Schaefer 43 times with a homemade shank. The motive for the murder remains unclear, though some suspect it was related to Schaefer's cooperation with the police. Other inmates reported that Rivera was also angry with Schaefer for taking two cups of hot water instead of one from the water fountain.

Rivera, already serving a life sentence, was found guilty of Schaefer's murder and received an additional 53 years and 10 months to his sentence.

Despite his brutal end and the mounting evidence against him, Gerard Schaefer continued to maintain his innocence, leaving the true scope of his crimes shrouded in mystery.

VACATION MURDERS

"I figure the person who did it is sitting back there laughing. They'll get caught eventually. There isn't anybody that smart."

HAL ROGERS, HUSBAND AND FATHER

Nestled in Van Wert County, Ohio, the Rogers family, Joan "Jo" Rogers and her husband Hal, lived a quiet life with their daughters Michelle and Christie. The hard-working family ran a 300-acre dairy farm.

Jo, a native of Van Wert County, met her soulmate Hal during high school. Following graduation, the couple exchanged vows, although Jo's teenage pregnancy with Michelle left her parents displeased. Jo faced several restrictions during her wedding, including the absence of a traditional dress and no friends or family in attendance. Nevertheless, the newlyweds embarked on their honeymoon in Fort Wayne, Indiana, staying at the Hospitality Inn Motel. Three years later, the family welcomed the arrival of Christie.

Known for her vivacious personality, Jo quickly made friends wherever she went, whereas Hal was more introverted. Yet, Jo's effervescence brought out the best in him, culminating in a tender and loving marriage.

Growing up on the farm, Michelle and Christie considered the animals their pets. Christie even named the cows and performed her cheerleading routines in front of them. An ever-optimistic and bubbly girl, she attended Crestview Junior High and loved sports, particularly softball and roller skating. Her connection with her father, Hal, was strong, and they were inseparable.

Michelle, the older and more reserved sister, often kept to herself or mingled with boys from her class. Shy by nature, she would sit silently at the back of the school bus, avoiding conversations with her peers. Despite her introverted tendencies, Michelle held a passion for jewelry, particularly rings. Aspiring to be a veterinarian, she dreamed of attending college.

Jo, motivated by the health insurance benefits for her family, worked a midnight shift at Peyton's Northern as a forklift driver. This often left her exhausted, and she struggled to get adequate sleep.

JOHN ROGERS

John Rogers, Hal's brother, co-owned the family farm and frequently lent a helping hand. Living in a trailer adjacent to the family home, neighbors perceived him as an eccentric individual with an obsession for the Army, CIA, and Secret Service. In March 1988, John's world unraveled when his girlfriend accused him of sexual assault, leading to his swift arrest. She asserted that John had attacked her in the trailer and recorded the incident.

When investigating the trailer, sheriff's deputies discovered a briefcase containing the incriminating tape. Shockingly, they also discovered photographs of Michelle Rogers, who appeared blindfolded and disrobed. Michelle reluctantly confirmed that her uncle John had been molesting her since the age of 15. Jo and Hal were devastated, as they had sensed something amiss with Michelle but had attributed it to typical teenage angst.

Michelle explained that she had remained silent because John threatened her life. The abuse occurred on weekends when her parents were away on business trips. Throughout the two-year ordeal, Michelle diligently protected her younger sister from John, ensuring they were never left alone together.

Hal plunged into a deep depression, burdened by his inability to recognize the abuse and protect his daughter. John denied the allegations and claimed he was being framed. John was found guilty of sexual assault and sentenced to seven years up to 25 years in prison.

In light of the family's recent turmoil, Jo believed her daughters deserved a reprieve. She decided to treat them to a vacation in Florida – a destination none of them had ever visited. Although Hal wished to accompany them, someone had to remain behind to manage the family farm.

On the evening of May 26th, 1989, Jo, Michelle, and Christie embarked on their road trip to Jacksonville, Florida. They arrived the following day, visiting the Jacksonville Zoo before heading to Silver Springs. There, the girls gleefully documented their trip with their Nikon One-Touch camera, capturing memories of their glass-bottom boat ride.

The family then traveled to Titusville, where they checked into the Quality Inn. On May 29th, they mailed postcards and set off for Sea World. By May 30th, they were lodged at Gateway Inn in Epcot, eager to explore Disney's MGM Studios. On June 1st, they arrived at Days Inn in Tampa and picked up a Busch Gardens brochure, though it remains uncertain if they visited the park.

Jo, Michelle, and Christie were last seen enjoying dinner together. They left the hotel around sunset, and the final photo taken with their camera depicted the bay from their balcony. Tragically, they were never seen alive again.

THREE BODIES FOUND

On June 4th, 1989, passengers aboard a sailboat returning to Tampa spotted a body floating in the water and promptly contacted the Coast Guard. The rescue boat discovered a partially clothed female with her hands and feet bound and a rope around her neck, tethered to a submerged heavy object. The rescuers cut the rope and transported the body to the Coast Guard station.

As the boat approached the shore, they received another call regarding a second body in the bay. Similarly, this female was bound and had a rope around her neck tied to a heavy object. Shortly after, a third call reported yet another body nearby. All three bodies were in advanced stages of decomposition, but the victims appeared young.

The Coast Guard retrieved two concrete blocks tied to the second and third bodies. Each victim had duct tape over their mouths and were bound in a similar fashion. Although water had washed away any DNA evidence, investigators from the Tampa Bay Police Department surmised that the women had likely been sexually assaulted, given their state of undress.

With no visible wounds on the victims, it was theorized that the women had been tied to the concrete blocks and thrown into the water alive. Autopsies later confirmed they had died of asphyxiation. The investigators struggled to identify the bodies, left with only the victims' clothing and jewelry as clues.

A week later, a maid at the Days Inn in Tampa reported that the personal belongings in Room 251 had been left untouched for several days. Detectives arrived to examine the room, lifting fingerprints that matched those of the bodies found in the bay. They also learned the victims' names from the registration form and contacted the Van Wert County Sheriff's Office in Ohio. Dental records confirmed the identities of the three victims. Hal Rogers, anxiously awaiting the return of his family, was informed they would never be coming home.

The registration form also indicated that the victims had been traveling in a blue Calais, which was later found parked near a boat ramp by the Courtney Campbell Parkway. Inside, police discovered handwritten notes on Days Inn stationery with directions from the motel to the ramp, indicating that the Rogers family had planned to meet someone with a blue and white boat.

A Clearwater Beach brochure with written directions to the motel was also found in the car, suggesting the family had made a stop before arriving at their accommodation. While liaising with detectives from the Van Wert County Sheriff's Office, Tampa investigators learned about the fraught relationship between Michelle and John Rogers, which raised the possibility that John had arranged the murders from prison. A special task force was formed to solve the case, but they were hindered by the lack of a crime scene or physical evidence on the bodies.

Tidal experts from the University of South Florida confirmed that the victims had been dropped from a boat in Tampa Bay, not from a bridge or shore. Investigators retraced the family's journey using receipts and credit card transactions, interviewing staff who had encountered the victims. The media helped publicize the case, informing the Tampa Bay area that Jo, Michelle, and Christie had been lured to their deaths by someone with a blue and white boat.

Two Florida detectives visited the Rogers farm to speak with Hal and gather more information about the victims. Although they soon determined that John Rogers had been unaware of the vacation and it was unlikely he had arranged the murders, they couldn't rule out Hal as a suspect. A few days after his family's disappearance, Hal had withdrawn $7,000 from the bank. He explained that he had planned to travel to Florida and search for them, and he still had the money in his possession.

Despite the ongoing investigation and his shock, Hal continued to run the farm with the help of friends. Detectives eventually concluded that Hal couldn't have traveled to Florida, committed the murders, and returned to Ohio in time to manage the farm.

SURVIVOR JUDY BLAIR

As the months passed without any leads, the special task force began to shrink. However, lead detective Jim Kappel remained determined. In October 1989, a fellow officer suggested he examine the monthly bulletin of unsolved cases, as one case of a sexual assault near Madeira Beach might pique his interest.

Detective Kappel discovered that on May 15th, 1989, a 24-year-old Canadian tourist named Judy Blair had been assaulted on a boat by a man she met during her vacation. He owned a blue and white boat, just like the one mentioned in the Rogers' case. Wanting to interview Blair, Kappel traveled to Canada. Blair recounted that she and a friend had met a man in his 30s, Dave Posner, at a parking lot in front of a 7-Eleven. He seemed polite and harmless, offering to take them for a boat ride the next day.

While Blair enjoyed the first boat trip, her friend declined to join them on the second outing. Everything seemed normal at first, but Dave suddenly began acting strangely, demanding sex and ultimately assaulting Blair. He then apologized, instructing her to get dressed, clean herself, and swim back to shore.

After interviewing Blair, Kappel became convinced that the same man had murdered the Rogers family. Blair helped detectives create a second sketch of her attacker, which was sent to the local media. Hundreds of tips poured in, but none led the detectives to the killer.

COLD CASE

As the first anniversary of the brutal murders of Jo, Michelle, and Christie Rogers approached in the spring of 1990, the case had gone cold. It was at this time that Glen

Moore, a newly appointed sergeant, requested a review of the case. Moore believed that retesting the evidence and involving new investigators might finally bring a resolution to the haunting crime.

Moore and his team meticulously sifted through the available files, focusing on a brochure found in Jo's car that contained directions to the motel. They discovered an unknown set of fingerprints on the brochure and requested assistance from the FBI's behavioral science unit to develop a profile of the killer. In the spring of 1991, the profile revealed that the killer was likely a serial murderer in his 30s or 40s, intelligent, charming, and friendly. He meticulously planned the murders and derived pleasure from his victims' suffering. The FBI deduced that he had probably assaulted or killed someone prior to the triple murder and was familiar with Tampa Bay, suggesting he was a local resident.

In the spring of 1992, almost three years after the murders, investigators theorized that the person who wrote down the directions to the motel on the brochure could be the killer. The handwriting didn't match Jo or her daughters. The police distributed photos of the handwriting to the media and placed it on billboards throughout Tampa Bay, hoping for a breakthrough.

Jo Ann Steffey, a Tampa resident, closely followed the case since the release of the sketches connected to the sexual assault in Madeira Beach. The drawings bore a striking resemblance to her neighbor, who owned a blue and white boat and lived just a couple of miles from the boat ramp where Jo's car was discovered. Though her neighbor appeared amiable and helpful, Steffey couldn't shake her suspicions about his darker side.

Steffey confided in a Hillsborough County sheriff's deputy, who attended an accounting class with her, and he promised to relay the information. As months went by, Steffey's convictions only grew stronger. In the summer of 1990, her neighbor moved away from Dalton Avenue, and the handwriting samples were published in newspapers on May 14th, 1992. Recalling that her former neighbor had built a porch for her friend Mozelle Smith, Steffey and Smith compared the handwriting on the contract to the sample, and it was a match.

Steffey and Smith contacted the task force and faxed the handwriting samples, identifying the neighbor as 45-year-old Oba Chandler. Despite receiving hundreds of tips, the police eventually followed up on Steffey and Smith's lead in July 1992.

OBA CHANDLER

Born in 1946 in Cincinnati, Ohio, Oba Chandler grew up with his parents and four siblings. Following his father's suicide when he was only 10, Chandler's life took a dark turn, and he began stealing cars at the age of 14. Throughout his life, he faced numerous criminal charges, including armed robbery, burglary, and kidnapping.

On May 14th, 1988, Chandler married Debra Ann Whiteman, and the couple bought a house on Dalton Avenue in December of the same year. In February 1989, they had a daughter. After verifying that Chandler owned a blue and white Bayliner in 1989 and sold it three months after the murders, the investigators started to piece together a clearer picture of their suspect.

In the summer of 1990, the family moved from Tampa Bay to Port Orange on Florida's east coast. Chandler continued working as an unlicensed aluminum-siding contractor.

After Judy Blair identified Chandler in a photo lineup as her assailant, and handwriting experts confirmed he wrote the directions on the brochure found in Jo's car, investigators placed him under surveillance throughout September 1992. On September 24th, they arrested Chandler and charged him with sexual battery. He immediately requested a lawyer. The palm print on the brochure also matched Chandler's, further proving his connection to the murdered women.

The state attorney's office demanded more evidence before charging Chandler with the murders, so investigators turned to his family. Kristal Mays, one of Chandler's children from a previous marriage, cooperated with the police. She revealed that her father had visited her in Cincinnati in 1989 and claimed he was wanted for murder in Florida. Kristal's husband corroborated the story, adding that Chandler confessed to rape and murder. This information was sufficient for a murder charge.

The trial began in September 1994. Chandler testified that

he had only given directions to the motel to the Rogers family and denied any further involvement. He claimed he had been fishing alone in Tampa Bay on the night of the murders.

The prosecution called Judy Blair and her friend to testify against Chandler. Blair once again identified Chandler as her assailant. Chandler's daughter Kristal also testified against her father.

On November 4th, 1994, the jury found Oba Chandler guilty of the murders and sentenced him to death. He maintained his innocence and continued to file appeals from prison.

On November 15th, 2011, Chandler was executed by lethal injection at Florida State Prison in Raiford. He claimed his innocence until the very end.

THE MURDER OF IVELISSE BERRIOS-BEGUERISSE

On February 25th, 2014, over three years after Chandler's execution, DNA evidence revealed that he was responsible for the murder of 20-year-old Ivelisse Berrios-Beguerisse on November 27th, 1990. She worked at the Sawgrass Mills Mall and didn't return home after her shift. Her car was found in the parking lot with slashed tires.

Her lifeless body was discovered hours after she was

reported missing and showed signs of bruising on her legs and arms. She had packing tape stuck in her hair, and she had been sexually assaulted and strangled. If it weren't for Chandler's execution, he would have been charged with her murder.

DIVORCE COURT

> "This was not a quick death. She clearly struggled for quite a while. This is not only somebody who wanted to kill her but wanted to make her suffer. It's clear to the medical examiner and to us that she was grabbing onto the murder weapon, and it's in desperation, and it almost cuts her fingers off."
>
> KELLY KONCKI, KENT COUNTY PROSECUTOR

In the warm month of August 2006, a teacher and nurse from Rockford, Michigan was brutally murdered in her own home as she recuperated from surgery. The case remained unsolved for almost 14 years before finally reaching its conclusion with a surprising twist in 2020.

Renee Beth Pagel, born on July 29th, 1965, in Grand Rapids, Michigan, was the daughter of Forrest and Doris DeMaagd. Raised in a devout Christian household, Renee regularly attended church and was known for her generosity, kindness, and enthusiasm for helping others. She initially worked as a nurse at Forest View Hospital before transitioning to a health instructor role at Kent Career Technical Center.

In 1995, Renee married Michael Pagel, and they settled in Rockford, Michigan, where they had three children—twins Sarah and Joel in 1999 and Hannah in 2003.

According to friends and family, Michael and Renee initially appeared to have a loving relationship. They doted on their children and were seemingly an ideal couple. After almost a decade of marriage, their relationship started to crumble.

Renee, as the primary breadwinner, held multiple jobs, while Michael chose to stay home with their children, only occasionally taking on part-time work. This disparity created tension between the couple, and in 2005, Michael served Renee with divorce papers in the middle of one of her classes. Despite this, the couple managed to successfully co-parent, with Michael moving out of the family home and living on a farm. He continued to take care of the children whenever Renee had to work long hours.

A SELFLESS ACT

In the summer of 2006, Renee discovered that one of her students was particularly interested in kidney disease due to her father's own battle with kidney failure. Renee, moved by the girl's plight, offered to get tested as a potential kidney donor for the girl's father. Days later, Renee found out she was a match and told her student that she would indeed donate her kidney to the student's father. In July 2006, her friends threw her a surprise 41st birthday party shortly before the scheduled surgery. During her recovery, Renee's children stayed with their father, while friends and family occasionally visited her to ensure she was doing well, as the surgery had been a success for both parties.

A HORRIFYING MURDER

On Saturday, August 5th, 2006, Renee had planned to meet a friend. When she failed to show up, the friend contacted Renee's father, Forrest, who, along with his wife, went to Renee's house to check on her. There, they discovered their daughter lying in bed, her sheets drenched in blood. Distraught, Forrest called 911. He initially thought that Renee's death was related to a complication from her recent surgery.

The Kent County Sheriff's Department arrived quickly. Officers noticed that there were defensive cuts on Renee's arms, hands, and even her feet. Items were knocked over close to the bed, and there was blood splatter on the walls.

Renee's body lay tangled in several blankets. They knew this was now a murder investigation, and they called in detectives.

Renee had been brutally murdered, with over 50 stab wounds covering her body. The medical examiner said the cause of death was multiple stab wounds, with the most severe being a deep incision to the carotid artery, leading to massive blood loss and, ultimately, Renee's death.

Renee's jewelry and money were untouched, so robbery was ruled out as a motive. There were no signs of forced entry, suggesting either that Renee had left her door unlocked or the killer had a key to her home. The murder weapon, later identified as a military-style knife, was not found at the scene. However, investigators discovered a seemingly new, clean orange flashlight behind Renee's home, which they believed the killer had dropped.

Family, friends, and neighbors were shocked by the news of Renee's murder. Renee had no known enemies. However, upon learning of her ongoing divorce from her ex-husband, Michael, investigators decided to question him.

A FAMILY ALIBI

Several hours after the gruesome discovery of Renee's body, detectives from the Kent County Sheriff's Department headed to Michael Pagel's farm. There, they encountered his mother, Patricia, who informed them that

Michael was attending an Alcoholics Anonymous meeting. She had traveled from nearby Saginaw to help care for the children. Detectives inquired about Michael's whereabouts the previous night without revealing that Renee had been murdered.

Patricia told them that Michael and the children had spent the evening at home, enjoying a bonfire in the yard before falling asleep together in the front room. She recalled waking up in the middle of the night and seeing Michael asleep, though she did hear the front door open and assumed someone had let the dog out.

While Patricia spoke with the detectives, Michael returned home and was told of Renee's death. Michael's alibi wasn't particularly strong, so he remained on the suspect list. However, the investigators learned that Renee had a tenant living in an apartment above the barn on her property.

This tenant had been on the property at the time of the murder and detectives heard from Renee's sister, Michelle, that the tenant had been late with his rent payments and had expressed romantic interest in Renee.

Renee's tenant claimed he hadn't heard anything the night Renee was murdered, which surprised the investigators. The attack on Renee and her death had been extremely violent and lasted several minutes as she fought her attacker. She had likely screamed multiple times for help.

The tenant willingly provided the police with a DNA sample and fingerprints and allowed them to search his apartment. He was brought to the police station for a four-hour interrogation, during which he passed a lie detector test. He admitted to having been unemployed for months and being late with rent payments for a few months, but Renee had been understanding and not upset with him for the delays. He was up-to-date on his rent at the time of the murder. Moreover, the tenant exhibited no bruises or scratches, which investigators expected to find on Renee's assailant. Lacking a motive or evidence to connect the tenant to the murder, the police removed him from the suspect list.

BO PAGEL

During conversations with Renee's friends, the police learned about her aversion to Charles "Bo" Pagel, her brother-in-law. Bo allegedly harbored animosity toward Renee, believing that his brother had made a mistake in marrying her. Renee sensed something off about Bo and refused to allow her children to be alone with him. Several days after the murder, Bo Pagel was interviewed by the police. At the time, he worked as a truck driver and claimed to have been in Saginaw on the night of the murder. Bo insisted he had slept through the night and then went kayaking with his children the following morning. The investigators noticed one scratch on his arm, which Bo attributed to a dog.

As the investigation unfolded, law enforcement gathered more information about Michael and the ongoing divorce. Renee's family and friends described how Michael's behavior had become increasingly hostile toward his ex-wife in the year leading up to her death. He sought to acquire the family home, which Renee had purchased, as well as full custody of their children and child support payments, effectively leaving Renee with nothing.

In June 2006, the couple appeared in court, where the judge informed Michael that he needed to get a full-time job, as he would be required to pay child support to Renee. She would retain the family home, and they would share custody of the children. Michael's fury was palpable, and Renee confided to her friends that she had never seen him so angry.

Despite interrogating several potential suspects, Michael remained the prime focus of the investigation. In the months following Renee's murder, police searched his house but found no evidence linking him to the crime. However, they did uncover journals in which he had written hateful things about Renee, dating back years before their divorce.

Investigators were aware of the weakness in Michael's alibi, so they attempted to glean more information from his mother, Patricia. Their second interview proved fruitless, as Patricia had altered her story entirely, now insisting that no one had left the house that night. It was evident she was protecting her son.

During an interrogation, Michael declined to discuss his relationship with Renee or their divorce. He reiterated his mother's version of events, maintaining that he had not left the house on the night of the murder. Despite appearing guilty, the police were unable to prove that he had been at Renee's home on August 5th. Consequently, the case went cold.

Years passed, but Renee's friends refused to abandon her memory. They continued to post flyers throughout Rockford, hoping someone would come forward with new information. One friend, Chris, called the Kent County Sheriff's Department weekly to inquire about the investigation's progress. Chris also created a Facebook page to keep the case alive. Meanwhile, Renee's children relocated to Saginaw with Michael to start anew.

TWELVE YEARS LATER

In 2018, a new lead detective was assigned to the case and decided to reexamine the evidence from scratch. The orange flashlight caught his attention, prompting him to investigate the manufacturer and serial number. It turned out that these flashlights were sold in two-packs in 2006, and Michael owned the matching blue flashlight. Although the serial numbers matched, this evidence was not conclusive.

Nearly 14 years after the murder, Bo contacted Renee's friend Chris on Facebook, claiming they needed to talk. The police advised her to record the conversation, which she did. Bo revealed that Michael carried a loaded gun and behaved erratically, adding that he was unsure of his brother's innocence and feared for his own safety.

In early 2020, as the police conducted interviews with everyone connected to the case, it seemed that Bo wanted to talk. Aware of his relationship with Michael, they didn't press him but encouraged him to reach out if he wished to disclose more information. Shortly after, Bo's attorney contacted the police, informing them that his client was ready to talk.

According to Bo, he and Michael were driving around Saginaw in August 2011. Bo was searching for deer while Michael relaxed in the passenger seat with a beer. They stopped at Birch Run Creek, where Michael pulled a rag from his pocket, which contained a large knife. He threw the knife into the creek, claiming that this act "finalized the divorce." Michael then threatened Bo to stay silent about the incident saying, “I f—ed her up, and if you tell anybody, I’m gonna f— you up too.”

Later that day, Bo spoke to their mother about what had transpired. She urged him to wait until she passed away before taking any action. Patricia passed away in September 2019, and a few months later, Bo finally opened up.

The police needed the murder weapon, so they asked Bo to pinpoint the exact location where it had been tossed into the water. A search team arrived at Birch Run Creek in February 2020 and used a large industrial magnet to dredge the creek. After three days, they successfully recovered the knife, which matched the wounds inflicted on Renee. On February 6th, 2020, Michael Pagel was arrested for Renee Pagel's murder.

Rene's friend Chris, who had supported the investigation throughout the years, said to the media when Michael Pagel was arrested:

> "This is a great day. I am overwhelmed with happiness that justice will be served and Renee will be able to rest in peace. I feel a huge weight has been lifted off of me."

Shortly after his arrest, Michael accepted a plea deal. He was charged with second-degree murder and faced a minimum of 25 years in prison. Michael pleaded guilty in May 2020 and surprised everyone with his version of events. According to Michael, he had paid his brother Bo $100,000 to kill Renee.

Although no one believed his claims, the police were obligated to investigate. They found no evidence to suggest that Bo had killed Renee or received the money from Michael. In October 2020, Michael Pagel was sentenced to 25 to 50 years in prison for the murder of Renee Pagel.

ECHOES OF INJUSTICE

"Kathy Page was not killed in her vehicle. She was killed at another location, cleaned up, redressed, and placed back in her vehicle, and after that, the vehicle had been rolled into the ditch."

DETECTIVE SERGEANT RAY MOSELEY, VIDOR POLICE DEPARTMENT

The brutal murder of 34-year-old Lucille Katherine Page, a devoted mother of two, in Vidor, Texas, prompted her grief-stricken father to erect billboards on the outskirts of the small town, accusing the only suspect in the case — her own husband. Despite his tireless pursuit of justice, the murder of Kathy Page remains unsolved.

Born in 1957 in Hollandale, Mississippi, Lucille Katherine Page, affectionately known as Kathy, was the daughter of Dorothy and James Fulton. Growing up in Vidor, Texas, Kathy shared a close bond with her siblings. It was in this close-knit community that she met her future husband, Steve Page, a charismatic insurance salesman from an affluent family who quickly won the hearts of Kathy's family.

The couple tied the knot on November 18th, 1978, and soon welcomed their two daughters, Erin Michelle and Monica Nicole. The family resided in a cozy house on a quiet, dead-end street near Interstate 10. Unfortunately, their marriage was tumultuous, marked by periods of separation. In May 1991, Kathy resolved to divorce Steve, who reluctantly agreed to move out of the family home. He rented an apartment close by, across the interstate from the Page residence, and committed to co-parenting their daughters.

Steve maintained that their separation was temporary, a mere hiccup resulting from the couple drifting apart. He was convinced they would reconcile shortly. However, Kathy's friends and family painted a different picture, asserting that she was ready to embrace life without Steve and was even dating someone new.

On May 13th, 1991, just one day after Steve relocated, Kathy asked her husband to care for their girls that night, as she planned to visit a bar in Beaumont with her friend, Charlotte. Earlier that day, Steve and Kathy had attended their daughters' baseball game together.

Charlotte later confirmed that Kathy called her between 9:30 and 10 pm, advising her to ignore her phone as Steve would likely be monitoring her. Kathy intended to rendezvous with her new boyfriend, Tom, and enlisted Charlotte to provide her with an alibi. Steve arrived at the house after 10:30 pm, finding Kathy preparing to leave. He stated that she departed between 11:15 and 11:30 pm.

Kathy met with Tom at a hotel in Beaumont, where the couple rented a room. She left at around 2:30 am. Charlotte received a mysterious phone call, but the caller disconnected without speaking. She presumed it was Steve calling to check on Kathy.

THIS WAS NO ACCIDENT

At 4:20 am on May 14th, 1991, a paperboy stumbled upon Kathy's Mercury Tracer submerged in a drainage ditch only 100 yards from her home. Kathy was in the car. The car was oriented away from the house and exhibited minimal damage. Investigators found no skid marks, suggesting that the vehicle had been deliberately rolled into the ditch.

Initially appearing as a tragic accident, the scene soon transformed into a chilling murder investigation. Numerous clues indicated that the crash site was staged. Kathy's feet were tucked tight against the seat rather than extended. She wasn't wearing a seatbelt, and her back was pressed against the seat, her lifeless body sitting upright.

When police visited the Page residence to inquire if anyone was home, Steve, clad in his boxer shorts, answered the door. Upon being asked about Kathy's whereabouts, he stated she wasn't home. Strangely, before learning about Kathy's death, he glanced in the direction of her car. When detectives entered the house, they informed Steve of Kathy's passing. At first, he reacted with tears and emotional outbursts, throwing himself onto the couch. However, he soon resumed speaking as if nothing had transpired. Steve's peculiar behavior and actions led investigators to suspect that he might be behind Kathy's staged accident and subsequent murder.

A meticulous examination of Kathy's vehicle unearthed several puzzling clues that strongly indicated the accident scene had been fabricated. For one, the rearview mirror was askew, leading detectives to surmise that the individual who positioned Kathy in the car had inadvertently bumped it. Moreover, blades of grass clung to Kathy's jeans, suggesting she had been dragged to the car at some point.

During the autopsy, the medical examiner found no external injuries except for a laceration at the back of Kathy's head. Her nose was fractured, and she sported a black eye, neither of which could be attributed to the car crash. The official cause of death was established as manual strangulation. Bloodstains were found on her underwear, yet her clothes remained unblemished.

Interestingly, Kathy was found without makeup or jewelry. According to her boyfriend, Tom, she had been wearing both when she left the hotel room at 2:30 am. Kathy's family attested that she habitually removed her jewelry before going to bed, leading them to believe that she had returned home and met her untimely end there. Semen was detected in her vagina, indicative of intercourse prior to her death. Shockingly, the sample contained no spermatozoids and originated from someone who had undergone a vasectomy. While Tom confirmed that they had been intimate before the murder, it was Steve who had had a vasectomy.

Confronted with this evidence, Steve insisted that he and Kathy had engaged in intercourse before she left for Beaumont. However, Kathy's family and friends disputed this claim, revealing that the estranged couple hadn't been intimate for some time, with Steve sleeping on the couch for months. Kathy's sisters expressed doubt that she would sleep with her ex-husband before meeting her new boyfriend.

THE BOYFRIEND

Tom, Kathy's boyfriend, fully cooperated with the police and immediately went to the station upon learning about her death. He wasn't a Beaumont native, having met Kathy while she worked at the Hoffbrau Restaurant. Tom typically stayed at the Best Western International Hotel when in town, and the couple decided to rendezvous there on the evening of May 13th. He consented to a polygraph test and passed it, leading to his elimination as a suspect.

The Fulton family approached the police several days after the murder to report a series of peculiar behaviors exhibited by Steve. One of Kathy's sisters claimed that he was doing laundry the morning after Kathy's body was discovered. He was also spotted cleaning the living room carpet, explaining that he had spilled fish grease on it.

Investigators also observed odd behavior. For example, Steve refused to allow the medical examiner to conduct an autopsy on Kathy's body. The autopsy was ultimately authorized by her father, James. Steve also denied investigators entry into the house, asserting that they might discover traces of Kathy's blood in the living room and misinterpret it as a crime scene. He explained that Kathy often shaved her legs on the living room floor.

Sherry, one of Kathy's sisters, spoke with Steve's sister-in-law and discovered that he had found two phone numbers on a piece of paper when Kathy left for Beaumont. He called both numbers on the night of the murder. The first belonged to Kathy's friend Charlotte, and the second was for the Best Western International Hotel. This led the Fulton family to deduce that he likely suspected Kathy had moved on and was seeing another man that night. They theorized that he confronted her upon her return home, sexually assaulted and strangled her, and subsequently staged the car accident to conceal the murder.

During police questioning, Steve claimed that a powerful member of the Beaumont mafia had conspired to frame him for the crime. The Fulton family, on the other hand, accused the Vidor Police Department of deliberately mishandling the investigation, alleging that they did so because Steve and his parents were close friends with the chief of police, and that Steve and Detective Ray Mosely, who was leading the investigation, had grown up on the same street. This theory may have some validity, as the police failed to collect photos of the crime scene due to an apparent lack of film in the camera. Furthermore, they searched the Page family home three years after the murder but found no physical evidence linking Steve to the crime.

After Kathy's funeral, the Fulton family hired a private detective who caught Steve on tape vandalizing Kathy's grave. James Fulton, Kathy's father, responded by putting up billboards on the side of the road, hoping to draw attention to his daughter's case and pressure the police into solving it. The billboards initially contained written statements aimed at the investigators but eventually included Steve's and Kathy's photos. James vowed to keep the billboards up until Steve was convicted, disregarding Steve's complaints that they were ruining his life.

Three small hand-painted billboards:

Vidor Police

Botched UP

The CASE

WAITING FOR

CONFESSION

THIS COULD

Happen To

You!

Large Billboard 1:

Steve Page

Brutally Murdered his Wife in 1991

Vidor P.D. Does not Want to Solve This Case

I Believe They Took A Bribe

The Attorney General Should Investigate

James Fulton-Her Father

Large Billboard 2:

In '91, Here in Vidor-He got by with MURDER

•Found Responsible for Wife's Death in Civil Court

•Appeals Court Upheld Conviction

•Pleaded "Guilty" of Desecrating her Grave

CRIMINAL CASE: NO ARRESTS

Did the Police Take a Bribe???

In 1995, Steve moved to Houston, Texas, and sent his two daughters to live with his parents in Huntsville, Alabama, cutting them off from Kathy's family. Steve was willing to co-parent with Kathy, but he wasn't ready to be a single father. He eventually remarried and became a carpenter.

In 1999, the Fulton family sued Steve in civil court, and after hearing all the evidence, the jury found Steve's version of the events to be untrue, ordering him to pay $261,780 to James Fulton.

In 2018, the film Three Billboards Outside Ebbing, Missouri, directed by Martin McDonagh, was released and was inspired by Kathy's murder case. The film garnered seven Oscar nominations and won two awards. This brought Kathy's case to the public's attention, giving it more publicity than ever before.

Despite efforts to reopen the case, no arrest has been made, and in 2021, Crime Stoppers increased the reward to $50,000. Erin Page, Kathy's older daughter, runs a blog called A Billboard in Texas, where she discusses the case. Tragically, Kathy's younger daughter, Monica, passed away in 2011 from a drug overdose.

THE FORT

"This case is about the defendant's lifelong pattern of sexually assaulting children. He has done nothing but leave a trail of victims throughout his life."

PROSECUTOR VALERIE SUMMERS

In March 1993, two boys were biking and having fun on a Saturday afternoon. Unfortunately, they never made it home. They were found brutally murdered three days after their disappearance. The families waited for eight years to get answers.

Charles Allen Keever, also known as Charlie, was born on November 1st, 1979, to his parents, David and Maria Keever. He had two older siblings, Lisa and Michael. Charlie was friends with the Sellers children and often spent time with Alton Williams II and his younger brother Jonathan.

Jonathan Lee Sellers was born on April 18th, 1983, to parents Dennis and Milena Sellers. He was the fourth of six children. Jonathan had a twin sister, Jennifer. Little Jonathan loved spending time on the basketball court and dreamed of becoming a professional player one day. In 1993, his mother bought him a bike as an early birthday present.

Charlie and Alton would often ride bikes together and explore their neighborhood. But now that Jonathan had a bike, too, he tagged along regularly. When they were out, the group would sometimes go to Otay River, where they biked on the riverbank. Nearby was an oddly shaped bush they considered their fort.

On the morning of March 27th, 1993, Charlie Keever arrived at the Sellers' house because he had planned to go bike riding with Alton Williams. It was Saturday, and the boys, both 13 years old, had the whole day ahead of them. However, Alton wasn't able to go out, so his younger brother, Jonathan, who was nine years old, stepped in. Before the boys rode off on their bikes, Jonathan's twin sister Jennifer asked if she could come. Jonathan insisted he didn't want a girl with them, so their mother, Milena, told Jennifer she could join them some other day.

The boys left the house around noon on their 20-inch bikes and headed straight to Imperial Beach. They ate at Rally's, a popular fast-food restaurant in San Diego, and spent some time in the arcade. Their next stop was a pet store, where the boys played with some of the animals and talked to the staff about the different breeds of dogs and cats. Once the boys left the pet store, they were never seen alive again.

Since they failed to return home by nightfall, Milena Sellers contacted Maria Keever to check if the boys were at their house. Suspecting they might be lost, the mothers contacted local law enforcement. Jonathan's older brother Alton mentioned to his mother that the boys usually biked on a riverbank trail by the Otay River.

The two went there to look for them, but there were no traces of the boys anywhere. Alton forgot to mention the igloo-shaped bush they usually crawled into. On March 28th, search parties combed the neighborhood in search of Charlie and Jonathan. Again, nothing was found.

On March 29th, 1993, a man riding a bike on the riverbank noticed something odd in the bushes. He stopped and went in to investigate. The man was shocked to see a boy hanging from a castor bean tree. Police officers arrived on the scene shortly, and they were also shocked by what they saw. The boy hanging from a branch was identified as Jonathan Sellers. His hands and feet were tied together, and he was gagged.

Charlie Keever was found on the ground nearby, lying on a neatly folded pile of clothes. His hands and feet were also bound. Both boys had been sexually assaulted, as evident by the deep bite marks around their genitals. The medical examiner discovered foreign tissue samples in Charlie's mouth and sent them for analysis. At that point, the police had tissue containing DNA from the killer, but they had nothing to compare it to at that time.

The police received hundreds of tips in the months following the murders, but they weren't any closer to finding the killer. Wanting to help, CrimeStoppers offered a $10,000 reward for any information that would lead to the person responsible for the murders, but the case went cold.

THE DNA MATCH

In March 2001, the San Diego Police Cold Case Unit reopened the investigation into the murders of Charlie Keever and Jonathan Sellers. The investigators went over the evidence collected from the bodies and the crime scene and sent it for DNA testing. Swabs from Charlie's mouth and cigarette butts from the crime scene had the same DNA profile.

Once that DNA profile was entered into CODIS, the investigators had a hit. The DNA belonged to Scott Erskine, who was currently incarcerated in San Quentin State Prison. Erskine had a long history of sexual assaults that began when he was only 10 years old.

ERSKINE'S BACKGROUND

Scott Erskine was born on December 22nd, 1962, and

spent his childhood in Southern California. When he was five, Erskine ran into traffic on the Pacific Coast Highway and was hit by a vehicle. He was in a coma for 60 hours. Erskine recovered from his injuries, but according to his mother, he sometimes suffered from blackouts.

When he was 10 years old, Erskine sexually assaulted his six-year-old sister. He then began abusing his friends. As a teen, he was sent to a juvenile detention center, but Erskine escaped and sexually assaulted a 13-year-old girl at knifepoint. The following morning, he attacked a female jogger.

By 1980, Erskine was out of the juvenile detention center and was trying to become a camp counselor. On his way to the interview, Erskine attacked a 14-year-old boy and attempted to assault him. Fortunately, he was stopped, arrested, and sent to jail, where he awaited trial. While there, Erskine assaulted a fellow prisoner.

Since Erskine was still a minor, his mother asked the judge to send her son to a mental institution because he needed help. However, the judge decided to send him to jail. He was sentenced to four years in adult prison and was released in 1984.

Soon after, he met a woman, and the two got married in 1988. The couple moved from San Diego to Orlando, Florida, and welcomed a baby boy, but Erskine's wife soon realized that her husband was a cruel person. He regularly beat her and had also attacked her while she was pregnant.

Soon after giving birth, Erskine's wife left him, and he moved back to San Diego, California.

In late 1993, Erskine invited a woman he saw at a bus station to his house. He imprisoned the woman and held her hostage for days. She was raped and sodomized during that time. Erskine let the woman go, and she didn't hesitate to go to the police and report what had happened to her. Erskine was arrested and found guilty of multiple charges. After being sentenced to 70 years behind bars, he became a registered sex offender. This required him to submit his DNA to CODIS, which eventually led cold case detectives straight to Erskine in 2001.

THE MURDER OF RENEE BAKER:

Erskine's trial was scheduled for September 2003, and during this time, investigators in Florida had a breakthrough in one of their unsolved cases – the murder of Renee Baker from June 1989. Detectives got a DNA match through CODIS.

In 1989, Erskine lived in Florida with his then-wife. He sexually assaulted Renee Baker, broke her neck, and left the young woman to drown. The medical examiner collected DNA samples from the murder scene, and the case was finally solved in 2001. Detectives from Palm Beach County suspect that Erskine is behind several more murders that occurred when he resided in Florida.

THE TRIAL

The trial for the murders of Charlie Keever and Jonathan Sellers began in September 2003. Erskine's defense lawyer argued that he committed the murders because of the brain injury he suffered when he was five years old. According to his lawyer, Erskine was unable to control himself and couldn't recognize that his behavior was not acceptable. Regardless, the prosecution asked for the death penalty.

The jury found Erskine guilty of murder on October 1st, 2003. However, they were unable to reach a unanimous verdict regarding his sentence. Eleven jurors were for the death penalty, and one juror was for a life sentence without the possibility of parole. In April 2004, Erskine appeared again in front of another jury, and they voted for the death penalty. He was sent to San Quentin.

> "I'm so happy. I'm so relieved. It's like a weight has been lifted off my chest. I knew this day would come. I never lost faith...I never gave up hope. I always knew they would catch him. It's just too bad he's going to die so easy."
>
> MARIA KEEVER, MOTHER OF CHARLIE KEEVER

Erskine filed several appeals since 2004, and all of them were rejected. He refused to speak to the families of his victims, even though Maria Keever tried to get in touch with Erskine for years. The mother wanted to know what really happened on the day of the murders and how he managed to lure the boys into the bushes. Unfortunately, she never got the answer.

On July 3rd, 2020, Scott Erskine died from COVID-19. He was hospitalized for days after contracting the virus. Ersk-ine's health had been in decline in the years before his death, and he had heart and lung problems long before the pandemic.

THE EYEBALL KILLER

"He was kind of a renaissance man. He could sing... he sung at churches and stuff. He played piano and organ. He painted. And oh, by the way, he might have been the one who killed prostitutes and cut their eyeballs out."

BRAD LOLLAR, CHARLES ALBRIGHT'S DEFENSE LAWYER

At the beginning of the 1990s, Dallas was terrorized by a murderer nicknamed the Eyeball Killer. This unknown individual frequented red-light districts and targeted sex workers for several months before being caught.

Charles Frederick Albright was born in 1933, in Amarillo, Texas. He was adopted two weeks later by Delle and Fred Albright, a middle-class couple from Dallas. The Albright family lived in Oak Cliff, a beautiful residential area. Fred worked in a grocery store, while Delle was a teacher. She adored her son and was often overprotective.

During his childhood, he received a lot of attention and care from his family. Delle was a germaphobe, so proper hygiene was a top priority in the house. On occasion, when Albright's aunt was around, he was dressed in feminine clothing and gifted with a toy. Albright was told by his adoptive mother that his birth mother was a 16-year-old law student who got pregnant, and her father forced her to give the baby up for adoption. It is unclear if this story was true or not.

Regardless, Delle expected Albright to be an exceptional student, and she worked with him daily. As a result, Albright skipped two grades. Delle talked to Albright about her relationship with his father, hoping her son would be a better man than Fred. When he was old enough to date, Delle wanted him to be respectful toward his girlfriends.

A CHANGE IN BEHAVIOR

Albright's parents got him a gun as a gift, and he used it to start shooting and killing birds in his neighborhood in his early teens. Delle spent a lot of time with Albright and was determined to stop the bird killing. She enrolled Albright in a taxidermy class. The teen enjoyed this new hobby, and

Delle displayed his work around the house. She was very proud of how skillful Charles was.

COLLEGE CRIMINAL

After graduating high school at 15, Albright applied to North Texas State College and was accepted. Since he was interested in anatomy, Albright took pre-med classes, hoping to become a doctor one day. However, Albright spent just a few months there because he was arrested for theft. Albright received a two-year sentence and served only six months. After his release, he continued his education at Arkansas State Teachers College.

Albright was a popular student at that college and had many friends. However, the teen was still burglarizing rooms on campus. He was caught with stolen items and expelled before earning his bachelor's degree. Since he wasn't interested in attending yet another college, Albright decided to forge his diploma. He also gave himself a fake master's degree.

CREATING A FAMILY

After Christmas 1954, Albright married his college girlfriend, Bettye Nestor. Nestor became a teacher and gave birth to a daughter. Meanwhile, Albright struggled to keep a job because he would usually get bored after several months.

Nestor worked hard as an educator while her husband

stayed at home and forged checks. The pair had two more children.

Throughout the 1960s, Albright continued to falsify documents and was even employed as a teacher with a fake license. Albright was discovered and arrested less than two years later and sentenced to probation. Nestor and Albright separated in 1975, but stayed married for another decade.

By the end of the 1970s, Albright was a member of St. Bernard's Catholic Church and sang in the choir. He enjoyed helping people and often gave out $100 bills to those who needed the money. Delle Albright passed away in 1981, and her adoptive son was shaken by the news.

Several months later, Albright was arrested for molesting a 14-year-old girl. The girl also attended St. Bernard's Catholic Church, and Albright helped her family financially. Both sides wanted the incident to resolve as quietly as possible. Albright pleaded guilty and received 10 years of probation. Afterward, he would claim that he never touched the girl and was innocent.

Albright's father, Fred, had a heart attack in 1986 and left his son $100,000, along with the family property in Dallas. Soon after, Albright met Dixie Austin, who became his girlfriend. The two moved in together into the Albright family home at 1035 Eldorado, and Austin supported Albright financially after he spent all of the inheritance money.

Albright was well known in red-light districts around the city, but his friends and family had no idea at that time. In October 1990, at the age of 57, Albright found a job delivering newspapers for the Dallas Times Herald. His wife later learned he visited sex workers while working.

MARY LOU PRATT

On December 13th, 1990, a 33-year-old sex worker named Mary Lou Pratt was found murdered on the side of a road in Oak Cliff. The body was discovered by a resident who covered her with a blanket after seeing she was only in a t-shirt and a bra. The woman was beaten and had a gunshot wound in the back of her head. It was later determined she was killed with a .44-caliber pistol.

The officers who arrived first immediately recognized Pratt since she often worked at the nearby Star Hotel. She lived with her parents in south Dallas, and they had no idea she was a sex worker. Unfortunately, Pratt was an addict and spent most of her money on drugs. The investigators didn't have witnesses, but they knew she was killed in another location.

During the autopsy, the pathologist discovered her eyeballs had been removed with surgical precision. The killer was skilled because there were no visible cuts around the eyes. The eyeballs weren't found at the scene, so the investigators assumed the murderer had taken them. The police didn't share this detail with the media, and the murder of Mary Lou Pratt wasn't big news in Dallas at the time.

SUSAN PETERSON

On February 10th, 1991, the body of 27-year-old Susan Peterson was found on the same road in Oak Cliff. Like Pratt, Peterson was a sex worker. She was shot twice in the head and once in the chest. The location of the body suggested there might be a connection between the two murders.

The pathologist confirmed these suspicions after examining the body. Again, the eyeballs were missing and were taken out cleanly. Not wanting to alarm the citizens, the police again withheld information about the killer removing the eyeballs from the victim. However, they posted flyers around Oak Cliff, warning sex workers to stay off the streets.

SHIRLEY WILLIAMS

On March 19th, 1991, Shirley Williams, a 45-year-old sex worker, was found on a road next to an elementary school. It was obvious the killer didn't want to hide the bodies. Williams' eyeballs were also removed, but this time, the murderer didn't do it as precisely as before. The investigators suspected he was interrupted or didn't have enough time to complete what he had started.

The pathologist noted cuts around the eye socket. Furthermore, they discovered a broken blade in her right eye. Williams had visible bruises around her nose and was shot in the head. The investigators theorized the killer got scared by the media attention and started looking for victims in another part of Dallas.

After the second murder, the police were often seen in the red-light districts of Dallas. Some officers were familiar with sex workers in certain areas and talked to them about their clients. Early in the investigation, Veronica Rodriguez told the officers she was attacked by a man who was a regular in Oak Cliff. Rodriguez said that a client named Axton Schindler saved her.

However, the officers encountered Brenda White on a street corner, and she told them about her recent experience with a well-dressed white man with gray hair. He refused to take her to a hotel and wanted to drive her to a secluded location. When Williams said no, the man attacked her, and she used pepper spray to get away.

Thinking there might be more to Rodriguez's story, the investigators looked into Axton Schindler and learned he rented a house at 1035 Eldorado in Oak Cliff. However, the owner of the property was named Fred Albright. They found out Fred Albright owned a house near the elementary school where Williams was discovered. But he couldn't be their suspect because Fred had passed away.

One of the officers remembered the surname Albright and said he had received an anonymous call from a woman claiming to be Mary Lou Pratt's friend. The woman said Pratt dated a nice man who was a bit strange and had a weird obsession with eyes. His name was Charles Albright.

The investigators soon learned he had a lengthy criminal record.

Albright's mugshot was shown to Brenda White, and she pointed him out of a photo lineup. Veronica Rodriguez was more hesitant because she initially claimed to know her attacker. But investigators managed to show her a photo lineup, and she pointed at Albright too.

Charles Albright was arrested on March 22nd, 1991, at his house in Oak Cliff and charged with three counts of murder. He was interrogated for hours but refused to confess to the murders. The police searched his properties in Dallas and didn't find anything to connect him to the killings. He had hidden guns and rifles behind a fireplace, but none was the murder weapon. Despite the lack of physical evidence, the police were sure they had the right guy.

THE TRIAL

Just a couple of days after Albright's arrest, the forensic lab reported that the hairs found on the victims belonged to the suspect. Furthermore, the hairs collected from Albright's vehicle were a match to Pratt and Peterson, and those from Albright's vacuum cleaner matched Williams. The trial began on December 2nd, 1991, and the prosecution used forensic evidence to prove Albright was the killer.

Albright's defense lawyer claimed the evidence was

circumstantial and that Axton Schindler, Albright's tenant, was the murderer. Albright didn't testify in court. On December 19th, 1991, the jury found Charles Albright guilty of the murder of Shirley Williams only, and he was sentenced to life in prison. Albright was incarcerated at the John Montford Psychiatric Unit in Lubbock, Texas. He died in prison on August 22nd, 2020, at the age of 87.

MALL MURDERS

"Why her? Who would kill a little girl like that? I don't feel safe here anymore."

NEIGHBOR SANDRA ROSSI ON THE BOCHICCIO MALL MURDERS

Shopping malls are usually bustling with activity, especially during the holiday season. So it came as a shock to the citizens of Boca Raton when a double murder occurred in broad daylight in one of its most popular shopping centers.

Nancy Bochiccio was born in 1960, in the Bronx, New York. She had an American-Italian upbringing and was known for her charitable nature. Nancy worked as a stock analyst and met her future husband, Philip Hauser, in the 1990s. The couple moved to Boca Raton around the turn of the millennium.

Nancy soon found out that she was pregnant and gave birth to her daughter Joey Noel Bochicchio-Hauser on December 17th, 1999. Although Philip and Nancy eventually divorced in 2006, they remained committed co-parents.

Nancy and Joey lived on Buttonwood Lake Drive in the Hidden Lake Community of Boca Raton. Joey was a polite girl who loved ballet, golf, and cheerleading. She spent her time playing around the family home with their dog, Lindsay. Nancy decided not to date after the divorce and gave all her attention to little Joey. She worked hard to pay Joey's tuition at St. Jude Catholic School.

~

It was the winter of 2007, and Joey had decided to grow out her hair so she could donate it to the *"Locks of Love"* charity organization.

On December 12th, 2007, Joey had a doctor's appointment, so Nancy picked her up from school earlier than usual. Joey was supposed to join her classmates that evening to practice lines for a Christmas play. Mother and daughter drove to the Town Center Mall in the afternoon to do some early holiday shopping.

The surveillance cameras showed they entered the mall at

2:19 pm through Entrance 4 between the Sears and Neiman Marcus department stores. Nancy and Joey exited at 3:11 pm using the same doors. Minutes later, the Palm Beach County Sheriff's Office received a call from Nancy's number. However, the line disconnected before anyone could pick it up. The dispatcher called back, but there was no answer.

The Town Center Mall had closed at 10 pm, and the security guard observed a black Chrysler Aspen SUV in the carpark just before midnight. He approached the vehicle to find its engine still running. It was parked near the Sears department store, adjacent to Entrance 4. An ominous feeling drove him to call Boca Raton Police Services' non-emergency line.

Officers arrived shortly after and found two bodies inside the car. Nancy and Joey Bochicchio were shot execution-style and bound with plastic zip ties and duct tape. Nancy wore goggles with black fabric over the lenses. The forensic team also uncovered handcuffs in the car.

Due to the lack of surveillance cameras at the parking lot, it was impossible to know when the car left or returned to the mall. The police recovered videos from when Nancy and Joey exited, but it seemed like no one had been following them. Therefore, investigators concluded that they were ambushed in the parking lot.

Detectives determined that some of Nancy's belongings were missing from the vehicle, namely her credit cards and cell phone. Several hours after the discovery of the bodies, the police learned that Nancy had withdrawn $500 from a nearby ATM. The security footage shows her pulling up at the ATM after 3 pm. The footage was grainy, but the police believed an adult was sitting in the back seat of Nancy's SUV.

Nancy's missing credit cards were found in Miami. Two homeless men picked them up on the side of the road and used one of the cards. They were questioned by the authorities, but the pair had nothing to do with the double murder.

The public was shocked that a double murder could happen in broad daylight in front of a shopping mall that was usually very crowded. Even though the police didn't have any leads immediately after the murders, they quickly realized they could be connected to two recent crimes that occurred in the Town Center Mall parking lot. One of them was eerily similar.

INCIDENT ONE: THE MURDER OF RANDI GORENBERG

On March 23rd, 2007, Randi Gorenberg, the 52-year-old mother of two, was in the Town Center Mall around noon. She purchased a pair of shorts and a new John Legend CD, then exited the shopping mall through the entrance between the Sears and Neiman Marcus stores. It is unknown what happened after she left because the parking lot wasn't covered by the surveillance cameras.

People in Lawton Chiles Memorial Park, just five miles

from the mall, heard gunshots at around 1:45 pm. The witnesses said they saw a woman being pushed from a black Mercedes-Benz GL450 SUV that sped away immediately after. A 911 call was placed, and the man who contacted law enforcement said the woman was dead.

A black Mercedes-Benz SUV was found at the nearby Home Depot parking lot. The surveillance video showed the SUV was followed by a white Chrysler sedan. The investigators were puzzled by this crime because it looked like a robbery since Randi's purse was stolen. However, she still had all her jewelry and an expensive watch.

The investigators focused on Randi's family first, suspecting that her husband Stuart Gorenberg or son Daniel had something to do with the murder. Daniel provided the police with a false alibi and wasn't very cooperative. However, after years of investigation, both were cleared as suspects.

INCIDENT TWO: THE KIDNAPPING OF JANE DOE

On August 7th, 2007, Jane Doe and her two-year-old son left the Town Center Mall at 1 pm. According to Jane, she placed her boy in the back seat and opened the trunk to put the stroller inside. After climbing into the driver's seat of her SUV, Jane noticed her son sounded scared. She turned around and saw a man sitting next to her son in the back.

He was wearing a floppy hat and wraparound sunglasses. The man had pointed a gun at her son and ordered Jane to drive to an ATM, where she withdrew $600. He told her to go to the Hilton Hotel. Once Jane parked the SUV, the man tied them up using zip ties, duct tape, and handcuffs. Terrified, Jane asked him not to kill them, and the man said they would be fine.

The man then placed blackout sunglasses on Jane and continued driving her vehicle for the next two hours. They returned to the Town Center Mall, where he told Jane he would dial someone from her phone and ordered her to inform them her car had broken down.

Before slamming the car door, the man told Jane to provide a false description of him to the police. Even though he instructed her to wait until her son's father arrived at the parking lot, Jane managed to free herself. She approached the valet and told him she was just kidnapped. He was confused until Jane showed him the handcuffs on her wrists.

The police arrived and didn't believe her story right away. However, after obtaining the traffic videos, they confirmed the movement of her vehicle. Meanwhile, Jane took a lie detector test and passed. Jane Doe's identity was never published. But she provided the investigators with a sketch of the suspect. So when Nancy and Joey Bochicchio were murdered in December 2007, the investigators had a feeling these two cases were connected.

Since Jane Doe had provided the police with the sketch of the man who kidnapped her in August 2007, they had a general idea of how their potential suspect looked. Unfortunately, no leads came in for years. The case was featured on America's Most Wanted three times, but the police weren't any closer to catching the killer.

A promising tip was received in June 2011 after an informant told the investigators about Michel Barrera. According to the informant, he overheard several gang members discuss the mall murders and said that Barrera was the person who killed Randi Gorenberg. The investigation revealed Barrera had access to a white Chrysler sedan at the time of the murder.

It was soon revealed that the police found an unknown DNA profile in Randi's vehicle, but it didn't match Barrera. According to law enforcement, they still haven't identified the person driving Randi's SUV on the day she was killed. The kidnapping of Jane Doe and the murder of Nancy and Joey Bochicchio remains unsolved to this day.

Cathy Strauss, a neighbor of the Bochicchios and an employee of the Town Center Mall in Boca Raton, wrote a letter to the Palm Beach Post one month after Nancy and Joey's murder. The letter, entitled, *Let Murder Victims' Legacy be More Secure Malls,* criticized what she called one of the most affluent malls in America for their lack of security cameras and security staff to protect employees and mall patrons. She was fired from her job at Town Center Mall.

JoAnn Bruno, Nancy's sister, continues to fight for justice.

She believes that the Boca Raton Police Department should release more information about the case to the public because JoAnn thinks someone out there knows something and might be willing to come forward after more than 15 years.

A DOUBLE LIFE

> "One can't even imagine the torture Mr. Merendino experienced. With David behind bars, Jake's loved ones mourn his loss, knowing that, in his final moments, he realized the man he loved had betrayed him. Sadly, the only thing David loved about Jake was his money."
>
> JUDGE JEFFREY T. MILLER

Jake inherited millions from his parents and was living a dream life. He also had a hot new boyfriend who worked in adult movies. Always seeing the best in people, Jake never suspected his boyfriend was living a double life and, from the beginning, had his eyes on Jake's wealth and how he could get all of it – without Jake.

Jake Clyde Merendino was born on September 22nd, 1963, in Beaumont, Texas. He grew up in a wealthy family and attended Monsignor Kelley High School in his teens. Jake's parents, Irene and Charles Merendino worked for Exxon-Mobil and flipped houses in their free time. As a result, the Merendino family earned millions. The money allowed Merendino to travel around the world and build an impressive art collection.

Known as kind and generous, Merendino was a true globe-trotter. In June 2013, he was in San Diego, California, and saw an ad online for a male escort. Merendino hired the young man, invited him to his hotel, and they spent an hour together. That's how Merendino met David Enrique Meza. Merendino fell in love with him immediately and wanted to have Meza in his life forever.

He paid for Meza's trip to Houston, where they spent several days together. Later that year, Merendino returned to San Diego and gave Meza money for his college classes. The two agreed they would start a long-distance relationship as Merendino was frequently traveling. He still took care of Meza by regularly sending him cash.

David Meza was from Imperial Beach, near San Diego. He worked as an escort and appeared in several adult films under the alias Mario Romo. While Meza was in a relationship with Merendino, he was hiding a huge secret from him. Meza had a fiancée named Taylor Langston. The two met when Langston was only 16. David managed to hide everything related to his job as an escort and appearances in adult films from her.

According to Langston, she did hear about Jake Merendino, but Meza explained that he worked as a personal assistant for the millionaire. He also said that Merendino's name was George. She didn't question the expensive gifts he received from Merendino or their frequent trips together.

When Langston discovered that she was pregnant, Meza was excited to become a father, and she believed they would be a happy family.

Merendino didn't have a clue that Langston existed. He continued to see Meza and plan their future together. Eager to share his happiness, Merendino told all his friends about Meza, and not everyone was thrilled. Some questioned the intentions of the young man. After all, Merendino was a millionaire and an easy target because he always saw the best in people.

In December 2014, Merendino was so in love with Meza that the young man managed to persuade him to write a new will on a piece of hotel stationery and leave all his fortune to him. Several months later, Merendino was planning to purchase a lavish waterfront apartment in Rosarito Beach, Mexico. He wanted to retire and live with his young boyfriend there.

However, Meza was still with Langston, who was due to give birth soon. They were also making plans of their own. Meza knew he could inherit a fortune and the waterfront apartment, but the only thing standing in his way was Merendino himself.

On April 29th, 2015, Merendino and Meza drove to Mexico in a rented car to finalize the purchase of the luxury $273,000 apartment. The deal was signed, and the two men were the new owners of the property. They arrived at the apartment the following day, but it wasn't ready. The couple returned to San Diego and rented a room at Hector Hotel in Chula Vista. Wanting to be closer to the new apartment, Merendino drove his Range Rover to a nearby hotel called Bobby's by the Sea on May 1st, and Meza followed on his motorbike.

According to the hotel manager, Merendino was in the lobby around 7 pm, asking for a bottle opener. Other guests heard Meza leave at around 10:30 pm on his bike. He entered the United States at 11 pm, which was confirmed by a border camera. Meza went home to his girlfriend in San Diego and returned to Mexico after midnight. He contacted Merendino after midnight and told him he was stranded on the road.

Without hesitation, Merendino left the hotel around 1 am. He told the security guard he was going out to help a friend. Unfortunately, that was the last time anyone saw him alive. His body was discovered by police at about 3:30 am on the road between Rosarito and Ensenada. The officers first noticed an abandoned Range Rover parked by the side of the road.

The interiors were soaked with blood, and the trail led to the edge of the ravine. There they found Jake Merendino. The evidence confirmed he was dragged and then pushed down the cliff. The autopsy revealed he was brutally attacked, stabbed 24 times, and his throat was slashed, which explained the blood all over his vehicle.

Meanwhile, David Meza was back in the United States. He crossed the border at 3:57 am and was picked up by surveillance cameras once again. At 7 am, Meza was back at Bobby's by the Sea, but this time, he was with his girlfriend, Taylor Langston. The two arrived in a black SUV, and Meza told the hotel staff he had forgotten some of his personal belongings in Merendino's room.

The staff recognized him because they had seen Meza with Merendino on May 1st and allowed him to go to their room. The couple wasn't there for Meza's things. They stole Merendino's Rolex watch, his iPad, and his laptop. The watch alone was worth around $15,000.

When the local police learned the identity of their murder victim, they suspected he was robbed by someone in the middle of the night. After all, he was a millionaire and was driving an expensive car. Meza and Langston were both questioned by the investigators, and they claimed the two were in Tijuana at the time of Merendino's murder. According to the couple, they were visiting their friend Joe. The police identified Joe as a man named Jose Aguilera. He said he hadn't seen Meza and Langston for more than two years. Furthermore, Meza contacted him several weeks before the murder and asked Jose to provide him with an alibi. Meza expected that Jose would help him cover up his involvement in the crime.

Additionally, several days after Merendino's murder, the

family lawyers were ready to go through his will. But Meza appeared with the new version of Merendino's will, which was handwritten on hotel stationery, and claimed he had the right to Merendino's millions, as well as the apartment. The investigators believed that David Meza was the killer, but they still needed evidence that placed him at the crime scene.

The police took a closer look at Meza's cell phone data and uncovered that he was at the scene of the murder after 1 am. He was called in for a second interview, and this time he confessed that he planned to rob Merendino at the side of the road. According to Meza, all he wanted was to steal the apartment keys, which he allegedly did. He told the investigators that Merendino was alive when he left him and that someone else probably saw him on the road and then murdered him.

The investigators didn't believe in this new version of the events and arrested both David Meza and his fiancée Taylor Langston for the murder of Jake Merendino seven months later. They couldn't tell where Langston was in the early hours of May 2nd but believed she helped Meza hide the crime. Langston gave birth to the couple's child soon after the murder.

In February 2017, Taylor Langston pleaded guilty to covering up the murder of Jake Merendino. Her attorney claimed that she was the victim of David Meza's lies because she didn't know the truth about Merendino. They also said Langston was abused by her fiancé and perhaps even forced to lie about the crime. But that didn't help her receive a lighter sentence.

In June 2017, Langston was sentenced to one year and nine months behind bars. The prosecution later said that she was almost charged as an accomplice, but they didn't have any evidence she was at the scene of the murder.

David Meza was charged with first-degree murder and pleaded not guilty. His trial began in late 2017, and the defense relied on the lack of physical evidence that placed Meza at the scene. He was sticking to his story that he robbed Merendino and left him by his Range Rover. Meza's lawyers also claimed their client was much smaller than the victim and couldn't drag him to the cliff by himself.

On December 11th, 2017, David Meza was sentenced to life in prison. Earlier that year, he received 20 years for conspiracy to obstruct justice.

DRUG OF CHOICE

"She was a very kind, giving old woman."

BRIDGET JOSEPH, ON 81-YEAR-OLD INEZ NOTTER

Addiction makes people do unimaginable things, and Billy Armentrout is the perfect example. He bludgeoned his loving grandmother to steal checks from her because he needed money for drugs. The police quickly arrested him, and Billy was sent to prison. However, it took him years to accept he was his grandmother's killer.

Charles "Billy" Armentrout was born in 1965 in St. Louis, Missouri. His parents separated when he was six, and Billy's mother, Gloria, soon remarried. The new family moved to Jonesburg, west of St. Louis. Billy's new stepfather was cruel toward the boy and often verbally abused him. He felt humiliated every day, and his self-confidence was low. As a result, Billy started acting out and often argued with his stepfather. When he was 18, things at home were getting even worse. That's when Billy's father invited him to live at his house. His father thought that Billy was now an adult and could make his own decisions.

Despite the change of scenery, Billy continued to hang out with a bad crowd and started using drugs. He also began robbing gas stations because he enjoyed the excitement and thrill. Soon after, Billy needed more money, so he began stealing from his father. Billy's dad caught him and was very angry at his son.

High on drugs, Billy believed his father would throw him out of the house. He was terrified to go back to his stepfather. So Billy patiently waited for his dad to return home and shot him through the door. Billy's father, Charles Armentrout Jr., was hit six times in the chest but survived the attack. Billy was arrested on June 19th, 1984. His father refused to press charges because he believed Billy needed help from a psychologist. Meanwhile, the police connected him to a string of gas station robberies. Several months later, Billy was sentenced to 19 years behind bars.

Billy was released from prison in August 1994 after serving 10 years for the robberies. He was 28 years old when he was paroled and needed a permanent address. His family refused to help him out. The only family member willing to accept him was his grandmother, Inez Notter. She was a woman with a kind heart who forgave him for shooting her son and believed her grandson could change.

Inez lived in the Bevo Mill neighborhood in St. Louis, a quiet part of the city where crimes rarely happen. Even though Billy was on parole, he quickly connected with other addicts, namely Roger Brannan and Rick Lacey. The trio hung out at the Brannan house and smoked marijuana around the clock. Roger was only interested in weed, but Rick was open to experimenting. Billy began dating Bridget Joseph, who introduced him to cocaine. He quickly became addicted and needed more and more money every day to feed his addiction.

Billy started taking money from his grandmother. He would tell her his friend was in trouble and needed cash quickly, and Inez always wrote him a check. In December 1994, he started stealing from Inez by forging the checks. She was contacted by her bank and informed about the forgeries. Inez confronted her grandson, who admitted he stole from her and apologized. According to Billy, he promised he would get a job and repay her. Unfortunately, he wasn't ready to turn his life around.

On February 20th, 1995, Billy tried to cash another forged check, and the police were called to the bank. He was arrested and taken into custody, but Inez again refused to prosecute him. The following day, Inez met with the bank manager and explained that she didn't want to pursue legal action against Billy Armentrout because she was scared of him. Inez even mentioned he might try to kill her.

On March 18th, 1995, Billy went to Inez's house to ask for money. She refused to write a check, which enraged him. He believed the only way to get the cash was to rob his grandmother. Billy followed Inez into her bedroom and attacked her with a souvenir baseball bat. Inez tried to defend herself, but it was useless against a bigger attacker. Billy hit her more than 12 times, and she died of a head injury. Inez also had eight broken ribs.

Billy then tied Inez up using a cord and wrapped her body in a blanket. He hid her body in a trunk in the basement and went out to meet with Roger Brannon and Bridget Joseph, who were waiting for him in front of Inez's house. He had $100 with him, which he spent on drugs that evening. Additionally, Bridget was given two bags full of things that belonged to Inez. According to her, Billy claimed his grandmother was reorganizing the house and was giving away some things.

The following morning, Billy was back at his grandmother's house. He told Bridget he was going there to get more money. His girlfriend had no idea Billy had killed his grandmother the day before. The bedroom was stained with blood, so Billy decided to clean the walls and throw away the evidence. The souvenir baseball bat was wiped clean and returned to its place.

In the afternoon on March 20th, Billy attempted to cash another forged check at the bank's drive-through window. He was with his friend, Shirley Mendez, who was arrested by the police. Billy managed to get away.

Inez Notter's relatives contacted law enforcement after not hearing from the 81-year-old woman for two days. Police officers arrived at her address and searched Inez's house. They found her body in the basement and noticed blood spatter in the bedroom. After examining her head wounds, the investigators searched for the potential weapon in the house and found the souvenir baseball bat. Blood and hair were visible on the bat. DNA testing later confirmed the blood belonged to Inez.

The investigators spoke to Inez's family, and they immediately pointed the finger at Billy. After learning about his criminal history, he became the prime suspect. The police were informed about his attempt to cash a forged check one day prior, which meant he was still in the area.

Police informants were contacted, and soon the police knew that Billy was at Rick Lacey's house. One police car was parked behind the house in case Billy tried to run. Officers knocked on Rick's door at 11:30 pm, and he said Billy was inside. Billy immediately tried to run by jumping out of a window. He was caught in the backyard and taken to the station, where he agreed to do a videotaped interview.

The detective leading the case quickly learned Billy was heavily addicted to crack cocaine because he asked him before interrogation if he could smoke one last time. During the interview, Billy kept mentioning his friend Rick Lacey as the person who killed his grandmother.

According to Billy, Rick was the mastermind behind the

murder. He wanted to bludgeon his grandmother Inez and steal her checkbook.

Furthermore, Billy said Rick suggested they throw the baseball bat into the river. Investigators believed Billy was lying and that Rick wasn't at Inez's house that day. Rick's DNA and fingerprints were not found in Inez's house. Detectives called him to the station, and Rick said he didn't even know where Inez Notter lived.

Their friend Brennan was called in for an interview, even though he didn't spend much time with Billy and Rick lately because they were now using heavier drugs. The investigators wanted to know more about his attempt to cash in one of Inez's checks for Billy several weeks ago. When he learned that his friend was involved in a murder, Brennan told them everything he knew.

MURDER CHARGE

On March 22nd, 1995, Billy Armentrout was charged with first-degree murder and robbery, and Rick was released. Oddly, Billy wanted to represent himself in court and waived his right to counsel. He was required to have a defense attorney with him as a stand-by counsel. On September 16th, 1996, Billy escaped from jail with another prisoner. The two of them sawed the cell bars and managed to get out. However, they were arrested again two miles from the jail.

THE TRIAL

The trial for the murder of Inez Notter began on January 26th, 1998. Billy continued to blame Rick Lacey for the crime. He refused to testify and didn't present any evidence to prove Rick's involvement.
Billy asked his mother to testify on his behalf but she refused to come to the trial so he had her subpoenaed. On the stand she answered Billy's questions but called him her former son. She wanted nothing to do with him.

On February 14th, 1998, the jury found him guilty of first-degree murder. Billy Armentrout was sentenced to death.

He spent eight years on death row, claiming he was innocent. In 2006, his sentence was reduced to life without parole due to a legal technicality, and he was moved to the general population. More than a decade after the murder, Billy finally accepted he was guilty of the death of his grandmother and that he killed her because of his addiction to crack cocaine. He is serving his sentence at the Potosi Correctional Center in Washington County, Missouri.

MILLIONAIRE'S MISTAKE

"Today, we hold our head high, as we have throughout the whole ordeal, because that is what our father would expect of his children...There were enough aggravating factors versus mitigating factors to sentence you to death, and unfortunately, some of the jurors couldn't come to terms with putting you to death. I accept their verdict and understand how some of them possibly couldn't kill like you did."

JAYE KLOS, JACK REID'S DAUGHTER

In the summer of 2005, a beloved community member went missing in Derry, New Hampshire. After a search that lasted more than one week, his body was found hidden in the back of his truck. This discovery launched a thorough investigation and led the detectives to an unlikely suspect.

Jack F. Reid was born in 1948, in Cambridge, Massachusetts. Reid ended up in foster care from a young age. He moved a lot during childhood and always longed for family stability. Reid enlisted in the army in the 1960s.

He finally settled in Derry, New Hampshire, where he became a part of the community through his business. In 1996, Reid started a company called Jack F. Reid Trucking and quickly found success. He met many people while helping them move or transfer goods, and everyone knew him as a hard-working man.

In 2005, Reid took on various projects to save as much money as possible for his retirement. He planned to move to Las Vegas, Nevada, in 2006 because he didn't like New Hampshire winters. His daughter, Megan, graduated from high school, and he was waiting for his youngest son to do the same the following year.

MISSING FROM WORK

On June 29th, 2005, Jack Reid didn't show up for a scheduled job. The client called Reid's family because that was unusual. Several members of Reid's family went to his house to look for him, but Reid wasn't there. His truck was also missing. Despite the efforts, Reid's family couldn't locate him, so they contacted the police around 6 pm and filed a missing persons report.

The police immediately started searching for Reid, and the family posted flyers all over Derry, but there was no sign of him. Then on July 5th, 2005, Megan Reid received a phone call from someone informing her they had seen her dad's truck in a Target parking lot in Saugus, Massachusetts. She contacted the police right away, and two detectives went there to check the vehicle.

The plates confirmed the truck belonged to Jack Reid, but he was nowhere to be seen. The detectives took a closer look at the abandoned vehicle and lifted the tarp at the back. Inside, they found an object rolled into a large piece of plastic. They cut the material and saw a human body.

The medical examiner confirmed that the victim's chest was caved in. There were also signs of blunt force trauma to the forehead and the side of the skull. The injuries were so severe that visual identification was impossible. The examiner used Reid's dental records to confirm his identity. After more than a week of searching, the police had finally found Jack Reid.

The investigators examined Reid's truck and found DNA that didn't belong to him on the stick shift. They also located Reid's work logbook, which contained the list of his clients and projects. The surveillance footage was checked, and the police had their first clue.

On June 27th, 2005, Reid's truck arrived at the parking lot and was followed by a white minivan. Two men exited the vehicle, one of them checked the tarp, and both got into the minivan. Unfortunately, the footage was grainy, and the investigators couldn't see the minivan's plates. However, they now knew that at least three people were involved in the murder.

The police also learned that Megan Reid, Jack's daughter, was in Saugus one day before the discovery of the truck. She was also seen on the parking lot surveillance on July 4th, accompanied by her boyfriend, Walter. They didn't see Reid's truck, but the investigators wondered if the two had something to do with the murder.

Megan and Walter were interviewed, and the couple revealed they were visiting Walter's sister in Saugus for the 4th of July celebration. Megan was under a lot of stress due to the search for her father, and Walter thought a change of scenery could help her. The two took a lie detector test, passed, and were cleared of suspicion.

The investigators now focused on Reid's logbook and learned he was at a waste management site around 2 pm on June 27th. The police checked Reid's phone records and saw he received a call from a man named Charlie Was at 2:07 pm. After failing to reach the caller, investigators learned that it was a prepaid phone that was activated on June 19th. The phone was last used on June 27th to contact Reid.

THE LAKE HOUSE

After checking Was' phone records, the police discovered that all the calls from that number were made to Reid. However, Was received one call on June 19th that came from the lake house of John "Jay" Brooks. Brooks was a local celebrity and a millionaire who was in the medical supply industry. He had hired Jack Reid several times in the last couple of years. Reid helped Brooks move to Las Vegas, Nevada, in the fall of 2003.

Detectives also found a random address scribbled in Reid's log book and assumed it was from Charlie Was. They visited 145 North Road and discovered it was a horse farm in Deerfield that belonged to a man named Michael Connors. After talking to Connors, detectives learned he was the overseer of the renovations at Brooks' lake house. Two workers confirmed he was there the whole day on June 27th.

The workers also mentioned that Brooks was in Derry that day with two men from Las Vegas. The group arrived on June 18th and left on June 29th. The police quickly learned the names of the duo – Robin Knight and Joe Vrooman. Since there were three men on the parking lot surveillance video, the investigators decided to take a closer look at Brooks.

The millionaire had several vehicles registered to his name. One was a minivan that looked exactly like the one in the surveillance video. The police needed to test the trio's DNA to confirm one of them was in Reid's truck, but they were in Nevada at that time. However, Knight returned to New Hampshire in October 2006, and the investigators saw it as an opportunity to learn what happened in June 2005.

PLANNING THE MURDER

Detectives had a warrant for Knight's DNA. But they told him the warrant was for his arrest, so Knight panicked and said he wanted to talk before Brooks and Vrooman did. According to Knight, Jack Reid helped Brooks move to Las Vegas in September 2003. Once the trucks arrived at their destination, Brooks noticed that several of his motorcycles were missing, as well as his wife's jewelry. He reported the theft to the police but never mentioned Reid's name.

Brooks blamed Reid for the missing items and felt very wronged by him. So instead of openly accusing Reid, he decided to punish him. Brooks approached Knight and Vrooman, who worked for him, and told them about his plans to hurt Reid. The millionaire started planning the murder in 2004 and had almost everything worked out.

Brooks, Knight, and Vrooman arrived in Derry in June 2005 and were joined by a local petty criminal named Mike Benton, a friend of Brooks' son. They were staying in Brooks' apartment in New Castle. Brooks remembered Connors' horse farm and thought it was the perfect place to commit a murder. He approached Connors and offered to remodel one of the barns in exchange for him supervising the renovation of his lake house. Connors gladly accepted.

Benton purchased the burner phone on June 19th, and Brooks called the number from the lake house. Knight posed as Charlie Was, contacted Jack Reid, and set up a meeting at Connors' horse farm on June 27th. Always punctual, Reid arrived on time, and Knight led him into a barn where Brooks, Vrooman, and Benton were waiting.

Benton started hitting Reid with a hammer, and he fell to the ground. Reid was bleeding from his head, and the men panicked. Brooks then hit Reid in the chest to kill him. That was the fatal blow, and Reid was dead. The men loaded Reid in the back of his truck and covered the body with the tarp. Knight and Vrooman drove the vehicle to the parking lot in Saugus while Brooks followed them in his minivan.

The men took off their bloody clothes in Brooks' apartment and threw them in the garbage. They returned to the horse farm later in the evening and removed the flooring to cover up the murder. When Connors came home, he thought the men were fixing up his barn and didn't ask questions. Benton received a large sum of money from the millionaire, and Knight and Vrooman were soon back in Nevada.

The police needed to confirm Knight's story, so they visited Connors' farm once again and examined the barn where the murder allegedly took place. They found only a tiny drop of blood, and DNA testing confirmed it belonged to Jack Reid. The investigators finally had all the puzzle pieces.

Brooks, Vrooman, and Benton were all arrested in October 2006. Both Vrooman and Benton agreed to testify against Jay Brooks. Vrooman also admitted he was approached by the millionaire and was offered $10,000 to kill Jack Reid. Benton confirmed that Jay's son Jesse recruited him, which led to yet another arrest in this case.

THE TRIALS

Vrooman received a lighter sentence because he cooperated with the investigation and was convicted of conspiracy to commit capital murder and hindering apprehension. Since he pretended to be Charlie Was and lured Jack Reid to the horse farm, Robin Knight was found guilty of being an accomplice to first-degree murder and conspiracy to commit murder. Benton was found guilty of second-degree murder and conspiracy to commit murder.

Mike Benton described at the trial how he and his co-conspirators murdered Jack Reid. Benton said he was waiting in a closet inside the barn, and another man pushed Reid inside.

"Immediately when he fell in, that's when I hit him with the hammer," Benton said.

In Joe Vrooman's testimony, he said was paid $10,000 to help kill Reid. He also said he watched Jesse Brooks, Jay's son, hit Reid with the hammer.

Vrooman testified that Jesse Brooks said, "Stop the heart, stop the bleeding," as he picked up the hammer. He said Brooks struck Reid twice in the chest, with one hit being directly in the center of Reid's chest.

Jesse Brooks was sentenced to 15 to 30 years in prison for conspiring to kill Jack Reid.

Jay Brooks' trial began in September 2008 and lasted for five weeks. On October 16th, 2008, he was found guilty of two counts of capital murder, first-degree murder, and conspiracy to commit murder. He was sentenced to two life sentences in prison without the possibility of parole.

Jack Reid's daughter Megan made a statement in court with the feelings of anger and loss of her father evident in her words:

> "To the coward that murdered my daddy: I hate you. He admired you, and look what you did to him. You're disgusting."

LETHAL LOVE

> "We had to helplessly watch her die again and again and again. The pain of that last day will haunt me and my family for the rest of our lives."
>
> WILLIAM YODER, MARY'S HUSBAND

Mary Yoder, a chiropractor who led a healthy life, suddenly felt ill and ended up in a hospital. Less than two days later, she was dead. A toxicology report found a deadly toxin in her system, but the investigators had no idea who would want to hurt the kind-hearted doctor.

Mary Yoder was born in 1955 in Buffalo, New York. She met her future husband, William Yoder, while they both attended college in the 1970s. They had three children, Liana, Tamryn, and Adam.

Mary and William were doctors and ran a well-known practice in Utica, New York, together. Mary worked as a chiropractor, and her patients loved her.

Even though she turned 60 in 2015, she had numerous hobbies like dancing, hiking, pottery, and gardening. Mary was very energetic and had an active lifestyle. According to her friends and family, Mary and William were very happy and had been planning a second honeymoon to Europe in the summer of 2015.

On July 20th, 2015, Mary went to work as usual, ready to see her patients. She had a protein shake for lunch and started feeling nauseous afterward. As time went on, Mary couldn't continue working. She told her receptionist that she was going home. When Mary returned to the house, she experienced sharp stomach pains and was vomiting the entire evening.

Since she was rarely sick, Mary assumed it was just a stomach bug. However, she was getting progressively worse and couldn't keep down liquids. William was worried, so the two agreed to go to the emergency room on July 21st. The doctors ran tests on Mary, and everything seemed to be fine. Several hours after she arrived at the hospital, doctors realized Mary's organs were failing.

She experienced three heart attacks just as her children reached the hospital. Mary Yoder passed away on July 22nd, 2015, less than a day and a half after she began feeling ill. The doctors at the hospital were perplexed by Mary's death because they couldn't find the reason behind the organ failure. A toxicology report didn't show cyanide or arsenic in her system.

The Yoder family requested an autopsy, hoping it might give them an answer. The medical examiner noted severe organ damage and suspected that Mary was poisoned. The hospital contacted a poison control expert who wrote a list of toxins that could cause similar damage. One of the listed toxins was Colchicine. Colchicine is typically used to treat gout and can produce excellent results, but patients are advised to be very careful with the dosage. An accidental overdose could be lethal.

Mary wasn't diagnosed with gout, and no one in her family used this toxin. But in October 2015, the second toxicology report confirmed Mary had a lethal dosage of Colchicine in her body. It meant she was poisoned by someone.

On October 15th, 2015, Oneida County Sheriff's Department got a call from one of Mary's sisters, who informed them about the toxicology results and told the officers Mary didn't die of natural causes. She urged the officers to investigate the case, which they did. The police were already familiar with the suspicious death of Mary Yoder and knew they had to talk to her husband, William.

Mary's sister revealed to the police that William was in a relationship with Kathy, their third sister, and she believed the two had been seeing each other before Mary's death. It led the investigators to think that since William was also a doctor, he ordered Colchicine and poisoned Mary. They suspected that Mary got poisoned during lunchtime.

The killer knew that drinking protein shakes was Mary's daily routine, and they mixed the poison with the protein powder. William came in for the interview and told the investigators that his relationship with Kathy began after his wife's death. Additionally, the police learned William wasn't at the clinic on the day Mary got sick. Soon after, he was eliminated as a suspect.

In November 2015, Oneida County Sheriff's Department received an anonymous letter that blamed Adam Yoder for the murder of his mother. The writer said they were friends with Adam and that he killed his mother with Colchicine. The toxin was ordered online by using prepaid credit cards. The rest of Colchicine was hidden under the passenger seat of his Jeep Wrangler. According to them, he resented Mary for not giving him enough attention and murdered her for financial gain.

The investigators realized that the person who sent the anonymous letter knew Mary's cause of death which wasn't made public. Therefore, they had to take a closer look at Adam. He was 25, and attended SUNY Polytechnic Institute in Utica. When he wasn't at school, he worked at his family's practice at the front desk.

He dated Kaitlyn Conley, a 23-year-old young woman from a wealthy family who also worked at the practice. Kaitlyn loved Mary and William and was especially close to Adam's mother. Her relationship with Adam was rocky, and the pair often broke up.

Adam was brought in for questioning and was shocked to

learn about the anonymous letter. When the investigators asked if they could search his Jeep, Adam said yes because he thought the letter was a hoax. However, the investigators found a small glass vial under the passenger seat. It was stashed in a box and also had a receipt with it. The investigators saw Adam's confused look when they showed him the vial. The slip had an email address, but Adam said it wasn't his.

Meanwhile, the anonymous letter and the vial of Colchicine were sent to the forensic laboratory for testing. Adam's sister Liana confirmed that Adam was visiting her on Long Island when their mother got sick. Both of them returned home on July 21st, 2015.

Since Kaitlyn Conley was very close to the Yoder family, she was invited to the police station for an interview. The investigators hoped they would learn more details about the day when Mary got poisoned. Kaitlyn was friendly and approachable but didn't tell the police anything they didn't already know. She also gave them her DNA sample.

The police looked into the email address that was written on the receipt and learned that three different devices were used to access it. The IP addresses confirmed that the email was accessed from the computer at the front desk of the Yoder family practice, Kaitlyn's home computer, and Kaitlyn's cell phone. They finally had the person who had ordered Colchicine online. But why would Kaitlyn poison Mary?

The investigators dug deeper into Kaitlyn's relationship

with Adam and learned it was very toxic. It seemed like Kaitlyn couldn't allow Adam to be with anyone else but her. After one of their breakups, Kaitlyn called Adam to inform him she almost bled to death because of an ectopic pregnancy and that the baby was his. Adam was on a date with another girl, and he left her to go and be with Kaitlyn.

In April 2015, Adam was studying for exams and had a hard time concentrating. Kaitlyn told him to try a new supplement called Alpha Brain. She was pushy, and Adam agreed. After taking a second pill, he got extremely sick. Adam experienced stomach cramps, diarrhea, and vomiting. He spent two weeks in the hospital. These symptoms were similar to Mary's, which led him to believe he was poisoned too.

The police seized all three devices that were used for the fake email account. Kaitlyn researched toxins on the office computer during her shifts. She also managed to delete thousands of files from her phone, but the police were working on recovering them. Meanwhile, the forensic laboratory confirmed her fingerprints were found on the Colchicine vial.

Kaitlyn was brought to the station, and she denied all accusations but admitted she wrote the anonymous letter, saying she was scared of Adam. The investigators lied to Kaitlyn and said they had surveillance videos of her purchasing the prepaid credit cards that were used for buying Colchicine. Kaitlyn broke down and confessed to poisoning Mary Yoder. She was charged with second-degree murder in May 2016.

The trial began in April 2017, and the prosecution had all the necessary evidence to prove that Kaitlyn Conley was the killer. The evidence included her DNA on the vial, the anonymous letter, prepaid credit cards, and a fake email account. The defense tried to blame William for the murder. However, it ended up as a mistrial because of a hung jury.
During the preparations for the second trial, Adam remembered Kaitlyn had plugged her iPhone into his computer. It created an automatic backup. The investigators were finally able to get their hands on the deleted files.

They discovered Kaitlyn had created the fake email in September 2014. She began researching various poisons and toxins in December of the same year. Then she ordered Colchicine in February 2015. Her notes also included calculations about the precise amount of Colchicine needed to kill a person who weighed around 180 lbs which fit Adam's description. He was given the supplement in April 2015.

On November 6th, 2017, Kaitlyn Conley was found guilty of first-degree manslaughter. She was sentenced to 23 years in prison. Kaitlyn's lawyers have filed several appeals, but they have all been rejected.

Adam made a statement in court:

> "I introduced her to my family, I got her a job with my parents and if I hadn't done those things, my

> mother would still be alive. Since this investigation began, I have seen three psychologists and one psychiatrist. I've now been prescribed multiple medications for sleep, for major depression, for severe anxiety and for PTSD, all of which have been prescribed for one simple reason: self-hatred."

Kaitlyn Conley's motive remains unclear, but the investigators theorized she wanted to hurt Adam by killing his mother. Even though the two had their differences, Adam and Mary were very close.

MURDER AND MORE

> "Our victim, in all likelihood, was alive when placed in the water."
>
> DAVID BABCOCK, NEWAYGO COUNTY SHERIFF'S OFFICE.

How can fear of a court appearance for a sexual assault charge spiral into what was likely serial murder? Although the full story has never been proven, a man was sentenced to death for the murder of a young woman, yet her infant daughter and all other possible witnesses have disappeared.

Rachel Timmerman was born in 1978 in Grand Rapids, Michigan. Her parents were very young when they had her and soon split up. Rachel lived with her mother, who was distant and didn't care for her daughter. Rachel often missed school because she had nothing to wear. A social worker got involved, and Rachel moved in with Tim and Lynn Timmerman.

As a high schooler, Rachel partied a lot and started using drugs recreationally. However, when she was 17, Rachel learned she was pregnant. The teen decided to change her life for the better and was excited about motherhood. Her daughter, Shannon Verhage, was born on June 15th, 1996. Even though they weren't together anymore, Rachel was thrilled to have her ex-boyfriend and Shannon's father in their lives.

On August 6th, 1996, Wayne Davis, a family friend, Mikey Gabrion, Rachel's classmate, and his uncle Marvin Gabrion stopped by Rachel's trailer and invited her to a card game. Rachel's sister Sara agreed to babysit little Shannon, so Rachel left her at home.

After a few hours, the group decided to go on a beer run. They all hopped into Marvin's vehicle. Suddenly, Marvin stopped his car and ordered Wayne and Mikey to get out. He drove Rachel to a remote location where he sexually assaulted her. Marvin also bit her nose, which resulted in an injury. Rachel was terrified but tried to make Marvin drive her home. He agreed and threatened to murder her and her baby Shannon if she told anyone what had happened.

When Marvin and Rachel arrived at her trailer, she ran inside and found a hammer. Marvin was banging on the door, and Rachel yelled at him to leave. Sara, who was napping on a couch, woke up and saw that her sister had a bloody nose. The man left, and Rachel told Sara she was sexually assaulted.

Sara and their brother Shane urged Rachel to go to the police, but she was scared of Marvin. Finally, she agreed and went to Newaygo County Sheriff's Office on August 8th, 1996. The police tried to reach Marvin, but instead, he faxed them his statement, saying that the intercourse was consensual. Marvin Gabrion was charged with third-degree criminal sexual conduct and arrested on January 20th, 1997. He was released on a bond in February.

~

On July 5th, 1997, two turtle hunters contacted law enforcement and reported a body in Oxford Lake. The police arrived at the remote location to discover a female floating in the water. She was dressed in a plaid shirt and blue jeans. The woman was weighted down by cinder blocks and had floated to the surface because of decomposition.

Her mouth and eyes were covered by duct tape, and she had chains around her body. The woman's hands were handcuffed behind her back. The police called in divers to retrieve the body, and they used a trampoline to pick up all the evidence underneath her.

An autopsy revealed that the woman died of asphyxia by drowning. After checking the list of missing persons from the area and not finding a match, the police weren't any closer to finding her identity. On July 12th, the Medical Examiner's Office managed to get her fingerprints, and the investigators learned the woman's name was Rachel Timmerman.

The police went to speak to Rachel's family, who were shocked by the discovery. According to Rachel's father, Tim, she was last seen on June 3rd, 1997. She went out on a date with a man named John and took Shannon with her. John spoke with Rachel over the phone for days and wanted to meet the little girl. The next day, the family received a letter from Rachel, who informed them she was head over heels in love with her new boyfriend and that she won't be coming home soon.

One week later, a letter arrived from Little Rock, Arkansas. It was from Rachel again, but this time she told them she had moved there permanently. Tim confirmed it was Rachel's handwriting. Since she was 19, the family couldn't do anything. Tim and Sara went to the police and provided a sketch artist with a description of the man who picked up Rachel.

Meanwhile, Newaygo County Sheriff's Office contacted the FBI, and they sent a special agent to help with the investigation. They had learned about Rachel's sexual assault that happened less than one year ago and wanted to gather more information about Marvin Gabrion.

THE COURT APPEARANCE

Rachel was scheduled to appear in court on June 5th, 1997, and testify against Marvin Gabrion. He showed up, but Rachel didn't, which led to the dismissal of the charges. Gabrion's last known address was in Altona, Michigan, and the police went there to interview him. However, Gabrion's house appeared to be empty. The investigators found cinder blocks in the garden, and they matched those found tied to Rachel's body.

The investigators obtained a search warrant and entered Gabrion's home. It was vacant, with various items and trash left in all rooms. However, they didn't find any trace of baby Shannon or evidence she had been in Gabrion's house. The suspect was missing, so the investigators started contacting his friends. Wayne Davis, one of those present on the night of Rachel's sexual assault, was on the list.

The police went to Wayne Davis' house, and it was also empty. A friend of his talked to the investigators and revealed they hadn't seen Davis in weeks. He left a note saying he couldn't be involved in the sexual assault trial and that he had gone to California. However, the friend was suspicious because Davis left his favorite jacket at home, which was unusual.

GABRION HAS ALIASES

In August 1997, the Michigan State Police tip line received

an interesting call from a woman named Elaine. She told them about her boyfriend, John Weeks, who talked to a girl named Rachel in May 1997. According to Elaine, Weeks often hung out with a friend named *Lance* at that time.

The investigators showed Gabrion's photo to Elaine, and she said that was her boyfriend's friend *Lance*. Elaine last saw her boyfriend at the end of June and he had been missing for more than a month. Elaine just assumed he had left town with Lance, but now she was worried that something had happened to John Weeks.

The FBI agent who worked on the case checked Gabrion's bank records and learned he had used another alias – Robert Allen. The local police knew the real Robert Allen, a disabled person from Grand Rapids who relied on social security checks. Allen was last seen in late 1995 by his family. Police discovered that Gabrion continued living at his address and regularly cashed the man's checks. However, the checks were now delivered to a post office in Sherman, New York. The FBI office in Buffalo was contacted, and agents talked to the post office employee. They identified Gabrion as the man coming in every month to pick up the social security check.

Meanwhile, Newaygo County Sheriff's Office talked to two campers who were near Oxford Lake in June 1997, around the time of Rachel's disappearance. One evening, a truck drove up to their camp, and two men asked them if they could leave their aluminum boat there because their campground didn't have available space. One of them had visible scratches on his face. The campers identified the men as Gabrion and John Weeks.

The FBI forensic laboratory examined the cinder blocks found behind Gabrion's house and determined that the red paint matched the one on the cinder blocks tied around Rachel.

On October 14th, 1997, the FBI was waiting at the post office in Sherman, New York, hoping Gabrion would show up to collect the social security check. Gabrion appeared, picked up his mail, and was arrested in front of the post office. He was soon extradited to Michigan.

Gabrion claimed he had nothing to do with the murder of Rachel Timmerman or the disappearance of her daughter Shannon. According to him, someone else must have taken them. It was clear Gabrion wasn't willing to reveal Shannon's location. The police were losing hope they would find the baby alive.

The investigators suspected baby Shannon was kidnapped to force Rachel to write the two letters to her family. Gabrion was convicted of social security fraud and was sentenced to 60 months in prison in 1998.

The trial for the murder of Rachel Timmerman started on February 25th, 2002. Marvin Gabrion claimed he was innocent and that John Weeks and Rachel's friend Eddie Start were involved, but not him. The prosecution's theory suggested that Gabrion killed baby Shannon in front of

Rachel and then threw the young mother into the lake to drown.

During the trial, Gabrion testified on his behalf and provided even more incriminating information that convinced the jury he was guilty. The defense blamed his behavior on head injuries and troubled childhood. Gabrion also tried to appear mentally unstable and even attacked his lawyer in the courtroom.

Since the murder was committed on federal land in Manistee National Forest, Gabrion faced the death penalty. The trial lasted for seven days, and Marvin Gabrion was found guilty of the first-degree murder of Rachel Timmerman. He was sentenced to death.

In July 2002, Wayne Davis' body was found in Twinwood lake in Manistee National Forest. He was tied with rope and weighted with rocks, which was eerily similar to Rachel Timmerman. Robert Allen and John Weeks were never found but are presumed dead.

The investigators never learned what happened to Rachel's daughter Shannon. One inmate said Gabrion told him he had killed the baby because he didn't know what to do with her. Her remains were never recovered.

BORN TO KILL

> "I've prayed about it. I've prayed to have the power to do what I need to do. I didn't sleep very well last night. It's disconcerting to have this responsibility. I suspect a lot of people won't sleep this night either."
>
> GOVERNOR BEN NELSON ON THE EVE OF THE EXECUTION OF JOHN JOSEPH JOUBERT

A TERROR FROM THE BEGINNING

As a teen, Joubert terrorized the residents of Portland, Maine. In the early 1980s, he was known in the area as the *Woodford Slasher*. By age 21, he'd murdered three boys and evaded the authorities for years. However, a sharp-eyed teacher found him suspicious and contacted law enforcement, which resulted in Joubert's arrest.

John Joseph Joubert IV was born in 1963 in Lawrence, Massachusetts. He grew up in a seemingly happy family home alongside his sister. But their parents would argue constantly, and Joubert's mother divorced his father when he was only six years old. His mother didn't allow Joubert to see his father, which over time, made him hate her.

While clever, Joubert was seen as an outcast by his peers. He didn't have many friends at school, so he joined the Cub Scouts. In elementary school, he started to have dark thoughts and fantasized about attacking and cannibalizing his babysitter.

MOVING TO MAINE

In 1974, Joubert's mother decided to start over in a new place, so the family moved to Portland, Maine. Joubert begged his mother to let him stay in Lawrence with his father, but she refused.

THE WOODFORD SLASHER

Being the new kid at school was a nightmare for Joubert, who had to find new friends. He did get close to one boy, and the two were inseparable. In the summer of 1976, Joubert stayed with his dad in Lawrence. When he returned to Portland, his best friend was gone. His family moved away, and the boy didn't leave a phone number or address.

When he was 13, Joubert attacked a six-year-old girl. He stabbed her with a pencil and felt ecstatic when she screamed. He replayed this scene in his head for days, and after a while, he wanted more. Since no one had seen him with the girl, Joubert grew more confident. He took a razor blade and biked past another young girl, slashing her along the way.

A gap of two years went by before Joubert, now in his mid-teens, attacked again. This time it was an eight-year-old boy. Even though the boy got away from him, Joubert felt powerful. He now understood why bullies always picked on those smaller than them. He continued to stab or slash people on the street, and the newspapers nicknamed him the *Woodford Slasher*.

The police tried to identify the *Woodford Slasher* and even stopped Joubert to question him after one of the attacks, but they didn't arrest him.

Joubert's attacks didn't stop him from being an excellent student in high school. He ran track and played clarinet in the band. He graduated from Cheverus High School as an honor student.

In the fall of 1981, Joubert started his freshman year at Norwich University in Vermont. Everyone expected him to succeed and get high grades, but Joubert started drinking and playing Dungeons and Dragons instead of going to class. He failed his first year in college and returned home to Portland completely defeated.

THE FIRST MURDER

Richard Stetson, also known as Ricky, was an 11-year-old boy from Portland. He left home on August 22nd, 1982, and went running on Back Cove Trail. Meanwhile, Joubert was on a bike, determined to find someone to kill. He spotted Ricky after 5 pm and followed the boy. Joubert grabbed him near Interstate 295 and tried to strangle him but eventually killed him by stabbing Ricky in the chest.

Ricky's body was found by a motorist who thought that Ricky had been hit by a car. When the investigators examined the body, it was clear they had a murder on their hands. When they moved Ricky's body, the investigators saw a bite mark on the boy's leg. Whoever killed him tried to conceal the bite mark by slashing it with a knife. Even though the boy was partially undressed, he hadn't been sexually assaulted.

While detectives searched for the killer, Joubert knew he had to leave Maine. Since he didn't have money to move away, he joined the Air Force and was sent to San Diego, Texas, for basic training. He was assigned to Offutt Air Force Base in Bellevue, Nebraska.

Joubert made a friend in San Diego, and they were always together. However, other airmen teased them by saying the two were a couple. It made Joubert's friend uncomfortable, and he asked to be transferred from Offutt Air Force Base, leaving Joubert alone. Once again, Joubert felt depressed, and he started searching for another victim.

Danny Joe Eberle, who was 13, lived in Bellevue with his parents and a brother. The boys had a paper route and delivered the Omaha World-Herald every morning. In the early morning of September 18th, 1983, the boys were delivering newspapers as usual. Joubert approached Danny Joe at the address of his fourth delivery and pulled out a knife. He ordered the boy to get inside his car, where he tied him up and placed the boy in a trunk.

Joubert drove to the outskirts of Bellevue and found a remote cornfield where he parked his car. Danny Joe was ordered to take off his clothes, which he did. Joubert tied his legs again and placed surgical tape on his mouth. He brutally stabbed the boy in his chest and back. Joubert bit Danny Joe several times and slashed the bite marks with the knife.

Bellevue police searched for Danny Joe for days but had few leads. They found his bike parked by the fourth house he visited that morning, and that was it. However, Danny Joe's brother remembered seeing a man following them in a tan car for the last few mornings. On September 21st, Danny Joe's body was discovered near a gravel road outside the town.

The FBI was called in because Danny Joe was kidnapped. The agents created a profile of the killer and interviewed several sex offenders from the area. Danny Joe's brother described the man to the sketch artist, and posters were made. However, no one came forward with the information that could lead to the arrest. There were no new leads months after the murder, and the case went cold.

Christopher Walden, a 12-year-old boy from Papillon, Nebraska, became Joubert's third victim. By November 1983, Joubert started following groups of boys as they walked to school in the morning. He tried to find out who was walking alone and memorized their routes. On December 2nd, 1983, he parked his car and approached Christopher Walden.

Joubert showed him the knife and told the boy to walk toward the vehicle. Christopher was placed on the passenger seat, and Joubert ordered him to lie down. He was driven past train tracks and then forced out of the car. The boy started crying, which annoyed Joubert, who ordered Christopher to take off his clothes.

Without hesitation, Joubert started strangling the boy who fought back. The killer then stabbed Christopher and slashed the boy's throat. Hoping that the police wouldn't connect the two murders, Joubert resisted biting his third victim. Instead, he tried using the knife to carve pictures of leaves into his stomach.

Christopher was reported missing in the afternoon, and the police began searching for him immediately. A woman who lived close to the location of the abduction reported seeing a man in a tan car with Christopher. He matched the sketch of Danny Joe's killer. Christopher's body was found by hunters two days after the abduction.

BELLEVUE KILLER

The residents of Bellevue and the surrounding communities knew there was a serial killer in their area. Posters of the wanted man were put up everywhere, but there were still no leads. Regardless of everything, Joubert was desperate to kill again. He knew his tan car was spotted twice, so he rented a new vehicle.

Following the same pattern, Joubert drove through Bellevue, searching for his next target in January 1984. But this time, a preschool teacher spotted him several times and grew suspicious. She called the police on January 11th, 1984, to give them a license plate number. According to the teacher, the man stopped the vehicle when he saw her writing something down and threatened her.

The plates of the rental car led to John Joubert, a radar technician at the Offutt Air Base. He owned a tan Chevrolet that was currently at a repair shop. His barracks room was searched, and the investigators discovered a rope similar to the one used in the murder of Danny Joe Eberle.

Realizing that lying was useless at that point, Joubert confessed to killing Danny Joe Eberle and Christopher Walden. He was charged with two murders on January 12th,

1984, and pleaded not guilty. Soon after, he changed his plea to guilty and went through psychiatric evaluations, which diagnosed him with obsessive-compulsive disorder, sadistic tendencies, and schizoid personality disorder. A panel of three judges found him sane when he committed the murders, and John Joseph Joubert IV was sentenced to death.

The FBI was involved in the investigation of the murders of two boys in Bellevue, Nebraska, and the cases were presented in Quantico during a lecture. A police officer from Portland, Maine, was present at the lecture and immediately connected the dots. Joubert lived in Portland at the time of Richard Stetson's murder, and the boy had a bite mark.

Bite mark comparison confirmed that Joubert murdered Ricky Stetson in 1982. The police revealed that Joubert was the Woodford Slasher and connected him to attacks on several individuals in the early 1980s. In 1990, Joubert was sentenced to life in prison in Maine.

On death row in Nebraska, Joubert developed a romantic relationship with a woman from Ireland named Theresa O'Brien. They wrote letters back and forth for four years. Theresa attended his execution and reportedly mouthed, *I love you* to Joubert after he was strapped into the electric chair.

Lt. Kent Woodhead from the Lincoln police department was outside the Nebraska State Penitentiary and commented to the Lincoln Star Journal about the 800-plus people who stood outside waiting for the execution.

"I'm surprised and dismayed that so many people would come out for the execution of a human being."

Before he was executed, Joubert apologized for the murders and asked the families of Danny Eberle, Christopher Walden and Richard Stetson to "try and find some peace." He also asked the people of Nebraska to forgive him.

At 12:15 am, July 17th, 1996, Joubert was executed in the electric chair at Nebraska State Penitentiary.

At 12:16 am, a phone rang in the family quarters of the governor's mansion, reporting that the execution had taken place without incident.

Gov. Ben Nelson, who once considered ministry as a career, said, "It's what the law requires. At times it's difficult to carry it out. A life has been extinguished but you have to conclude it's just, even though that doesn't mean it's easy."

CATFISHED

"It's doubtful this was his first time. There weren't a lot of missteps made or sloppiness on his part. There was some planning done here."

MAJ. MARK ELSINGER, CONWAY POLICE

In the early 2000s, the internet seemed like a great place to meet friends around the world. Despite the warnings from the grownups, teens rarely questioned the identities of the people they were chatting with. Unfortunately, a 13-year-old girl from Arkansas met an online predator posing as an 18-year-old surfer from California. He traveled across the United States to kidnap and murder her.

Kacie Rene Woody was born in 1989 in Little Rock,

Arkansas. She grew up in Holland, Arkansas, where she lived with her parents, Rick and Kristie, and two older brothers, Austin and Tim. Unfortunately, Kacie lost her mother when she was only seven years old. On June 19th, 1997, the family was driving home from Tim's baseball game when a horse ran into the road. Rick, who was driving the car, hit the animal, and it went through the windshield. Everyone in the vehicle was unharmed except for Kristie, who died at the scene.

Just like her two brothers before her, Kacie attended Greenbrier Middle School. She was well-liked because her older siblings had been school football stars before going to college. Kacie had a large group of friends, and all the girls were very close. She was a member of the school band and sang in a choir. Kacie learned to take care of herself early, and her father, Rick, knew he could rely on her. She did her homework on time and cooked meals for herself.

In 2002, Kacie lived with her father, Rick, a police officer, her brother Tim, and Tim's college friend, Eric Betts. Austin, the eldest, had already moved out. Kacie's aunt Teresa Paul lived next door to the Woody family. Their house was on Griggers Lane in a rural part of Holland, surrounded by thick woods. Rick often worked nights, but he wasn't worried about Kacie. Tim and Eric were usually at the house by midnight, and Kacie herself kept busy by talking to her friends online.

Kacie's dad allowed his daughter to use the internet to communicate with her friends because the calls from their landline were sometimes billed as long distance. Kacie and her school friends frequented the Yahoo! Messenger chat rooms for Christian teens. Kacie's username was *modelbehavior63* because it was her favorite Disney movie.

In the summer of 2002, Kacie started talking with a 17-year-old boy from San Diego, California, whose username was *jazzman_df*. His profile photo showed a long-haired surfer guy, and Kacie soon learned his name was David Fagen, also known as Dave. The two talked about everything and soon started calling each other on the phone.

Kacie opened up about the death of her mother and how it changed her life completely. Dave told Kacie about his aunt, who also lived in Arkansas, and how she was in a coma after a car accident. It created a strong bond between them, and Kacie decided to introduce Dave to her real-life friends, Sam and Jessica. The girls added Dave to their Yahoo! Friends list but were still unsure about him.

Sam talked to Kacie about her chatting with Dave and told her not to fall in love with someone she had never seen live before. But around the same time, Kacie started communicating with a 14-year-old teen from Alpharetta, Georgia. His name was Scott, and he went by the username *Tazz2999*. Scott enjoyed football and wrestling and soon became a part of Kacie's group of friends.
Kacie talked to Scott over the phone too, and she introduced him to Dave. When Dave called Scott's house one time, Scott's dad picked up and told Dave not to call anymore. Scott's dad told his son that Dave wasn't a teenage boy but a grown man.

Kacie's friend Sam was also doubtful regarding Dave's age because he used words like *groovy* and *far out,* which were outdated in the early 2000s. Naively, Kacie assumed that teens in California talk like that. By the end of the summer of 2002, Kacie told her father, Rick, that her online friend Dave had just turned 18. Rick was shocked and told her Dave was too old to be chatting with 13-year-old girls. He told her to stop talking to him, but Kacie didn't listen.

Kacie continued to communicate with her online friends and had crushes on both Dave and Scott. However, she decided to have an online relationship with Scott. They started dating on October 3rd, 2002, and exchanged photos in the mail. Dave learned about the relationship and said he wanted to remain friends with Kacie. He allegedly enjoyed talking to her over the phone and needed someone to be there for him because his aunt was getting worse and could pass away soon.

One evening in November 2002, Kacie was hanging out with Jessica, and the girls were on the phone with Dave. They heard strange noises outside Kacie's house and ran to the bedroom. Kacie barricaded the door with a dresser, and the girls listened for footsteps. They heard a floorboard squeak in the kitchen, and Kacie knew someone really was in the house. She whispered this to Dave over the phone, and he calmly replied that she shouldn't be scared because no one was inside. Shortly after, the noises stopped.

On December 3rd, 2002, Sam and Kacie were at school. When Kacie opened her locker, Sam noticed Scott's Yahoo!

Profile photo and commented that he looked hot. Kacie misheard her friend and thought that she said Scott looked fat. The two started arguing, and Sam learned that Scott had mailed the photo to Kacie, meaning he had her address.

Sam was worried for her friend, so she went to the school counselor to tell her that Kacie had given her address to people she had met online. The counselor called Kacie to her office and warned her about the dangers of talking to strangers on the internet. As a response, Kacie said her father knew all about her online friends and approved of them communicating via phone.

After school, Kacie asked Sam if they could have a sleep-over at her house. Since it was a school night, Sam knew her mother would not be okay with it, so she declined. Kacie asked Jessica and another friend if she could spend the night at their houses, but both said no. All three girls were confused by Kacie's suggestion because they usually had sleepovers on weekends.

Kacie returned home after school on December 3rd, 2002, and saw her brother around 6 pm before he went to the library to study. His friend Eric was also out of the house, attending an evening class. As usual, Kacie was on her computer, talking to Scott. The two had been dating for two months and chatted about Kacie's day at school. Kacie was also on the phone with Dave. She told Scott that Dave's aunt was unwell and he was on his way to Arkansas.

THE RESPONSES STOP

At 9:41 pm, Kacie suddenly stopped responding to Scott's messages. Scott sent dozens of them over a 30-minute period. Kacie had stopped chatting, but she hadn't logged off.

Tazz2999: r u ok sweetie?

Tazz2999: r u busy baby?

Tazz2999: ... hehe guess so...

Tazz2999: u there baby?

Worried, he called Kacie's home, but nobody picked up. He even emailed Kacie's friend Jessica, but she didn't check her inbox that night.

Tazz2999: please GOD let her be ok

Tazz2999: why isn't anyone answering the PHONE!

Tazz2999: UGH

Tazz2999: PLEASE PICK UP KACIE

Tazz2999: GOD PLEASE LET HER PICK UP

Tazz2999: please be ok Kacie...

Eric came home at 10:15 pm and saw that Kacie wasn't in the living room. He assumed she'd gone to bed. Tim arrived at 11:40 pm and checked Kacie's bedroom. He was shocked to see she wasn't there.

Not knowing what was happening, Tim called his dad Rick who was on patrol that night. Rick rushed home and saw that something bad had happened. Kacie's glasses were on the couch, and one of the lenses was missing. Her shoes and two jackets were still in the house, but the weather outside was freezing.

Rick alerted the police right away, and other officers came to the Woody house after midnight. While investigators were searching the house, Eric saw the chat window on Kacie's computer. He messaged Scott, who instantly replied even though it was close to 3 am. The teen kept his computer on because he sensed something was wrong with Kacie. Scott told Eric the two were chatting, and Kacie was talking to their friend Dave on the phone. Nothing seemed off about their conversation.

By the morning, the police knew Kacie had been kidnapped. Local law enforcement called the Arkansas State Police and the FBI to help them find the missing teen. Kacie's computer was searched, and the investigators talked to Sam and Jessica at school, hoping the girls would give them a lead. When asked who could've kidnapped their friend, Sam and Jessica blamed Scott.

The FBI traced Scott's IP address, and the agents were sent to his home in Alpharetta, Georgia. They confirmed that Scott was 14 years old and lived with his parents, who didn't even know he had an online girlfriend. He was home on the night of Kacie's disappearance and wasn't their suspect. But the police were still searching for Dave.

The investigators learned from Scott that Dave was allegedly driving to Arkansas, so they checked the local motels for a guest called Dave Fagan or anyone with those initials. Patrols were also on the lookout for vehicles with California plates, and they found one in front of a Motel 6 in Conway. The clerk told them the car belonged to a guest named David Fuller.

The man arrived on December 2nd and requested no maid service. He also argued with the clerk because he couldn't connect to the internet from his room and needed to go to the library. Suspecting this was the kidnapper, the officers entered his room and discovered camouflage clothing and rubber gloves. The bed was neat, and the suitcase was unpacked.

Since his vehicle was still in front of the motel, the police checked the local Rent-A-Car and learned that David Fuller had rented a silver Dodge minivan. The paperwork listed his phone number and credit card. The number confirmed that Dave Fagan and David Fuller were, in fact, the same person. He also used the credit card to rent a unit at a storage facility in Conway.

On December 4th, 2002, at around 6 pm, a police sergeant and two FBI agents arrived at the storage unit rented by Fuller. The door wasn't locked, so they looked inside and saw the rented Dodge minivan. Suddenly, they heard a shot, and the three retreated and called for backup. The police were trying to get Fuller to surrender but didn't get any response from the inside.

The SWAT team was called, and they entered the unit at 8:30 pm. Fuller's body was beside the minivan. He committed suicide by shooting himself in the head. Kacie was found tied up to the minivan floor. Fuller had removed the back seats to make more room inside the vehicle. She had been shot in the head.

The medical examiner determined Kacie was sexually assaulted before death, but Fuller had used chloroform to kidnap her, and she was likely unconscious for the entire time. He likely kept her alive for hours but heard on the radio that the police were looking for him. That's when he decided to kill Kacie.

David Fuller was born on January 18th, 1955, in Salt Lake City, Utah and 47 years old at the time of Kacie's murder. Fuller grew up in a Mormon family and was married twice. Fuller had a son and a daughter with his second wife, Sally Krens. The family moved around frequently because Fuller was in the Navy. In 1997, they decided to stay in La Mesa, California and bought a house.

Soon after, Fuller started spending all his time online in different chat rooms. His wife sensed something was wrong, and by 2002, Krens was ready to divorce her husband. In June of that year, she got the paperwork, and Fuller was furious when he found out. In August 2002, Child Protective Services questioned Fuller because he allegedly had inappropriate showers with his seven-year-old daughter. He moved out of the family house afterward.

He was arrested for spousal abuse and indecent exposure to two young girls. During that time, Fuller worked as a car salesman but was fired because he used the work computer to watch pornography. His life was falling apart, but Fuller remained focused on Kacie.

The FBI searched Fuller's apartment in La Mesa and discovered shocking things. Beside his desktop computer were photos of Kacie and her friends. He had their street addresses and phone numbers written on paper. The investigators found chat logs that confirmed he had tried to groom three other girls while using the name Dave Fagan. He had been visiting teen chat rooms for two years.

The investigators carefully tracked his movements in the months leading to the murder of Kacie Woody and found out Fuller was in Arkansas twice before December 2002. The first time he arrived on October 11th and checked into the same motel. Fuller was likely there to confirm Kacie's address and see the house. The second visit to Arkansas was in November, and he rented the storage unit. Investigators believe he planned to kidnap the teen then, but something prevented him.

Kacie's friend Jessica remembered the evening when the girls heard strange noises outside and inside Kacie's home. The police suspected Fuller was in the Woody household but didn't expect to find two teens there.

According to Fuller's credit card records, he purchased chloroform, zip ties, duct tape, and chains in late November. Therefore, he was fully prepared to abduct the teen on December 3rd. Because of all the planning, the police believed that Kacie wasn't his first victim. But his DNA didn't match any unsolved cases in the databases.

Kacie Woody was laid to rest in South Crossroads Church Cemetery in Rose Bud, Arkansas. Her grave is next to her mother's. Kacie's family and friends started a non-profit organization called the Kacie Woody Foundation to teach kids and their parents about online safety. Rick Woody allowed the FBI to use Kacie's story in their training programs.

MURDERER FOUND

"I don't think so much about the guy who did this as I do about Rita, and my parents and what they went through."

TOM CURRAN RITA'S BROTHER

In 1971 a young school teacher was murdered in her apartment. There were very few clues, but circumstantial evidence pointed to notorious serial killer Ted Bundy. Bundy always denied the murder. Decades later, DNA evidence would reveal the truth.

Rita Patricia Curran was born on June 21st, 1947, in Brooklyn, New York. In the summer of 1971, Rita turned 24 years old. She worked as a second-grade teacher at

Milton Elementary School and rented an apartment on Brooks Avenue in Burlington, Vermont.

Rita had two female roommates, Beverly Lamphere and Kerry Duane. The young women didn't know each other before renting the apartment together. Wanting to move out of her family home, Rita answered an ad for a room near the University of Vermont campus. The location was perfect because she was taking graduate classes there. Since Rita was a teacher, the whole summer was ahead of her, so she found a second job. Rita worked as a maid at the Colonial Motor Inn in South Burlington.

On July 19th, 1971, Rita returned to the apartment around 10 pm from choral group rehearsal. Her roommates, Beverly and Kerry, were home, but they were getting ready to leave. The women planned to go out with Beverly's boyfriend and get something to eat. They invited Rita to join them, but she declined. She was supposed to get up early and go to work. Beverly and Kerry left the apartment around 11:20 pm, and that was the last time Rita was seen alive.

They were back at 17 Brooks Avenue with Beverly's boyfriend around 12:30 am. Rita wasn't in the living room, so they assumed she was sleeping. The group talked for a bit, and then Beverly returned to the room she shared with Rita after 1 am.

As soon as she opened the door, Beverly saw Rita lying on the floor. She was partially naked and had curlers in her hair, suggesting she was attacked while getting ready for bed. Beverly's boyfriend attempted to resuscitate Rita, but she was already gone.

Murders were uncommon in this part of the state, and police immediately started thinking that one of the students at the University of Vermont had something to do with this crime.

The medical examiner determined that Rita was beaten, strangled, and sexually assaulted. She probably died around midnight. The wounds on her hands suggested that Rita fought with her killer. The investigators found traces of blood near the back door, meaning the killer fled the scene after hearing Rita's roommates return. The young women kept their doors unlocked, and there were no signs of forced entry.

Rita's purse was in her room, and money was in her wallet. No valuables were missing from the apartment, so robbery wasn't the motive. The police found several clues at the scene, namely a cigarette butt near Rita's right arm. The evidence was collected and carefully preserved by the Burlington Police Department.

The investigators interviewed people connected to Rita and the residents of the apartment building. William DeRoos, who lived on the second floor in the apartment above Rita's, was questioned by the detectives. He had a record, and the police believed he might be the suspect. However, DeRoos' wife Michelle provided him with an alibi for the night.

Even though the police conducted a thorough investigation, they couldn't solve Rita's case. Despite hundreds of tips coming in after the murder, the suspect remained unidentified. Decades later, Rita's murder became the oldest unsolved crime in Burlington.

After the arrest of well-known serial killer, Ted Bundy, retired FBI agent John Bassett suspected he was responsible for Rita's murder. Bundy was born in Burlington at the Elizabeth Lund Home for Unwed Mothers. The Colonial Motor Inn, where Rita worked, was located on the same street. The investigators were interested in this theory because Rita looked similar to Bundy's then-girlfriend.

Additionally, the modus operandi was like Bundy's. It prompted Rita's sister, Mary Curran Campbell, to write to Bundy and directly ask him if he had any involvement in the crime. Bundy refused to answer the question. However, in an interview with a detective, Bundy claimed he murdered a woman in Burlington in 1971. According to him, he was there to get his birth certificate.

However, the police confirmed Bundy wasn't in Vermont at that time. The serial killer denied killing Rita Curran on the night of his execution. While Ted Bundy was a promising lead at one point, the murder remained unsolved.

The advancement of DNA testing opened new doors for the investigators working on this case. Even though the crime happened in the 1970s, the evidence collected at the scene remained sealed and properly stored. In 2014, the cigarette butt found next to Rita was sent for testing. Soon after, the investigators had a complete DNA profile of their suspect. It was entered into several databases, but unfortunately, there were no hits.

Several years later, genetic genealogy became incredibly popular, and the investigators saw it as something that could help them finally solve this crime. In 2019, a team of detectives and experts started working on Rita's murder. They reexamined the evidence and went through the list of possible suspects, as well as individuals who were interviewed in connection to the case.

Their best lead was still the cigarette butt, and it was sent to a private DNA testing company for genetic genealogy testing. Soon the sample was connected to four individuals related to the killer. Further testing of Rita's robe revealed that the collected sample belonged to the same man. His name was William DeRoos.

To make sure they had their suspect, the police tracked down William DeRoos' half-brother, who agreed to provide them with a DNA sample. It matched, and the investigators were certain DeRoos killed Rita in the summer of 1971. But there couldn't be an arrest because DeRoos died in 1986.

William DeRoos was questioned by the police immediately after Rita's murder. He was one of the people living in the apartment building where the crime took place. His wife of two weeks provided him with an alibi back in 1971, and the police continued to pursue different leads. DeRoos left the United States shortly after the murder.

He moved to Thailand to become a Buddhist monk and ended his marriage to his wife, Michelle. He spent several years abroad and returned to San Francisco sometime in 1974. By then, he was calling himself guru Dutch. Soon after, he married a woman named Sarah Hepting.

According to Hepting, she experienced several violent outbursts from DeRoos during their marriage. Once, she was talking to a female friend when DeRoos approached them, took a knife out of his pocket, and stabbed Hepting's friend. He was arrested after the attack, but Hepting's friend declined to press charges. He later told his wife he was imagining that he was stabbing her.

Hepting left DeRoos and filed for divorce after he tried to strangle her in a restaurant several weeks later.

Investigators talked to DeRoos' first wife, Michelle, in 2022 after the DNA results came in. Fifty years later, she was finally ready to tell the truth. The couple had a fight on the night of Rita's murder, and DeRoos stormed out of their apartment. When he returned, she was sound asleep. In the morning, DeRoos told her to say they were together in the apartment the whole night.

He explained that since he already had a record, the police would blame him for the murder. Michelle lied to the investigators, later saying she was young and naïve. Not to forget that she didn't know DeRoos well since the two had been married for only two weeks at the time of the murder.

Investigators said they think Michelle did believe DeRoos back in 1971 and had no idea he was the killer. When DeRoos left for Thailand, Michelle didn't reveal to anyone that he wasn't with her when Rita was murdered. William DeRoos died in a hotel in San Francisco in 1986 from a morphine overdose.

Rita's parents passed away before the murder was solved. Her siblings, Tom and Mary, expressed gratitude to Burlington Police Department and their detectives, who continued investigating the murder decades after it happened. Even though DeRoos couldn't face justice, Rita's family finally had closure.

SECRET PHOTOS

"When I think about what happened that night, Dylan looking up at his dad... What were you thinking when you saw his big blue eyes? I don't think it even fazed you. I think you need the maximum sentence — you have a lot of soul-searching to do."

ELAINE HALL, DYLAN'S MOTHER

The teenage son of a divorced couple visited his father to spend a weekend at his remote cabin. The next day he went missing and searchers could not find him. Most of the evidence pointed to a runaway teen who got lost in the woods, but further investigation revealed the boy disappeared because he knew a secret.

Dylan Nicholas Redwine was born in 1999, in Denver, Colorado. He lived with his parents, Mark and Elaine, and an older brother named Cory. Mark had two kids from a previous marriage. According to those who knew him, Dylan was a polite and quiet kid who enjoyed playing baseball, hanging out with his friends, and playing video games.

After 18 years of marriage, Elaine filed for divorce from Mark, and this created a lot of tension within the family. Mark worked as a truck driver and was away from home often. It didn't stop him from trying to get full custody of Dylan and Cory. During the custody battle, the judge asked Dylan where he wanted to live, and he said he wanted to stay with his mother.

Elaine was granted custody of Cory and Dylan, and Mark still had visitation rights. The boys didn't have the best relationship with Mark after the divorce because they saw how he treated their mother. Elaine soon started dating again and got into a relationship with Mike Hall. The boys and Elaine relocated to Colorado Springs, Colorado, while Mark stayed in Bayford, Colorado.

Since Mark had visitation rights, he booked a flight for Dylan on November 18th, 2012. He wanted them to spend Thanksgiving together. Dylan wasn't happy about it because this was the first time visiting his dad without Cory, who had turned 18. Mark lived in an isolated cabin, and Dylan didn't like it because he was far away from all his friends.

Elaine drove Dylan to the airport, and he sent her a

message once the plane landed. It was clear he was still feeling miserable because he included a sad face emoji. Mark picked Dylan up from the airport at around 6 pm, and the two stopped at Walmart to pick up a few things for the cabin. They bought dinner at McDonald's and drove to Bayford.

As soon as they arrived, Dylan asked his dad if he could sleep at his friend's house. Mark said no, and the boy texted his friend asking if they could meet tomorrow at 6:30 am. Dylan's friend agreed. It was the last activity on Dylan's cell phone.

According to Mike, Dylan slept until 7:30 am and didn't meet with his friend. He found him on the couch before exiting the house to run errands. Mike returned at 11:30 am, and Dylan was gone. The TV was on, playing the Nickelodeon channel. A bowl of cereal was left on the table. Dylan's backpack, cell phone, and fishing rod weren't in the house, so Mike assumed he had gone out to meet his friend.

Mike took a quick nap and woke up at 1:30 pm. Dylan wasn't home yet, so Mike texted him to ask where he was and got no reply. He went to look for him at 3 pm and stopped by his friends' houses. One of them lived nine miles away from the cabin, and Mike thought his son went to see him. Since the fishing rod was missing, Mike checked the nearby campground but had no luck.

No one had seen or heard from Dylan, so Mike drove to Bayfield Marshall's Office to tell law enforcement what was happening. Meanwhile, he contacted Elaine to ask her if she had talked to Dylan. Sensing something was wrong, Elaine, Cole, and Elaine's boyfriend immediately hopped in their car and drove to Bayfield. They arrived before midnight and met with the police. All three searched for Dylan around Mike's cabin at 2 am but found nothing. Mike refused to join them and decided to stay in.

Law enforcement suspected that Dylan was a runaway, but his mother was worried he was hurt because he hadn't texted anyone since 9 pm on November 18th. Like most teens, Dylan was always on his phone, typing messages to his friends or playing games. Elaine was suspicious of Mike and his story.

However, the police confirmed he was running errands from 7:30 am to 11:30 am on November 19th, but they couldn't verify his whereabouts during the night. Elaine was still thinking about the details provided by Mike and realized that Dylan hadn't watched Nickelodeon for a while. The teen was more into MTV.

Since Mike lived close to San Juan National Forest, rescue teams and volunteers signed up to search the area. They walked miles and miles of trails but found no traces of the boy. The police used drones to look for Dylan from the air. The family and friends printed posters offering $50,000 for any information about the missing teen. They also set up a Facebook page and used social media to organize searches in the Bayfield area.

Brandon, Dylan's half-brother, drove with his family from

Gilbert, Arizona, to help with the search. He wasn't on good terms with Mike, their dad, but felt like he needed to help his brother. Several days after Dylan was reported missing, a K-9 unit picked up his scent at Vallecito Lake, the nearby campground. Thinking he might have drowned while fishing, divers searched the waters but found no signs of the teen.

As days went by, the police were now sure that Dylan wasn't a runaway. They interviewed the family members, focusing on Elaine and Mike. Mike's cabin was searched, and the forensic unit found a couple of drops of Dylan's blood inside. Mike's girlfriend explained that the teen had cut his finger last summer. The police asked Elaine and Mike to take a polygraph test. Elaine passed, while Mike failed. However, the investigators still didn't see him as a suspect.

DR. PHIL

In the spring of 2013, Elaine, Mike, and Cory appeared on Dr. Phil. Elaine didn't hold back and openly said she believed Mike had something to do with Dylan's disappearance. Dr. Phil offered Mike the opportunity to take another polygraph test right there in the studio, and he agreed. Once everything was set up, Mike changed his mind.

REMAINS FOUND

La Plata County Sheriff's Office scheduled a search of

Middle Mountain Road for June 25th, 2013. It was a path that ran parallel to Mike's street. In the afternoon, the police found Dylan's partial remains just eight miles from Mike's cabin. The area where the remains were located was difficult to access. The police didn't find Dylan's backpack or cell phone near the remains.

The medical examiner couldn't determine the exact cause of death because he didn't have the entire body. On November 1st, 2015, a hiker discovered a human skull and contacted law enforcement. The skull was Dylan's. It was only one mile away from where Dylan's remains were discovered. The medical examiner found evidence of blunt force trauma and a fracture above Dylan's left eye. These injuries weren't from animal activity, and the cause of death was changed to homicide.

Mike was a person of interest from the summer of 2014 because the investigators noticed a lot of inconsistencies in his statements. By the summer of 2017, they had gathered enough evidence to arrest him for the murder of his son, Dylan Redwine.

On July 22nd, 2017, he was taken into custody by officers from Bellingham Police Department in Washington, where he was at the time. Mike still worked as a truck driver and was on the road often.

He was extradited to Colorado and charged with second-degree murder and child abuse resulting in death on August 15th, 2017. Mike Redwine pleaded not guilty. The trial was rescheduled 10 times for various reasons, including the COVID-19 pandemic.

In June 2021, the trial finally started in La Plata County. The prosecution believed that Dylan was killed in the living room on November 18th, 2012, with a sharp object, most likely a knife. The teen was probably decapitated. Mike then left his remains in two different locations within the forest. The investigators found his blood on the couch, and cadaver dogs picked up a scent in Mike's truck.

The defense claimed that the boy ran away from the house because he didn't want to spend the holiday with his dad, got lost in the wilderness, and was killed by an animal. According to them, the blood in the living room had been there since the summer of 2011.

Elaine and Mark's previous wife, Betsy, also testified and provided more insight into their relationships with Mike. Betsy was married to him for six years and experienced constant abuse and violence. Mike also threatened to kill their two kids during divorce proceedings.

Cory, Dylan's older brother, provided the potential motive for the murder. According to him, the boys went on a road trip with their dad in 2011, and he allowed them to use his laptop. Dylan and Cory found disturbing images on the computer and photographed the screen with their phones. The photos showed Mike wearing makeup and red lingerie, as well as him eating human feces out of a baby diaper. Both Cory and Dylan were disgusted and terrified of the photos.

In 2012, Cory asked his father about the images, and Mike got angry. He was scared the boys might show the photos to someone. This testimony led the prosecution to believe Dylan had also confronted his dad about the disturbing photos, which made him violent. The defense claimed that the images were photoshopped by Elaine to embarrass him during the divorce proceedings.

Cory Redwine said in a prepared statement in court, "I can't bring Dylan back. I can't talk to Dylan, so I pray to him. I dream of him... Dylan is my hero and became more of a man in 13 years than Mark became in 60."

In July 2021, Mark Redwine was found guilty of second-degree murder and child abuse resulting in death. On October 8th, 2021, he was sentenced to 48 years in prison.

Judge Jeffrey Wilson said at the sentencing hearing, "I have had trouble remembering a criminal defendant who has shown such an utter lack of remorse. This leads me to believe that you need significant punishment... and you need to be removed from society for a long period of time."

DRUNKEN CONFESSION

"I just slowly cooked it and I ended up cooking her for four days."

DAVID VIENS, POLICE RECORDING

A seemingly perfect marriage between Dawn and David Viens fell apart suddenly in October 2009 when Dawn mysteriously disappeared. Her friends and family knew she wouldn't just leave without telling them, but it took weeks for law enforcement to take their concerns seriously. Two years later, the investigators finally learned the gruesome details behind Dawn's death.

Dawn Marie Viens was born on March 16th, 1970, in Burlington, Vermont. She graduated from Burlington High School in 1988 and attended Trinity College. In the early

1990s, she began working as a food server and met a man named David Viens, who worked at the same restaurant as a cook.

David was also from Vermont and was 10 years older than Dawn. He was going through a divorce at that time. He had three kids from his first marriage, and the separation was difficult for him. However, Dawn and David fell in love and began dating soon after. The couple got married in 1997 and moved around quite often. After working at several restaurants together, they decided to open their place in Florida.

In 2008, the couple moved to Lomita, California, just 30 miles south of Los Angeles. They opened a restaurant called Thyme Contemporary Café on Narbonne Avenue, close to other small local businesses. David was a chef, and Dawn worked as a manager and hostess. The guests loved her because she was cheerful, optimistic, and approachable.

The restaurant soon got excellent reviews, and the business was booming. In public, Dawn and David appeared to be a happy couple, but things were completely different behind closed doors. They had financial issues, and David was violent toward Dawn.

Karen Patterson, one of Dawn's friends and an interior designer, said she saw bruises around her neck in August 2009, and Dawn said her husband had choked her during an argument. One month later, Dawn told the same friend she had to lock herself in the bathroom the night before to keep her husband, David, from attacking her.

CLOSING THE RESTAURANT

From May to September 2009, David decided to remodel the Thyme Contemporary Café, so the restaurant was closed. Dawn worked at another place and financially supported the family while David was in charge of renovations. In October the restaurant reopened and during that time, Dawn asked her friend Joe Cacace who owned a motorcycle repair shop near the restaurant, if she could leave some money at his office. According to Joe, Dawn gave him around $700 but never picked up the cash.

On October 18th, 2009, Richard Stagnitto, a family friend, arrived at Thyme Café to help David install a rack in the kitchen. After 10 pm, David was going through restaurant receipts and sounded angry. Richard heard him say that Dawn was stealing from him. Since David complained earlier about Dawn's drinking habit, Richard suggested that he should send her to rehab.

Meanwhile, Dawn called Joe Cacace around 11 pm to tell him she would bring more money to his office tomorrow. However, she never showed up. On October 19th, 2009, David gathered the employees of Thyme Café to inform them that Dawn was gone and wouldn't be working as a manager anymore. David asked Kathy Galvan, a part-time server, to take over as a hostess.

Dawn's friend, Karen Patterson, expected to see Dawn on October 20th, 2009. The two agreed that Dawn would come to the hospital where Karen was being treated for cancer. However, Dawn never showed. Karen drove to the restaurant to see where her friend was. David was there, and he seemed nervous answering questions about Dawn. He told her the two had had a fight two days prior because she didn't want to go to rehab. According to him, Dawn stormed out of their apartment. David also mentioned that Dawn was stealing from the restaurant. Karen reviewed the same receipts and saw that only $25 was missing.

Before entering the restaurant, Karen saw Dawn's car in the parking lot. When she asked David about it, he explained the vehicle didn't work, and as far as he knew, she left on foot. Three days later, David told Karen he had been texting with Dawn. On the afternoon of October 23rd, Karen received a text message from Dawn and noticed unusual spelling errors. Dawn said she was moving east and changing her phone number.

Joe also realized that Dawn was missing. He spoke with David and got the same explanation. Two weeks after his last communication with Dawn, Joe was shocked to see David and Kathy Galvan, the new hostess, holding hands. The two had started dating and Kathy was preparing to move in with David.

Around that time, David contacted his youngest daughter Jacqueline, also known as Jackie, and asked her to come to California to help him at the restaurant. Jackie was 19 and living in South Carolina, so she was happy to move to the west coast. Jackie arrived in Lomita at the beginning of November 2009 and was sad to learn Dawn was gone. Jackie loved Dawn and thought of her as a mother.

A MISSING PERSON

On November 8th, 2009, Dawn's sister Dayna contacted the Los Angeles County Sheriff's Department and filed a missing persons report. The police started investigating and checked the activity on her bank account and cell phone records. It was clear Dawn hadn't used her credit card since October 18th.

David Viens was interviewed on November 11th, 2009, and stated that the couple had many problems because of Dawn's substance and alcohol abuse. David said the two argued about him working too much at the restaurant and that Dawn had left him. He didn't report his wife missing because he believed she was with her friends, using drugs.

A NEW STORY

Then on December 9th, 2009, David changed his story. During his second interview, he said that Dawn was drinking too much and was rude to the restaurant staff. She was also stealing from the restaurant, which was unacceptable to David. On October 18th, 2009, he went to the restaurant in the evening to help his friend install a rack. When he returned to the apartment, Dawn was gone. She appeared seven days later in a disheveled state.

Dawn urged David to sell the restaurant, so the two could move to the mountains. Wanting her to get better, David told his wife to go to rehab first, and she agreed. Dawn allegedly continued communicating with him in the following weeks and said she needed more time to think about their marriage.

Dawn's family found it strange she didn't tell them about rehab, so they urged the police to continue investigating. However, law enforcement decided to wait and see if Dawn would contact someone. By August 2010, the lead detective on the case determined that Dawn wasn't coming home. He sent her case to the homicide unit.

Los Angeles County Sheriff's Department was now investigating a potential murder, so they began by searching the Viens' apartment in October 2010. David and his girlfriend Kathy weren't living there at the time. The forensic team found blood in the bedroom and bathroom, but the samples couldn't be tested.

JACKIE'S QUESTIONING

In February 2011, the detectives finally talked to Jackie, David's daughter, who revealed her father's secret. According to her, she got drunk and smoked marijuana with her dad in December 2009. During the evening, Jackie asked him about Dawn. She wanted to know if her stepmother was okay. David began sobbing and said that she would never see Dawn again.

He told her the two had an argument in October, and he needed to go to sleep because he was working early in the restaurant. However, Dawn wouldn't leave him alone. David said he tried to barricade the bedroom door but she still tried to get in. He took her to the living room, tied her up, and covered Dawn's mouth with duct tape. David took a sleeping pill and didn't hear anything the whole night. He realized in the morning that Dawn had suffocated on her vomit.

David claimed it was an accident and asked Jackie to keep his secret because he would end up in jail. She asked her dad what he had done with Dawn's body, and he didn't want to tell her. The investigators also learned about David's previous encounters with law enforcement and his involvement in drug trafficking at the beginning of the 1990s. Dawn's family confirmed he was also a recreational drug user when he met Dawn.

THE DRIVE

On February 23rd, 2011, David and Kathy went on a car ride, and he told her nobody would believe that Dawn's death was an accident. He was aware that Jackie talked to the detectives. He suspected that his daughter might have told them about their conversation. David was followed by a police car while the couple drove towards Rancho Palos Verdes cliff. He stopped the vehicle and jumped off the cliff after apologizing to Kathy. David survived the fall and was taken to the hospital but his suicide attempt left him in a wheelchair.

As he was recovering from the injuries, the police searched David's current apartment and the restaurant. They didn't find any evidence at David's residence. But a cadaver dog indicated that something had happened at the restaurant. The dog reacted in a couple of areas behind the building and around the shed.

In March 2011, David was ready to be interviewed by the police. He repeated the story told by Jackie but added a few more details, such as that Dawn was high on drugs on October 18th, 2009. According to him, the two argued about the stolen money. He was under a lot of stress because of the restaurant and bound Dawn's hands and legs. Her mouth was covered with duct tape. When he woke up, Dawn was dead, so he put her body in a bag and left her in the dumpster behind the restaurant.

The detectives didn't believe his story about leaving Dawn's body in the trash, but they soon got the answer they were looking for. David revealed even more details in the second interview claiming he realized he could get rid of the body in the kitchen. So he placed Dawn in a barrel with boiling water and cooked her body for four days. Her remains were placed in garbage bags along with grease and left in the dumpster. David claimed he saved Dawn's skull and left it in his mother's house. However, the detectives didn't find the skull during the search.

Karen Patterson, Dawn's friend, confirmed she had seen bruises on Dawn a couple of months before the disappearance. Jackie Viens confessed that she texted Dawn's family and friends from her stepmother's phone because she was trying to cover for her dad. Cell phone data confirmed that the texts were sent from California.

The trial for the murder of Dawn Viens began in the late summer of 2012. Jackie testified against her father and recounted his drunken confession to the jury. The defense tried to paint Jackie as an unreliable witness as she had been drinking and taking drugs.

The prosecution was hoping for a first-degree murder conviction and sought to prove Dawn's murder was premeditated.

David, who was displeased with his defense attorney, fired him after he rested his case. He stood up from his wheelchair and yelled, "Your Honor, I object!" when his attorney asked the jury to return a verdict of the lesser charge of second-degree murder.

The trial was over and the jury received instructions from the judge. They deliberated for five hours and found David Viens guilty of second-degree murder. They didn't believe Dawn's death was accidental but they also didn't think it was a premeditated murder.

In March 2013, David Viens was sentenced to 15 years to life. During the sentencing, David said he didn't remember speaking to the police in the hospital and that he was heavily medicated. He claimed he was innocent. David was eligible but was denied parole in 2021. He is serving his sentence in California State Prison in Corcoran.

WAGES OF SIN

> "The mortician stayed up all night trying to figure out what to do after they recovered as much as they could of her body."
>
> JEFF UNDERWOOD, JERALEE'S FATHER

When an 11-year-old girl was abducted from her neighborhood in Pocatello, Idaho, the community came together to help bring her home. But one week later, their hopes would be shattered because the police captured a man who confessed to her brutal murder.

Jeralee Underwood was born on January 9th, 1982, in Greeley, Colorado, to parents Jeffery Dean and Joyce Browning Underwood. She had five siblings – two brothers and three sisters. Jeralee was only four months old when her family decided to relocate to Pocatello, Idaho. Since she was the second oldest child in the Underwood family, Jeralee often babysat her younger siblings and did her best to help her parents.

She went to Indian Hills Elementary School and became the vice president of the student council in fifth grade. Jeralee loved studying and reading books. She was very friendly, outgoing, and religious. Her family was a part of the LDS Church, also known as the Mormon Church, and Jeralee was an active member.

Her older brother had a paper route, and Jeralee wanted to work as well. When she turned 11, she got a job delivering newspapers for the Idaho State Journal. Her parents were impressed with how many tips Jeralee got on her paper route. Neighbors loved the cheerful girl, and she even managed to enroll a large number of new subscribers for the Idaho State Journal. As a result, Jeralee was awarded a trip to Yellowstone National Park.

A TYPICAL SUMMER DAY

On the afternoon of June 29th, 1993, Jeralee left her family home and went on her paper route to collect the weekly subscription money. Since it was summer, she liked walking around the neighborhood. Her parents were at home, gardening, when they received a call from a woman they knew from the church. She asked them if someone was helping Jeralee on her paper route because she saw her getting inside a vehicle with a man.

Jeralee's parents were immediately alarmed, so they hopped into their car and drove to the neighbor's house. The woman told them she saw an unknown man put Jeralee into his vehicle. Jeffrey Dean used the neighbor's phone and contacted the Pocatello Police Department right away. The officers talked to the neighbor, who gave them the description of the man and his car.

The police were searching for a light cream vehicle driven by a man wearing a plaid shirt and a dark cap. They set up roadblocks and stopped every car that fit the description. However, the police couldn't locate the missing girl. Days went by, and there was no news about Jeralee.

A cash reward was offered to anyone who provided the police with information about Jeralee's whereabouts. The case was soon picked up by TV stations across the United States. On July 7th, 1993, police received a tip and arrested a man named James Edward Wood in connection with Jeralee's disappearance. According to the officer who took him in, Wood didn't resist the arrest and immediately confessed to killing Jeralee Underwood.

JAMES EDWARD WOOD

James Edward Wood was born on December 9th, 1947, in Pensacola, Florida. His father, Sherman, was in prison at the time of his birth. Sherman was an alcoholic who regularly abused his wife, Hazel, and Wood's older brother. Hazel decided to take her two sons and run away from Sherman to Idaho. The family lived in Rupert, and Hazel was able to give her boys a better life.

However, Wood's life changed completely when he was eight years old. Hazel worked at a potato warehouse close to his school, and one day the warehouse caught fire. His mother died because she tried to save other workers. She managed to pull out two but didn't get out in time. Wood watched the flames, not knowing if his mother was alive or dead.

Wood would later say that as he stood by the warehouse, he tried hugging a woman close to him. She pushed him away, and that moment remained with him forever. He started hating women who looked like her. Wood was adopted by his aunt and uncle from Idaho Falls. According to him, they abused him physically and mentally, which led him to act out.

A LIFE OF CRIME

In 1961, Wood stole a car and set fire to a trash can. He was sent to the Idaho Youth Training Center in St. Antony, where he continued to misbehave. Wood tried to escape eight times. In 1963, he was contacted by his father, Sherman, who had been released from prison.

Sherman offered to take him in, so Wood moved to Shreveport, Louisiana. In 1966, Wood decided to enroll in flight school in Missouri. There he met Angie Bell, and the two got married soon after. The couple had one child together.

In 1967, Wood moved in with his older brother, who lived in Bossier City, Louisiana. Months later, he was arrested after breaking into an apartment. During the break-in, Wood stabbed two women and tried to sexually assault one of them. They managed to call for help, and Wood escaped. After providing the police with a description of Wood, he was taken into custody.

When his wife Angie discovered what had happened, she filed for divorce from Wood. He was found guilty of aggravated battery and sentenced to 10 years behind bars. Wood was paroled in August 1971 for good behavior.

After his release from prison, Wood started working as a truck driver. He stayed in touch with his brother, and the two were involved in several robberies in Texas, Arkansas, and Louisiana. In 1977, Wood began a relationship with his ex-wife Angie, and the couple married for the second time. Soon after, Wood was arrested for sexual assault. Realizing her husband was a serial rapist, Angie divorced him again. He was found guilty and sent to prison, where he stayed until November 1986.

In 1987, he was back in Shreveport to live with his father. Wood soon met his second wife, Yvonne Anderson, and the two had a son in 1989. The couple moved to Grand Cane, where they lived until 1992. Wood worked at a photo lab and seemingly kept a low profile. However, a 14-year-old relative of his wife reported Wood to the police for sexual assault. Knowing he would end up in prison, Wood fled Louisiana.

He headed to Idaho because he knew he could stay with his relatives who lived in Chubbuck, a suburb of Pocatello. While on his way there, Wood kidnapped 18-year-old Jamie Masengill from the suburbs of St. Louis, Missouri, on November 28th, 1992. Wood sexually assaulted the teen and then tried shooting her in the head. His gun misfired, and the teen survived. Wood told Masengill it was her "lucky day."

ARRIVING IN POCATELLO

On December 1st, 1992, Wood arrived in Idaho.
Dave Haggard, Wood's cousin, lived close to the Underwood family. Wood asked if he could stay with him for a while, and Haggard reluctantly agreed. On June 29th, 1993, Haggard and Wood were eating when Jeralee knocked on the door. Haggard wrote a check and handed it to Jeralee, who placed it in her bag and continued walking to the next house.

According to Haggard, Wood got up several minutes later and said he was going to the store to buy some alcohol. However, he had other plans. Wood started driving through the neighborhood, looking for the girl. He saw her walking down the street, parked his car on the corner of Carter and Main Street, and approached Jeralee.

Wood told Jeralee that the check given to her by Haggard wasn't good and that he came out to find her and give her cash instead. While the girl searched her bag, Wood grabbed Jeralee and dragged her into the car. He drove south towards Preston. Jeralee was scared but continued to talk to him. She spoke of the church and her clogging class. The girl even asked Wood why he had taken her.

They were on the road for one day, and Wood stopped several times to sexually assault Jeralee. On the second day of the abduction, Wood headed toward Idaho Falls. He stopped the car near Snake River because Jeralee needed to go to the restroom. Wood followed the girl to a bush and shot her in the head. He drove back to Pocatello and returned to the crime scene shortly after.

Wood sexually assaulted Jeralee's lifeless body and then severed her arms, legs, and head to conceal what he had done. Jeralee's body parts and her clothes were thrown into the Snake River. He also removed her sex organs.

After the description of the kidnapper and his vehicle was published in the local newspapers, Haggard contacted the police and told them about his cousin, who vanished after Jeralee came to his door and didn't come back for more than a day.

Wood confessed to kidnapping, attempted sexual assault, and murder of Jeralee. He took the detectives to the crime scene, and the police started searching for Jeralee's body parts in Snake River. They managed to find everything except for the right hand and right calf.

The Underwoods chose not to view their daughter's remains and arranged her funeral.

MORE SEXUAL ASSAULT AND MURDER

While interviewed, Wood confessed to several rapes in the Pocatello area, an attempted murder on his way to Idaho, and a murder he committed in 1976.

According to Woods, he abducted Shirley Coleman from a parking lot when she was walking to her car after Christmas shopping. Coleman was 33 years old and lived in Greenwood, Louisiana. Woods drove Coleman's car to the General Electric Industrial Plant and sexually assaulted her. Afterward, Wood shot Coleman in the head. Her body was found on January 7th, 1981, outside Shreveport, Louisiana. While his confession regarding the murder of Shirley Coleman seemed probable, the investigators didn't find any physical evidence to confirm Wood was involved.

On July 12th, 1993, Wood was charged with first-degree murder and kidnapping, two counts of rape, and robberies. He pleaded not guilty. However, he changed his mind in September 1993 and pleaded guilty, reportedly saying, "The wages of sin are death."

James Edward Wood was sentenced to death on January 14th, 1994. A few weeks later, Wood's lawyers filed an appeal to overturn his sentencing because of ineffective counsel. His request was denied.

Wood was transferred to death row in the Idaho Maximum Security Institution in Kuna.

The Underwood family relied on their faith and focused on moving forward. Both Joyce and Jeff decided to attend professional counseling sessions and Jeff Underwood discussed his therapy with the KSL news network in Salt Lake City.

> "There was one session that was especially therapeutic for me. We made a scarecrow replica of James Wood to get my anger out. Then I actually did exactly what he did to Jeralee. I went through the whole process, and it was really helpful to get rid of the anger and not continue to harbor it."

While Wood was on death row, the Underwoods found out he was going to be resentenced. His case was impacted by a ruling from the U.S. Supreme Court. The court's decision stated that individuals facing capital punishment should be sentenced by a jury rather than a judge.

On February 1st, 2004, Wood, now age 56, said he was having trouble breathing. He was taken to the prison medical unit and passed away before the ambulance arrived. Wood died of natural causes.

HIGH EXPECTATIONS

> "I told her (Jennifer) that I wasn't going to do it, that I didn't want any part of it. But, you know, she was insistent."
>
> DANIEL WONG, DRUG DEALER AND MURDERER

In November 2010, residents of the tranquil city of Markham, nestled northeast of Toronto, were disturbed to learn about a lethal home invasion in one of its residential neighborhoods. The unsuspecting Pan family found themselves victims of this violent act, and a police investigation soon revealed that the real threat was lurking much closer to home.

Born on June 17th, 1986, in Markham, Canada, Jennifer Pan was the daughter of Vietnamese immigrants Bich Ha (pronounced *bick ha*) and Huei Hann Pan. Hann arrived in Canada in 1979 and eventually met Bich Ha in Toronto. The couple married and settled in Scarborough, Ontario. They went on to have another child, Felix, in 1989.

Both Bich Ha and her husband were employed at Magna International in Aurora and shared a common dream of relocating to a more upscale neighborhood closer to their other family. Their hard work and determination enabled them to purchase a home in Markham in 2004 and acquire two luxury vehicles—a Lexus and a Mercedes-Benz. They were also prudent savers, accumulating over $200,000 in their bank account.

PAN FAMILY LIFE

Hann and his wife were no strangers to hard work and perseverance and expected their children to follow suit, particularly Jennifer, as she was the oldest. They planned for Jennifer and Felix to attend college, with the University of Toronto as their top choice of universities.

JENNIFER'S BACKGROUND

Jennifer began taking piano lessons at the age of four and devoted herself to daily figure skating practice, aspiring to secure a place on Canada's Winter Olympic Team. Although she demonstrated talent in figure skating, she never quite reached the extraordinary level needed for Olympic success.

She attended Mary Ward Catholic Secondary School, where she was a diligent student but not a top achiever. Bich Ha and Hann imposed strict rules on Jennifer, forbidding her from participating in parties, school dances, or sleepovers and prohibiting her from dating until after she graduated from college.

Being a gifted musician earned Jennifer a spot in the school orchestra. So her parents let her go on a two-week trip to Europe with the orchestra in 2003. While she was away from her parents, Jennifer started a relationship with a fellow member of the orchestra, Daniel Chi-Kwong Wong. They continued to see each other when the pair returned home but kept the relationship a secret from Jennifer's parents.

JENNIFER'S FAILURE AND DECEPTION

Jennifer and her parents received the exciting news that she had been accepted to Ryerson University through early admission, a path that would lead her toward a successful future. However, her journey was soon derailed when she failed her high school calculus class. Rather than telling her parents, Jennifer kept the setback hidden, fearing their disappointment and disapproval. She pretended that everything was proceeding as planned, but she failed to graduate from high school.

TWO YEARS OF LIES

Bich Ha and Hann were sure that Jennifer was attending classes at Ryerson University. They supported her financially and even drove her to the university buildings. Once she was dropped off, Jennifer spent her time in cafés, worked part-time at a restaurant, and gave piano lessons. She told her parents she had won a scholarship and would transfer to the University of Toronto after completing two years at Ryerson.

Her parents wanted to give her more freedom because she was working hard on her degree, so they agreed to let her sleep at her friend's place near campus several times a week. Instead, Jennifer was at Daniel Wong's house. Their relationship was still going strong even though Wong was a drug dealer, and Jennifer disapproved of it.

To make her lies more believable, Jennifer purchased second-hand textbooks and spent hours online filling out notebooks with information related to pharmacology. She told her parents she had transferred to the University of Toronto and became a volunteer at The Hospital for Sick Children. After several months, Bich Ha and Hann were suspicious because Jennifer didn't have a hospital uniform or a badge.

Bich Ha followed Jennifer to the hospital one day and discovered she had been lying to them. Realizing she was caught, Jennifer admitted to everything. Hann was angry when he heard she hadn't even completed high school and wanted to throw Jennifer out of the house. Bich Ha remained calm and told Jennifer she should pass calculus, graduate and apply to college.

Jennifer wasn't allowed to leave the house except for piano lessons. That included seeing her boyfriend Wong, but the two continued to talk to each other in secret. Since his 24-year-old girlfriend was essentially grounded, Wong decided to move on and start dating other people.

THE EVENTS OF NOVEMBER 8TH

On the morning of November 8th, 2010, Jennifer was studying for a test. Bich Ha dropped by Jennifer's grandfather's house and then ran errands. She was home by 3 pm and started making dinner for the family. Hann came home from work at 4:30 pm and called his brother to see if he wanted to go with him to Home Depot.

Bich Ha got ready for her line dancing class after she and Jennifer ate dinner. Meanwhile, Hann returned home around 6:15 pm, ate dinner, and went to his study to read the news on the computer. He went to sleep shortly after. Jennifer's friend Adriane arrived at 6:30 pm, and the two young women went to the basement to watch television. Adriane left at 9 pm, and Jennifer went to her room upstairs.

She continued watching TV until her mother came back

home at 9:15 pm. Jennifer went downstairs to greet her, and then she returned to her room. She then called her former co-worker and chatted with him until hearing unknown voices in the house.

Bich Ha yelled for Hann, who was sleeping in the bedroom. Jennifer listened carefully to what was happening outside her bedroom door. Someone was coming up the stairs, and she was scared they might come to her room. Instead, the footsteps went straight to the main bedroom.

Hann woke up, and a man in a baseball cap was standing next to his bed, demanding to know where he kept his money. Before Hann could answer the question, he was taken downstairs and placed next to Bich Ha, who was on the floor crying.

Not sure what was happening in the house, Jennifer peeked out of her bedroom and was seen by a man with dreadlocks.

He ran up the stairs, grabbed Jennifer, and tied her hands. She was asked about the money, and Jennifer took the man to her room, telling him to take the $200 she had saved. Thinking Jennifer would know about her parents' stash, the man dragged Jennifer to the bedroom. Jennifer couldn't tell him where the money was, so the man tore the room apart looking for money and valuables. Jennifer was taken downstairs to her parents.

Hann said he had $60 more in his jacket, so Jennifer was

sent again to the bedroom to help find the money. She remembered one of her mother's stashes and gave the intruders $1100. Jennifer was then tied to a banister with a shoelace while her parents were taken to the basement. The intruders forced them to sit on a couch and covered their heads with blankets.

Hann was shot twice, with one bullet to his face and the other into his shoulder. As Bich Ha screamed, she was shot three times in her shoulder, neck, and head. She died instantly. Miraculously, Hann was still alive, but unconscious. Jennifer had heard the shots and was trying to untie her hands. Then she remembered her cell phone was in the waistband of her yoga pants. She managed to reach the device and dialed 911.

She stayed on the line as the police drove towards the house on Helen Avenue. As Jennifer talked to the dispatch, Hann regained consciousness and managed to climb the stairs from the basement. Even though he was in pain, Hann ran out of the house and saw his neighbor walking to his car to go to work. Hann collapsed in the driveway as the police vehicles reached the house.

Officers approached Hann, who was wailing on the ground. He told them his wife was in the basement, and his daughter was still inside the house. Not sure if the intruders had fled the scene, the officers entered the Pan residence with guns drawn. They went downstairs to the basement and discovered Bich Ha covered in blood.

One of the officers went up the stairs to Jennifer and checked the rooms on the upper floor. Once he was sure nobody was hiding in one of the rooms, he used scissors to cut the shoelace. Jennifer was taken out of the house and saw her dad in an ambulance. She was informed her mother had died. The officer who untied her hands asked Jennifer to tell him what had happened, and she replied that three men armed with guns had broken into their home. She could only remember that one of the intruders had dreadlocks, and that was it.

AFTERMATH OF THE INVASION

After the home invasion, Jennifer was taken directly to the hospital. She wasn't hurt but was feeling shaky. While there, she asked about her dad and was told he was in surgery. Doctors weren't sure if he would survive. Hoping Jennifer could provide more details about the incident, she was driven to the police station at 1:30 am.

Jennifer talked to one of the investigators who met her on the scene and did her best to describe the men who had broken into her family home. She remembered an African American man with dreadlocks, one shorter man wearing a bandana over his mouth, and another intruder with a Jamaican accent. Since Jennifer said she hung up on her friend when she heard the commotion downstairs, the police took her phone as evidence because it would tell them when the break-in happened.

Several hours after the home invasion, the police theorized

someone had followed Bich Ha from her dance class and attacked the family.

Jennifer was taken to her cousin's house because she couldn't go home. The investigators were still searching for clues and evidence at 240 Helen Avenue. Meanwhile, Hann was out of surgery and in an induced coma. He was lucky to be alive because a bullet fragment was still lodged in his skull. Regardless, the doctors expected he would recover.

One day after the home invasion, the police held a press conference, and the descriptions of the intruders were all over the media. Investigators started talking to the family, friends, and neighbors who knew the Pans, hoping they could provide more details about their everyday life, which could help them solve the crime. They quickly learned that Jennifer was dating a drug dealer named Daniel Wong. His background check confirmed he had a criminal record.

Daniel Wong was called in for an interview on November 10th, and he openly talked about his drug dealing past. He told the investigators about his secret relationship with Jennifer, which lasted until her parents gave her an ultimatum in 2009. They blamed him for all the lies she had told them and considered Daniel a bad influence.

According to him, Jennifer's dad Hann didn't like that he was part Filipino. Daniel started dating a young woman named Christina in February 2010 but kept in touch with Jennifer. He believed her parents were too strict and that she was a prisoner in her own house. By now, the police suspected that Jennifer had something to do with the home invasion. Earlier, when a police officer had informed Jennifer that they would check all the calls she'd made in the last nine days, she became visibly uncomfortable.

She was invited for a second interview with the investigators on November 11th. As soon as she entered the room, Jennifer was anxious. She was asked to recall the incident and provide as many details as possible. It was apparent that she was changing her story. The interview lasted for hours, and they talked about her parents and the relationship she had with them. She also admitted to owning more than one cell phone.

A REVELATION

Hann woke up from a coma on November 12th, 2010, and told the investigators that on the night of the home invasion, he saw his daughter Jennifer talk to one of the intruders like they were friends. It is why he ran out of the house without checking on her. Hann knew Jennifer was involved in the crime.

Jennifer was interviewed for the third time on November 22nd, 2010, and the detectives decided to use a different approach. The investigator told her he had software capable of analyzing speech and saying if statements were true or not. Of course, this was a lie, but Jennifer believed him and finally broke down. According to her, she had hired three men to kill her, not her parents.

Investigators soon learned Daniel Wong introduced

Jennifer to Lenford Roy Crawford, also known as *Homeboy*. Jennifer and Daniel planned to pay $10,000 for the murder of Bich Ha and Hann Pan. Jennifer was supposed to inherit the family money afterward, which she wanted to use to buy an apartment for her and Daniel.

Crawford contacted Eric Shawn Carty, also known as *Sniper,* and David Mylvaganam. Jennifer had used a phone given to her by Daniel to communicate with Crawford and organize the home invasion. On the evening of November 8th, she left the front door open before going upstairs to her room. She called Mylvaganam to let the group know they could enter the house. Daniel Wong and Lenford Crawford were at work during the home invasion. Carty later claimed he was the getaway driver. It is unknown who was in the house besides Mylvaganam.

Jennifer Pan was arrested on November 22nd, 2010, and transported to Central East Correctional Centre in Lindsay, Ontario, to wait for her trial. David Mylvaganam was arrested on April 14th, 2011. Eric Carty was already in prison on a different charge and was arrested on April 15th, 2011. Daniel Wong was arrested on April 26th, 2011. Lenford Crawford was taken into custody on May 4th, 2011.

The trial began on March 19th, 2014. Jennifer Pan, Daniel Wong, David Mylvaganam, Lenford Crawford, and Eric Carty were charged with first-degree murder, attempted murder, and conspiracy to commit murder. All five of them pleaded not guilty. The prosecution introduced the data collected from Jennifer's cell phones, her communication with Daniel, and the interviews with the York Regional Police.

THE TRIAL

According to the prosecution, Jennifer had planned the home invasion so that she could be with Daniel Wong. During the trial, Jennifer's brother Felix, now an engineer, testified that he had believed his sister's lies before her arrest. He said, like his mother and father, he thought Jennifer was attending university.

Felix also testified that his strict and traditionalist father was furious when he found out that Pan was with Wong and had ordered her to return home, confiscated her phone, and kept her in isolation. He added that his father's behavior was "tough love."

Jennifer's father, Hann, testified against his daughter and told a story that contradicted his daughter's statement about the home invasion. He pointed out that she communicated with the intruders in a friendly way and that she wasn't tied up.

Pan, Wong, Crawford, and David Mylvaganam were found guilty on December 13th, 2014. All four received a life sentence with a chance of parole after 25 years.

In December 2015, Carty pleaded guilty to the conspiracy to commit murder and was sentenced to 18 years behind bars, with the possibility of parole after nine years.

Jennifer Pan is serving her sentence at the Grand Valley Institution for Women in Kitchener, Ontario.

Hann and his son Felix filed a court order that forbids Jennifer from contacting any members of her family, and it was approved by the judge. Furthermore, Jennifer is not allowed to be in contact with Daniel Wong ever again.

HELPING CRIME VICTIMS

It's important that victims are not forgotten by the world. Victims deserve a voice even though they may not be able to speak for themselves. By telling and sharing their stories, we keep their stories alive. I liken it to lighting a candle in your window. They will not be forgotten.

Killer Case Files was written in part to benefit crime victims. A portion of the revenue from the sale of every volume in the *Killer Case Files* series goes to charities that fund DNA reconstruction to solve cold cases and to charities that support the families of murdered victims.

We often feel compelled to do something when we encounter the details of a horrible crime. This is my way of feeling helpful, and by purchasing the book, you've helped too.

I offer my heartfelt thanks to all of my readers of *Killer*

Case Files who are helping do something positive in a world that so urgently needs it.

Much appreciated!

Sincerely,

Jamie Malton

FREE VOLUME AND MORE

AS A THANK you to my readers, I created a special volume, ***Killer Case Files: 20 All New True Crime Stories.*** You can download it in audio format and e-book format right now for FREE at JamieMalton.com.

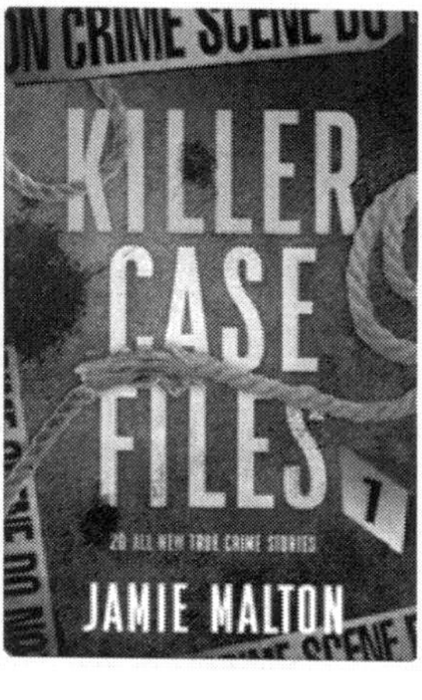

Would you like to join my **Launch Team** and receive a free volume before it's published?

If you are a reviewer on any of the well-known platforms like Amazon, Goodreads, or Instagram, you could receive an advance review copy of future volumes. I'd love to have you on my official launch team!

Sign up on my mailing list at JamieMalton.com for more info.

You might also love our new series of ***Curated True Crime***. This is a specialty series where each book has a theme. ***Volume #1: Ritual Killers*** contains crimes committed by people who felt compelled to perform malign rituals, sometimes over and over. It's an amazing look into the psychosis of ritual killers.

After Ritual Killers is Volume 2: Holiday Hell and Volume 3: Family Annihilators.

This series is available at Amazon.com

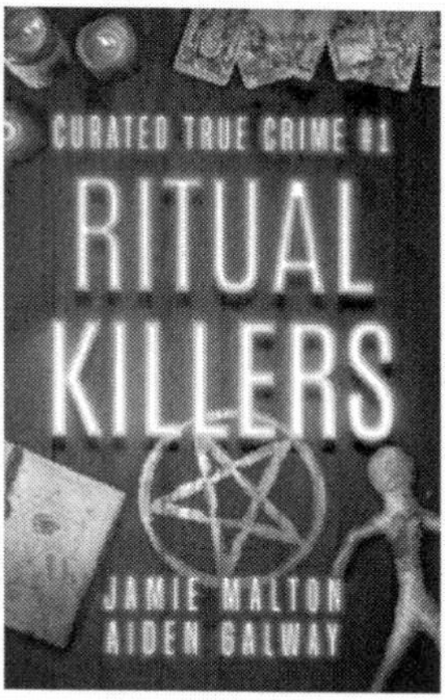
CURATED TRUE CRIME #1
RITUAL
KILLERS
JAMIE MALTON
AIDEN GALWAY

ABOUT THE AUTHOR

Jamie Malton is an award-winning author of true crime literature, known for her gritty, fact-driven narratives. Her books with their uncompromising portrayals of real crime have captivated readers of the genre.

Interested in real-life crime investigations, Malton writes about the intricacies of police work, DNA reconstruction, and genetic genealogy.

In her fifteen years as a digital nomad, she has traversed the globe, often venturing to the very locations where the crimes she details have unfolded. Her international journeys add layers of depth and authenticity to her writing.

Dedicated to the pursuit of justice, Malton goes beyond storytelling. She contributes a portion of her book sales to charities that aid in the DNA reconstruction for unsolved cases and provide support for the families of victims.

To delve into the world of true crime with Jamie Malton, visit her website at JamieMalton.com.

Printed in Great Britain
by Amazon

36186161R00335